Language and Gender
Second Edition

Language and Gender

Second Edition

MARY M. TALBOT

polity

First edition published in 1998 by Polity Press
This edition published in 2010 by Polity Press

Reprinted 2011 (twice), 2012, 2013, 2014

Polity Press
65 Bridge Street
Cambridge CB2 1UR, UK

Polity Press
350 Main Street
Malden, MA 02148, USA

ISBN-13: 978-0-7456-4604-6
ISBN-13: 978-0-7456-4605-3(pb)

A catalogue record for this book is available from the British Library.

Typeset in 11.25 on 13 pt Dante
by Servis Filmsetting Ltd, Stockport, Cheshire
Printed and bound in Great Britain by TJ International Ltd, Padstow, Cornwall

The publisher has used its best endeavours to ensure that the URLs for external websites referred to in this book are correct and active at the time of going to press. However, the publisher has no responsibility for the websites and can make no guarantee that a site will remain live or that the content is or will remain appropriate.

Every effort has been made to trace all copyright holders, but if any have been inadvertently overlooked the publisher will be pleased to include any necessary credits in any subsequent reprint or edition.

For further information on Polity, visit our website: www.politybooks.com

For my granddaughters, Tabitha and Madeline Talbot

Contents

Figures and tables

Figures

Tables

Acknowledgements

First edition

I am grateful to the students studying English at Odense University who took the course on language and gender from which this book developed. I am also deeply indebted to Marilyn Martin-Jones and Norman Fairclough, with whom I co-taught a similar course on separate occasions in the linguistics department at Lancaster University. Thanks are due to the following for commenting on parts of the work while it was in progress: Shoshana Blum-Kulka, Romy Clark, Margaret Deuchar, Gretchen Fortune, Susan Herring, Barbara Johnstone, Hans Jørgen Ladegaard, Keith Marsland, Joan Pujolar I Cos, Kathryn Remlinger and my husband, Bryan Talbot. Thanks also to Chris and Sylvie Toll for tolerating having their oral narratives scrutinized in chapter 4. Finally, thanks to the Southampton Institute for the research fellowship which gave me the time to write this book.

Second edition

I am grateful to Liz Morrish and Angela Smith for their supportive comments and valuable suggestions as I prepared this second edition. Thanks too to the anonymous cartoonist who inspired the 'It's a lesbian!' cartoon in chapter 11. My source was Judith Butler's *Bodies that Matter* but, sadly, she supplies no name.

The author and publishers wish to thank the following for permission to use copyright material:

D. Fortune and G. Fortune, 'Karajá literary acquisition and sociocultural effects on a rapidly changing culture', *Journal of Multilingual and Multicultural Development* 8(6): 469–78 (1987) © Multilingual Matters Ltd.

Peter Trudgill, 'Sex, covert prestige and linguistic change in the urban British English of Norwich', *Language in Society* 1(2): 179–95 (1972) © Cambridge University Press 1972.

Peter Trudgill, *Sociolinguistics: An Introduction to Language and Society* (1974, revised edn 1995) Penguin Books.

Transcription conventions

(.)	pause of up to half a second
(..)	pause of up to one second
(2.5)	approximate timing of longer pauses
=	latching (immediate follow-on)
heh heheh	laughter
(h)	laughter in speech
hhhhh	exhales
.hhh	inhales
(( ))	paralinguistic features and other business
(xx) (word)	indistinct utterances
> <	more rapid than surrounding speech
⌈	start of simultaneous speech, top
⌊	start of simultaneous speech, bottom
⌉	end of simultaneous speech, top (not always marked)
⌋	end of simultaneous speech, bottom (not always marked)
[ ]	indicates simultaneous speech
:	vowel lengthening

PART I

Preliminaries: Airing Stereotypes and Early Models

1

Language and gender

This opening chapter establishes the agenda by considering such key questions as: why do we need to distinguish between sex and gender, and why is language study important for feminists?

Gender is an important division in all societies. It is of enormous significance to human beings. Being born male or female has far-reaching consequences for an individual. It affects how we act in the world, how the world treats us. This includes the language we use, and the language used about us. I want this book to make you more conscious of the social category of gender, of the divisions made on the basis of it and, not least, of the part language plays in establishing and sustaining these divisions.

About this book

This first part, 'Preliminaries: Airing Stereotypes and Early Models', is looking at some early work on sex differences in language use and at stereotypes about women. Its three chapters provide a grounding in early work in the field and its central, but problematic, distinction between sex and gender.

Part II, 'Interaction among Women and Men', introduces a range of studies in the Anglo-American empirical tradition working within what is often called the 'difference-and-dominance' framework. This second part covers research into specific aspects of spoken interaction, including claims that have been made about large-scale gender differences. Two of the chapters present research into men and women's language grouped under a variety of speech situations and genres. These chapters take up some of the more minor issues and problems arising from the various studies presented, such as the difficulties arising from accounting for gender differences in terms of dichotomies like public versus private and informational versus affective. Part II finishes by considering more major problems, its concluding chapter examining some of the theoretical underpinnings underlying research presented so far and the problems they pose for researchers in language and gender. It focuses chiefly on the preoccupation with 'difference' and includes discussion of the reception among feminist linguists of Deborah Tannen's popularizing work on male and female 'interactional styles' (1986, 1991, 1995).

Part III, 'Discourse and Gender: Construction and Performance', turns to critical perspectives on gender and language. This last part introduces a contrasting approach to the study of language and gender, one that is grounded in a different theoretical background and asks different kinds of questions. It begins to try to explain how languages, individuals and social contexts 'interact', and how this interaction sustains unequal gender relations. In particular, it presents work in critical discourse analysis, an approach to the study of language in social context which is grounded in European theories of discourse and subjectivity. Looking at studies of the construction of a variety of feminine and masculine identities, the chapters in this final part of the book reflect both the high degree of interest in mass media and popular culture found in language and gender research within critical discourse analysis and the preoccupation with discourse and social change which is central to critical discourse analysis more generally.

Linguistic sex differentiation

The earliest work on men, women and language attended to 'sex differentiation'. Studies of such differences were carried out by Europeans (and other 'Westerners') with an interest in anthropology. They have tended to concentrate on phonological and lexicogrammatical 'exotica' (sound patterns, words and structures). A great deal of this kind of study has focused on the existence of different pronouns or affixes specific to men and women, whether as speakers, spoken to or spoken about. Sex differentiation of this kind is uncommon in languages of European origin. The pronoun systems of Germanic languages – such as English and Danish – only distinguish sex in third person singular reference (he/him, she/her or it). That is, when one individual is speaking to a second one about a third, the sex of the third person is specified. The pronoun systems of Romance languages – such as French, Italian and Spanish – are similar, except that they mark sex in the third person *plural* (**ils/elles**, etc.) as well. Colloquial Arabic also has sex-marking in the second person singular (**you**) so that, in addressing a person as **you**, the pronoun you use will depend on whether that person is male (**ʔinta**) or female (**ʔinti**). (The symbol **ʔ** represents a glottal stop.)

Other languages have very different pronoun systems. The Japanese one is complicated by the existence of distinct levels of formality and the need to take into account the status of the person you are talking to in deciding which level to use. There is a range of different words for the first person pronoun, **I**, for instance. There are formal pronouns which can be used by both women and men: **watashi** and the highly formal **watakushi**. Less formally, **atashi** is used only by women, **boku** traditionally only by men (there is also another form, **ore**, available to men if they want to play up their masculinity). Choice of pronoun depends here on the sex of the speaker, not the addressee. That is, if you are a woman you must use the 'female' pronoun form and if you are a man you must choose from the 'male' forms. Japan does appear to be undergoing change. Girls in Japanese high schools say that they use the first-person pronoun **boku**, because if they use **atashi** they cannot compete with the boys (Jugaku 1979, cited in Okamoto 1995: 314). Feminists have been reported using another form, **boke**, to refer to themselves (Romaine 1994: 111).

In some traditional, tribal societies, men and women have a whole range of different vocabularies that they use (while presumably understanding 'male' and 'female' forms but not using both). An extreme example of this phenomenon was in the language used by the Carib Indians (who inhabited what is now Dominica, in the Lesser Antilles). When explorers from Europe first encountered these people, they thought the women and the men were speaking distinct languages. A European writer–traveller in the seventeenth century had this to say about them:

> the men have a great many expressions peculiar to them, which the women understand but never pronounce themselves. On the other hand, the women have words and phrases which the men never use, or they would be laughed to scorn. Thus it happens that in their conversations it often seems as if the women had another language than the men.
> (Rochefort, cited in Jespersen 1922: 237)

This linguistic situation is more likely in stable, conservative cultures, where male and female social roles are not flexible. However, a contemporary tribal people in Brazil, the Karajá – whose language has more differences between male and female speech than any other language – are currently coping with rapid and profound cultural changes affecting every aspect of their society. In Karajá speech, sex of speaker is marked phonologically. There are systematic sound differences between male and female forms of words, even occurring in loan words from Portuguese. There are some examples in table 1.1. Notice the absence of /k/ and /ku/ in male speech.

Table 1.1 Differences in male and female speech in Karajá

Male speech	Female speech	Portuguese	English
heto	hetoku		house
out	kotu		turtle
bisileta	bisikreta	bicicleta	bicycle
nobiotxu	nobikutxu	domingo	Sunday

Source: Fortune and Fortune 1987: 476

Traditionally, the Karajá speakers have very clearly defined social roles for women and men. The distinct male and female forms contribute to marking these two domains, a central aspect of Karajá tribal identity. Since young people are now learning to read and write in their mother-tongue of Karajá, these distinct forms will be retained. As a consequence, they will be less likely to lose their sense of cultural identity in the process of assimilation into the larger, Portuguese-speaking Brazilian society than if they had to acquire literacy through Portuguese.

Sex differences in language of the kind we have been considering were grouped together as *sex-exclusive* differentiation in the 1970s. A distinction between sex-exclusive and *sex-preferential* differentiation – first suggested by an American linguist, Ann Bodine – became popular for labelling two different kinds of feature under investigation. Unlike sex-exclusive differences, sex-preferential differences are not absolute; they are matters of degree. While sex-exclusive differentiation is fairly uncommon in languages of European origin, the same cannot be said of sex-preferential differentiation. In later chapters of this book, I will be concentrating on sex-preferential patterns of language use, rather than sex-exclusive ones of the kind I have been talking about so far. This will involve, among other things, examining claims that women use forms of language that are closer to the prestige 'Standard' than men do (that is, speak more 'correctly'), and claims that women use a cooperative style in conversation while men use a style based on competitiveness.

Both sex-exclusive and sex-preferential differences are highly culture-specific. Acquiring them is an important part of learning how to behave as 'proper' men and women in a particular culture. Failure to acquire appropriate forms and their usage can have serious, even devastating, consequences for the individuals concerned. Gretchen Fortune, an American linguist in Brazil who co-produced the original writing system which is still used by the Karajá, has told of one young Karajá speaker whose use of women's forms was not corrected by his parents (Fortune 1995). This individual's collision with the linguistic norms of his community meant that he became a type of 'misfit' and source of ridicule within the community. For him, as a 'misfit', Portuguese provided a new identity and a kind of liberation.

Linguistic sex differentiation can become a location of social struggle within a society, not just the struggle of one individual. Japanese men's and women's forms are ceasing to be sex-exclusive, that is, forms used exclusively by one sex.

Sex versus gender

This brings me to the distinction between sex and gender. It was a conceptual breakthrough for second-wave feminism that was first articulated in detail by a British feminist in the early seventies (Oakley 1972). It does not exist in all languages – it's absent from French, Norwegian and Danish, for example – but for us, as language scholars, it is an important distinction.

According to the sex/gender distinction, sex is biologically founded, whereas gender is learned behaviour. Basically, sex is a matter of genes and the secretion of hormones and the physical developments that result from them. In this account, whether you have ended up male or female is all down to whether your father gave you an X or a Y. It is these chromosomes which determine the development of the gonads (embryonic sex glands) into either ovaries or testes. At around eight weeks old, the gonads of a foetus with one X and one Y chromosome start to produce the 'male' hormone testosterone, after which the foetus begins to develop male genitalia. Without the production of this hormone, the foetus continues as normal; that is, it carries on developing as a female. This assumption of a biological female-as-norm was an appealing idea for many feminists in the seventies and eighties, since it was a refreshing contrast to androcentric assumptions about the male-as-norm that permeated much scholarship (there are various examples of this assumption in operation in chapters 2 and 3). It has since been contested (Fausto-Sterling 2000: 204) and the account I give here is necessarily simplistic. The basic point, however, is that sex is a matter of bodily attributes and essentially dimorphic (that is, it has two forms). One is either male or female (intersexuals confuse the picture and I'll come to that issue in the next section).

Gender, by contrast, is socially constructed; it is learned. People acquire characteristics which are perceived as masculine and feminine. In everyday language, it makes sense to talk of a 'masculine' woman or a 'feminine' man. Unlike sex, gender is not binary; we can talk about one man being more masculine (or feminine) than another. This contrast is reflected in the grammar of English. Grammatically we can have **masculine**, **more masculine**, **most masculine** but not **male**, ***maler**, ***malest** (the asterisk is marking the ungrammatical forms, a convention in linguistics). People are 'gendered' and actively involved in the process of their own gendering, as I will argue in part III, where I will also consider some of the many possible kinds of masculinity and femininity.

From the above it is clear that what have been called sex-exclusive and sex-preferential differentiations are in fact ways of *doing gender*. They are part of behaving as 'proper' men and women in particular cultures. If they were genuinely matters of biological sex, they would not display the extraordinary diversity that they do. They would be the same everywhere.

So it would be misleading, and not at all helpful, to conflate sex and gender. Accounts differ, however, over the extent to which differences between the sexes are biologically determined or learned. For instance, there is a good deal of evidence indicating that men tend to be more aggressive than women. There are many more men than women convicted of violent crime. The presence of higher levels of testosterone in men than in women is often used to account for this difference (testosterone is known as the male hormone and is crucial in the development of the male foetus, but it is found in women as well).

The research evidence is far from being conclusive, however. There seems to be a connection between high testosterone levels and aggression, but it certainly is not possible to claim a definite *causal* link between them. That is, we cannot say for sure that testosterone makes people aggressive. After all, there is a lot of research evidence documenting boys' tendency to be more aggressive than girls, even at pre-school age; different levels of aggression between boys and girls cannot be put down to hormone differences, since children's hormone levels are negligible. In fact, there is some research to suggest that it might be the other way around: a person's aggressiveness might cause an increase in their testosterone level. We have a chicken-and-egg situation, in fact. And the problem doesn't end there. What do we mean by aggression anyway? The term is notoriously imprecise (see, for example, the Australian feminist Lynne Segal's account of it being used synonymously with 'dominance' (1994: 182)). It can be used to refer to very different phenomena, from assertiveness in seminars to serial killing.

So, is men's tendency for greater aggression a biological (that is, sexual) characteristic, or is it an aspect of masculine gender and therefore socially constructed? Or is it perhaps both? Well, it is probably best to concede that people's behaviour patterns come about in an interplay of biology and social practices, so that ultimately it is not really possible to separate the biological from the social. For the record, a causal link between testosterone and aggression has been established in rats and mice, not in humans or other primates. In some primate species, but not all, greater levels of aggression have been found among males than among females. Even where this is the case, there is no need for a biological explanation (Bem 1993: 34–5). As Segal observes:

> The biological alone is . . . never wholly determining of experience and behaviour. For example, all people must eat, but what we eat, how, when and where we eat, the phenomena of vegetarianism, dieting, dietary rules, obesity, anorexia, indeed any human practice or problem surrounding eating cannot even be adequately conceived of, let alone understood, only by talk of biological propensities. (1994: 186)

In making claims about the relation between sex and gender, then, we need to be careful. When gender is mapped onto sex, as it frequently is, there is an implicit assumption that socially determined differences between women and men are natural and inevitable. The confusion of sex and gender has political underpinnings: it often accompanies a reassertion of traditional family roles, or justifications for male privileges. Consider a few examples. Here are some comments I have heard fairly recently. They probably sound all too familiar:

> Women aren't allowed to do what's natural these days. Normal women want to have babies, they want to stay at home, but they can't.

> Well, I suppose the boys do dominate in class. Oh, they hog the computers, naturally. No, the girls just aren't interested.

> You women always complain. So now it's 'competitive work environments', is it? You get what you want and you're never bloody satisfied. Always whingeing about something. 'Competitive work environments', 'harassment in the workplace' – what a load of crap! Not up to the job, more like.

> If you can't take the heat, sweetheart, go back to the kitchen.

And so on. The last one was intended as a witty put-down, of course. (See Spender (1995) for Australian equivalents of the remark about boys in classrooms.) When the distinction between sex and gender is erased, restricted possibilities open to women and girls may be excused as biologically necessary, and received ideas about differences in male and female capacities, needs and desires left unchallenged.

So claiming that sex and gender are essentially the same is a conservative argument. As Ann Oakley has observed, 'in situations of social change, biological explanations may assume the role of an ethical code akin in moral persuasiveness to religion' (1982: 93). An extreme, and hence comical, expression of this in operation was in a magazine article in the late seventies dealing with a perceived threat to humanity in enormous numbers of women choosing the independence of a working wage over domesticity and dependency. The article was headed 'Ambition, stress, power, work – IS IT ALL TURNING WOMEN INTO MEN?' In it a 'top endocrinologist and Professor of Medicine' appealed to women to 'recognize their limits before it's too late' (cited in Kramarae 1981: v–vi). Too late for what, I wonder?

I wish it was always so easy to laugh at, though. There is a popular and influential field of research devoted to reducing human behaviour to biology. Sociobiology and evolutionary psychology try to establish a genetic basis for behaviour. A contribution to this field in the nineties claims to provide evidence that black Americans' relatively poor educational achievement is genetically based (Murray and Herrnstein 1994) – in other words, that black people are genetically inferior. A recent development is a genre of popular science books on 'brain sex' that places 'an extraordinary insistence on locating social pressures in the brain' (Fine 2008: 69). Critics of the genre have called it 'neurosexism'.

Claims about direct biological influences on language are just as contentious. There has been a huge amount of research attempting to establish sex-related differences in brain capacity. It is politically highly sensitive. Disputed claims about cognitive differences are that women are born to be better with language than men, and men are innately better than women with visual and spatial things. There are indeed some slight but fairly well-documented differences (Philips, Steele and Tanz 1987; Halpern 1992):

1 It has been claimed that girls statistically go through the stages of language development a little earlier than boys.
2 Girls have been said to be less likely to have language-related disturbances, such as stuttering and reading difficulties.
3 It has been claimed that the right and left hemispheres of the brains of girls and women tend to be less specialized in function than in boys and men (less lateralized). This means that the speech centres are not so exclusively established in the left hemisphere; women process speech on the right side more than men do. The upshot of this is that if a woman's left hemisphere is injured (through a stroke, for example), she will probably show less impairment of speech than a man would.

Difference 3 is often used to account for 1 and 2. There is a major problem with this, however. We have a chicken-and-egg situation again. How can we assume that the difference in lateralization is innate? Newborn babies don't fit the pattern at all. In fact, some researchers have discovered that *boys'* brains tend to be less lateralized. Environmental influence seems a far more plausible way of accounting for the differences. There is plenty of evidence indicating that boys and girls are spoken to differently. Apparently we talk to baby girls more, for instance. Might this not stimulate greater facility with language? It seems highly likely. To cut a long story short, after vast amounts of research trying to prove fundamental biological differences in the mental capacities of women and men, results have been inconclusive (see Hyde and McKinley 1997). Claims about lateralization, for example, have not been upheld in recent research using modern, non-intrusive methods that have made it possible to examine healthy subjects rather than relying on observation of people who've suffered brain damage (Frost et al. 1999; Knecht et al. 2000).

What intrigues me is that people want to find such differences at all. As British linguist Deborah Cameron has observed, 'studies of "difference" are not just disinterested quests for the truth, but in an unequal society inevitably have a political dimension' (Coates and Cameron 1988: 5–6). More recently, a feminist biologist, Anne Fausto-Sterling, has argued that 'biology is politics by other means' and stresses the need to continue to 'fight our politics through arguments about biology'. In this process, she urges us to never 'lose sight of the fact that our debates about the body's biology are always simultaneously moral, ethical, and political debates about social and political equality and the possibilities for change. Nothing less is at stake' (Fausto-Sterling 2000: 255).

In dealing with learned kinds of activity, such as linguistic interaction, we can only speak with any certainty about gendered behaviour. Linguistic interaction is obviously behaviour which has been learned, and there is little point in trying to account for it by talking about innate qualities. In societies with sex-exclusive differences in language use, choice from among a range of lexicogrammatical options is part of gender performance. The word 'choice' is perhaps not the right one, since the forms for use by women and men are enforced by prescriptive rule. They can be compared with prescriptive rules in English such as 'two negatives make a positive', 'never end a sentence with a preposition' or 'don't say "him and me", say "he and I"'. Speakers are corrected, one way or another, if they produce inappropriate forms. The consequences of transgressing the rules are probably more dire than they would be for an English speaker these days, however. Occasionally there are exceptions when speakers are not corrected and suffer as a result, as we know from Fortune's research among the Karajá in Brazil.

Gender, then, is not biological but psycho-social; it should always be considered in the context of social relations between people. The sex/ gender distinction has been contested, however, as have other nature/ nurture arguments. The next section considers why.

Sex and gender as troublesome dichotomies

A collection on language and gender research opens with the observation that 'Just as we rarely question our ability to breathe, so we rarely question the habit of dividing human beings into two categories: females and males' (Bergvall, Bing and Freed 1996: 1). The authors of this first chapter, American linguists Janet Bing and Victoria Bergvall, go on to consider how human beings need to impose categories and boundaries on experience in order to understand it. This is something very familiar to linguists. Boundaries in our experiences can be quite fuzzy and vague; language puts things into clear-cut categories, imposing boundaries, limits and divisions on reality. Bing and Bergvall observe, for example, that we have the distinct categories of 'day' and 'night', but the actual boundaries between them are indistinct. We cannot identify precisely when it stops being daytime and becomes night. Day and night are bipolar categories that language imposes; the reality is a continuum. Similarly, sociolinguists interested in dialect continua are used to dealing with indistinct boundaries. It can be very difficult to determine where one variety of a dialect or language ends and another begins. The point Bing and Bergvall are making is that a lot of experience is best described as a continuum and bipolar categories are not always accurate.

I have already observed that gender is a continuum. It makes sense to talk about degrees of masculinity and femininity. We can say that one person is more feminine than another. But surely male and female are clear-cut categories, aren't they? Well, usually yes, but not always. It turns out that sex is also a continuum. In the last section I presented the basic determinants of foetal sexual development. Sometimes things happen differently, however. For instance, a foetus with X and Y chromosomes may not receive its crucial dose of the 'male' hormone testosterone at eight weeks. It may not be enough. Or, if enough, it may be at the wrong time. 'Mistakes' like these mean intersexed development of the foetus. Not all individuals are born male or female. Some are born as both, some as

'Right. Tall ones at the back, short ones at the front!'
A drawback of bipolar categories

neither, and some are indeterminate. According to figures cited by Bing and Bergvall, for every 30,000 births there is 1 intersexed infant. Other accounts put the figure very much higher. 'Although the birth of inter-sexed individuals is not rare', as they observe, 'it *is* unmentionable, even in tabloids that regularly report such outrageous topics as copulation with extraterrestrials and the reappearance of Elvis'. In industrialized societies, the binary distinction between male and female is medically enforced. Exceptions are 'corrected', surgically and with hormone treatment. Since this is the case, it should be no surprise that physicians acknowledge that sex as well as gender is socially constructed (Bing and Bergvall 1996: 8–9).

In some writing on language and gender there is a tendency to treat the social categories of masculine and feminine as bipolar. This is particularly true of work on distinct interactional styles of men and women, especially the popularizing versions (see chapter 5). Such studies put essentialism out through the front door, only to let it in again at the back. That is to say, they do away with biological essentialism, just to replace it with a kind of social essentialism, which is just as bad. This problem of an obsession with bipolar difference is a theoretical concern that I return to in chapter 6, at the end of part II. Some of the studies presented in parts I and II treat sex/gender as unproblematic, establishing their research objective as identifying differences in linguistic behaviour between members of each bipolar category: men speak like this, women like that. Other studies avoid this, setting out to investigate not so much correlations of language and gender per se as of language and gendered social roles (such as position in a family group). Bing and Bergvall pessimistically predict that, despite our increasing awareness of the problems of gender polarization and stereotyping, 'there will probably be no decline in the number of students who begin their term-paper research with the question, "How is the language of men and women different?" Such questions strengthen deeply held certainties that mere facts cannot dislodge' (1996: 6). I sincerely hope they are mistaken. Refreshingly, a recent textbook includes a section headed 'It's Not about Sex Difference' in each of its chapters dealing with family, education, work, religion and media (DeFrancisco and Palczewski 2007).

But it is not just that sex and gender both need to be seen as continua. Ultimately the distinction between them simply doesn't hold up. The dualism that the sex/gender distinction implies breaks down, when you consider that cultural and environmental factors crucially influence the potential for foetal development even before the moment of conception (in fact, long before, if advisory texts for would-be parents are to be believed). In an article on the formative influence of culture on the development of the human skeleton, Fausto-Sterling convincingly argues that 'our bodies physically imbibe culture' (2005: 1495). 'The sex–gender or nature–nurture accounts of difference', she goes on to say, 'fail to appreciate the degree to which culture is a partner in producing body systems commonly referred to as biology' (2005: 1516). So which comes first: sex or gender? Neither.

There is also another kind of problem with assumed correspondences between sex and gender. In *Female Masculinity*, Judith Halberstam (1998) undermines the assumption that there are inevitable links between maleness and masculinity, or between femaleness and femininity. Her book-length study of 'masculinity without men' has one overarching objective: to render visible the widespread but studiously ignored phenomenon of female masculinity. In doing so, she uncouples masculinity from maleness altogether, challenging the powerful gender ideology that weds 'masculinity to maleness and to power and domination' (1998: 2).

Why is language study important for feminism?

In this book, I want to avoid too much exclusive attention to women's language use. There is a tendency to assume language and gender is all about women and language, or even to equate the study of language and gender with women's studies. If language and gender is part of women's studies it is because of woeful neglect of the field elsewhere, not because it is the natural preserve of women. It is a sad reflection on the many gaps in academic investigation that women's studies has been left to fill. In an ideal world, gender issues would be addressed in every discipline and there would not have to be a women's studies to make up for their absence.

What modern language and gender study does have a close connection with is not so much women's studies as feminism. The two are closely related, of course, but they are not the same thing. As I take a look at some early ideas about men, women and language, as I will in chapters 2 and 3, I think it will become apparent that the assumptions underlying the equation of 'gender and language' with 'women and language' are decidedly dodgy.

So, you may be wondering, what is the relationship between language and gender, and why is it of interest to feminists? Well, there are various answers to the first of these questions, and I think a brief airing of them will answer the second question as well.

One view of the relationship between language and gender – which might be called the 'weak' one – is that language simply reflects society, so that social divisions on gender grounds are reflected in patterns of language use. Let me consider some examples. Women in work settings are frequently subordinate in status to men, and this is reflected in their greater use of politeness strategies. Also, the existence of two traditional honorific titles for women (**Miss**, **Mrs**), in contrast with the single honorific **Mr** for men, reflects the importance society puts on women's marital status. The way a shopkeeper addresses an adult man as **sir**, but an adult woman as **dear** or **love**, reflects society's unequal treatment of men and women. According to a 'stronger' view, language does not just reflect gender divisions; it actually creates them. Things like differences in the use of politeness strategies, the asymmetry of the titles **Miss** and **Mrs** in relation to **Mr** and asymmetrical usage of terms of address for women and men are not just reflecting society – they actively create and sustain inequality. So the two extremes are language-as-mirror and language-as-reproductive.

I think we probably need to negotiate a position somewhere between the two. You may have come across the 'strong' view in some form or other. In this view, languages embody different world-views and our con-sciousness is constrained, even created, by the language we have. An early version of this is what is often known as the Sapir–Whorf hypothesis (we must bear in mind, though, that the linguists this hypothesis was named after were attending solely to grammar and vocabulary, not linguistic interaction). Edward Sapir has this to say:

> Human beings do not live in the objective world alone, nor alone in the world of social activity as ordinarily understood, but very much at the mercy of the particular language which has become the medium of expression for their society. . . . The fact of the matter is that the 'real world' is to a large extent unconsciously built up on the language habits of the group. No two languages are ever sufficiently similar to be consid-ered as representing the same social reality. (1929: 209–10)

This idea that different languages effectively provide different realities for their speakers is an intriguing notion, and quite appealing, I think. At its most extreme, though, it is a deterministic view: language determines what we are and there is nothing we can do about it. If people's lives are totally shaped by the language of their society, what can they possibly do to bring about change? What is the point of even trying? A less extreme version is what has motivated language reforms: movements promoting non-racist, non-sexist language use, and so on. The 'weak' view – that lan-guage simply reflects – stops us from getting absurd about the importance of language. Consider: it isn't enough to eliminate racist language and still behave in the same old racist ways. The point of it is to raise people's awareness and stimulate social change. This point is nicely expressed by Nan van den Bergh:

> To change language may not be to embark on drastic social changes directly, but it does involve consciousness-raišing; that is, bringing awareness of a problem to the public's attention. The assumption under-lying consciousness-raising is that before a behavior can be changed, there must be awareness that a situation exists warranting alteration. (1987: 132)

With all this in mind, feminists' interest in language and gender is understandable. Feminism is a form of politics dedicated to bringing about social changes, and ultimately to arresting the reproduction of systematic inequalities between men and women. Feminist interest in language and gender resides in the complex part language plays, alongside other social practices and institutions, in reflecting, creating and sustaining gender divisions in society. It is this role played by language that is the subject of this book. This will involve us in a wide range of issues, from expectations about how women and men ought to speak, to restrictions on women's access to public forms of talk, the division of conversational 'labour' among couples, representations of masculinity and femininity in the mass media, and much more besides.

Further reading

Sex-exclusive and sex-preferential differentiations

Most introductions to sociolinguistics tend to have a bit on these, although the actual terms may not crop up. A good survey of early sex-exclusive differences research is the article in which the two terms first appeared: Bodine (1975). An alternative is the chapter called 'Language and sex' in Trudgill (1995).

'Brain sex' / evolutionary psychology

Two popular science books on 'brain sex' are Baron-Cohen (2003) and Brizendine (2006). There is a critique of the former in ch. 6 of Cameron (2007). For a detailed biologist's account of just how tenuous research on 'brain sex' is, read ch. 5 of Fausto-Sterling (2000).

Sex/gender

Useful readings on sex and gender are Connell (2002) and chapter 1 of Eckert and McConnell-Ginet (2003). For issues of gender polarization and sex/gender continua, the source already mentioned is essential reading (Bergvall, Bing and Freed 1996). See also Bem (1993) and the websites of the Intersex Society of North America (www.isna.org) and the UK Intersex Association (www.ukia.co.uk). Fausto-Sterling (2000) is also insightful, but its detail may challenge some non-scientists.

2

Talking proper

This chapter looks at sociolinguistic survey work on English speakers that shows women consistently using 'Standard' forms more than men. It examines the influence of existing stereotypes on the survey results and their interpretation. It also briefly examines gender differences in pitch and other aspects of voice quality, in which the impact of stereotyping is also important.

Women, men and 'Standard' English

Like all languages, English is not homogeneous. It varies according to the circumstances in which it is spoken or written. To put it another way, the variety of English used depends on *where* it is being used, *why, when, how* and, of course, *who by*. A single individual's language will vary according to the needs of the social context, in terms of level of formality required by the relationship between speaker and hearer and what they are talking about, as well as other aspects of the social setting. The English you might use in a news broadcast is very different from the English you would use to gossip about the last film you saw or, for that matter, to conduct a lecture on astrophysics.

English also varies according to geographical location, both within and across national boundaries. In the British Isles there is enormous diversity; people in different regions speak varieties – *regional dialects* – with very distinctive differences. The United States also has distinct regional varieties, although they are not as strikingly diverse as in Britain. Other countries have distinctive national varieties: Nigerian English, South African English, etc. As well as varying according to geography, language also varies vertically, so to speak. Education and the socioeconomic opportunities of a person's family influence their language. For example, regardless of what part of the country they come from, university students in Britain are all likely to speak and write 'Standard' British English, rather than their local vernacular. Students from Belfast, Birmingham and London will sound rather different; in fact, they may initially find it hard to understand one another. But they will use very similar grammar and vocabulary; they will all have the same *social dialect*. As they get to know one another, their accents will converge; that is, they will start to iron out differences in pronunciation, almost certainly without realizing it. A lot of students report that when they go home in the holidays, their old school friends accuse them of 'talking posh'.

Social stratification studies

A substantial body of early, non-feminist work on language and gender came out of wider studies of social dialects. These were the sociolinguistic surveys of the sixties and seventies which, among other things, claimed to establish a rather intriguing difference between the language used by women and men: namely that, across social classes, women consistently tend to use more of the features associated with the prestige 'Standard' variety of a language than men do. A lot of this research was on English, but there are similar findings produced more recently for a range of other languages (see Further Reading for some examples).

The best-known survey work of this type was conducted by the American linguist William Labov, and examined language variation in New York City (Labov 1966). This kind of research involved study of large-scale patterns of language use, with a central interest in the processes of language change (What brings about linguistic change? In particular communities, who initiates it and why?). The field as a whole is sometimes known as *variationist sociolinguistics* or *variation theory*. It was far more rigorous and systematic than early work in dialectology. The social stratification studies of the sixties and seventies were concerted attempts at representative sampling of demographic groups. Early dialectology was far less systematic and was riddled with sexist assumptions. In traditional dialectology, women informants were virtually non-existent and, if justification for their absence was required at all, it was claimed that women were a poor source for authentic dialect. For example, Harold Orton claimed, without offering any evidence, that 'men speak vernacular more frequently, more consistently and more genuinely than women' (Orton 1962: 15).

The starting point for sociolinguistic study of this kind is identification of certain linguistic features which are known to vary in general: linguistic *variables*. In theory these could be any kind of feature; in practice sociolinguists have focused mostly on elements of pronunciation. A variable occurring in a lot of varieties of English is (ng), the final sound in words like

walking and **laughing**. This (ng) sound has two *variants* – that is, it can be pronounced in two different ways:

variable: (ng)
variants: [n] [ŋ]

The first of these two variants, [n], is the pronunciation that is often represented as **n'** in spelling: **walkin'** and **laughin'**. It is a common pronunciation of (ng) in the vernacular. The second variant, [ŋ], is the Standard form.

The amount a person uses one variant rather than the other depends on their social background and on the formality demanded by the situation. In order to collect data that would cover both these factors, Labov contacted a sample of the New York population intended to represent different social classes and devised a sociolinguistic interview. The interview was designed to elicit a range of 'styles' of speech, from highly self-conscious and formal to relaxed and informal. Labov found that, as he expected, the higher up the social scale and the more formal the speech style, the more often prestige variants occurred. He also found that in each social class women were consistently producing more of the prestigious forms than men in the same class.

Peter Trudgill, a British linguist, conducted a survey in Norwich which was modelled on Labov's New York survey. Trudgill taped a sociolinguistic interview from each of his informants. As in Labov's study, this was intended to elicit different degrees of formality. They were asked to read out a passage and a list of words. They were also asked some fairly formal interview-type questions, then asked some other questions that were designed to make them relax and forget to monitor their speech (such as 'Was there ever a teacher at school you were really scared of?'). The responses to these different sections of the interview were taken to be samples of four speech 'styles': 'wordlist style', 'reading passage style', 'formal' and 'casual'. For the social dimension in processing his findings, Trudgill assigned people to a class category. For this he used the Registrar General's Scale, on which they were allocated to a particular class on the basis of a range of factors, including place of residence and education. Men were also allocated according to their own occupation and earnings. For women, husbands' occupation and earnings were used, or their fathers' if they were not married.

The elaborate-looking table 2.1 presents Trudgill's findings for the (ng) variable in his Norwich sample. It states the occurrence of the non-Standard variant [n] as a percentage (0 means none at all; 100 means always). As you

Table 2.1   Variations of (ng) in Norwich by sex, class and style (frequency of non-
Standard variant [n])

	Reading wordlist	Reading passage	Formal	Casual
Middle middle class				
Male	0	0	4	31
Female	0	0	0	0
Lower middle class				
Male	0	20	27	17
Female	0	0	3	67
Upper working class				
Male	0	18	81	95
Female	11	13	68	77
Middle working class				
Male	24	43	91	97
Female	20	46	81	88
Lower working class				
Male	60	100	100	100
Female	17	54	97	100

Source: Trudgill 1972

can see from the table, in most cases women are using a lower percentage of the vernacular, non-Standard variant [n] than men in the same social class category. (There are three exceptions: upper-working-class women in the wordlist reading, middle-working-class women in passage reading and lower-middle-class women in casual speech.)

This kind of information is often presented in a more easily accessible way by condensing the findings for the different styles, as in table 2.2. The condensation of the figures makes it easier to interpret at a glance but actually oversimplifies the picture, since it irons out the wrinkles. The exceptions to the overall trend are not included. Trudgill found a similar pattern with other variables. Sociolinguistic surveys like Trudgill's mapped out general trends, but a lot of exceptions were hidden in the presentation of results. His sample was taken from fifty people. Given the size of the sample, any generalizations must be tentative.

In addition to the elements of the sociolinguistic interview mentioned above (taken from Labov), Trudgill also asked his informants to self-evaluate. He found that women more often over-reported (that is, claimed to use Standard forms when they did not), while men tended to under-report (claimed to use more vernacular, non-Standard forms than they actually did).

Table 2.2 Variations of (ng) in Norwich by sex and class only (frequency of non-
Standard variant [n])

	Middle MC	Lower MC	Upper WC	Middle WC	Lower WC
Male	4	27	81	91	100
Female	0	3	68	81	97

Source: Trudgill 1995: 70

Accounting for the differences

How can we account for this pattern of differences? Trudgill points out that, like the so-called 'sex-exclusive' kinds of difference in traditional societies (the kind we looked at in chapter 1), these differences in language use are the result of social attitudes about the proper behaviour of women and men. Trudgill's own suggested explanations centre around notions of status consciousness. It is worth quoting him at some length here, because the points he raises are among the problems with sociolinguistic survey work that I will be considering in the next section. These are his early speculations (expanded in his later work):

> Women informants, then, use forms associated with the prestige stand-ard more frequently than men. How can we explain this phenomenon? What follows is necessarily speculative, but there would appear to be perhaps two interconnected explanatory factors.
>
> 1 Women in our society are more status-conscious than men, generally speaking . . . and are therefore more aware of the social significance of linguistic variables. There are two possible reasons for this:
>
> (i) The social position of women in our society is less secure than that of men, and, usually, subordinate to that of men. It may be, therefore, that it is more necessary for women to secure and signal their social status linguistically and in other ways, and they may for this reason be more aware of the importance of this type of signal. (This may be particularly true of women who are not working.)
>
> (ii) Men in our society can be rated socially by their occupation, their earning power, and perhaps by their own abilities – in other words by what they *do*. For the most part, however, this is not possible for women. It may be, therefore, that they have instead to be rated on how they *appear*. Since they are not rated by their occupation or by their occupational success, other signals of status, including speech, are correspondingly more important.

2   The second, related, factor is that WC speech, like other aspects of WC culture, appears, at least in some Western societies, to have connotations of masculinity (see Labov 1966: 495), probably because it is associated with the roughness and toughness supposedly char-acteristic of WC life which are, to a certain extent, considered to be desirable masculine attributes. They are not, on the other hand, considered to be desirable feminine characteristics. On the contrary, features such as refinement and sophistication are much preferred. (Trudgill 1972, see Thorne and Henley 1975: 91–2)

According to Trudgill, then, women use the prestige variants more often than men because they are more status conscious. This is because they are less secure socially and more likely to be judged on appearances than men. Men, on the other hand, are judged by what they do, so that they are not under pressure to use the prestige variants. Moreover, the non-Standard forms found in the vernacular, used predominantly by the working class, have masculine connotations which motivate men to use them, but not women.

To account for the over- and under-reporting that he discovered in his informants' self-evaluations, he drew upon Labov's distinction between *overt* and *covert prestige*. Women liked to think they used forms associated with the prestige Standard, and tended to report that they did more often than was actually the case. This showed their desire for overt prestige. Men, on the other hand, liked to think they used the vernacular more than they actually did. They found the non-Standard forms carried another, hidden kind of status, or covert prestige.

Some problems
The first thing to note is that the phenomenon requiring explanation, according to Trudgill in the extract quoted above, is women's greater use of prestige Standard forms, rather than men's lesser use of them. Why is it the behaviour of those using the Standard forms more often that needs to be explained, and not the other way around? Feminist critics of stratificational studies have taken issue with this apparent example of the male-as-norm in operation, an underlying assumption that men's behav-iour is 'normal' and where women's differs it is a deviation that needs to be accounted for (Cameron and Coates 1988; Holmes 1992).

Trudgill's point 1 relates to what he terms overt prestige. From a contemporary perspective, the initial observation – that women are more 'status-conscious' than men – sounds distinctly odd. Are women really more preoccupied with keeping up with the Joneses than men are?

Certainly a claim like this needs backing up with evidence. Several British linguists have demonstrated that the work he refers to in order to substantiate the claim is very shaky indeed (Deuchar 1987: 305; Graddol and Swann 1989: 53–5). It is claimed that because women lack status, particularly those women who are not in paid employment, they try to acquire it through the way they speak – by using prestigious Standard forms. If there were any evidence for this happening – if, that is, working women could be shown to use fewer Standard forms than women working in the home – then it would quite plausibly back up the claim that women are using Standard forms to gain overt prestige. However, what research there has been on variation between women with and without jobs has not provided such back-up. In fact, women who worked in the home used *fewer* Standard forms than women in paid employment (see next section, on 'Market forces and social networks', for discussion).

Moreover, if it is covert prestige which motivates men to use vernacular forms, then clearly men are also being 'status-conscious'. In making his ill-substantiated sweeping generalization about women, Trudgill was exercising an old male privilege that has since come under a barrage of criticism from feminists. (We will come across other linguists who have done the same in chapter 3.)

He makes an interesting suggestion that women's greater use of Standard forms compared with men stems from the fact that they are rated on their appearance while men are not. Women certainly need to spend more time on their appearance, and they are judged on the basis of it to an extent that men are not. Trudgill presumably does not mean visual appearance, however, but something rather more nebulous, and the basic distinction between 'doing' and 'appearing' that his suggestion rests on is a difficult one to sustain in any case. This becomes particularly clear when we look at his point 2. If men can acquire covert prestige by using vernacular language with masculine connotations, then they must be rated on how they 'appear' as well as what they 'do'.

The association of working-class speech and masculinity comes from Labov's New York City survey work. But among women and men from most social backgrounds, use of vernacular forms increases in informal situations. When people are in relaxed settings they speak less formally and tend to slip into the vernacular. Why should use of the informal vernacular be thought of as masculine? It is an association which has the effect of making the speech of working-class women disappear from view, as feminist linguists have observed: '*Why* should the vernacular be associated with masculinity? There is a strong implication here that working-class women are *outside working-class culture*: whereas men have in-group (vernacular) norms, women are perpetual "lames" deferring to the norms of the super-ordinate class' (Cameron and Coates 1988: 17).

In Trudgill's account, women are said to use non-Standard forms less frequently because they convey working-class 'roughness and toughness', which are acceptable in men but not 'considered to be desirable feminine characteristics'; in women, 'refinement and sophistication' are 'much pre-ferred'. Here again we have the male-as-norm in operation. Working-class men's language is the real thing: working-class women's deviates from the norm, which is male. There is indeed evidence that people in some com-munities consider non-Standard speech more appropriate for men, tending to associate it with masculinity (James 1996: 113–14). Trudgill simply reit-erates this commonsensical association and notion of appropriacy.

It is not just the status-based explanations for sociolinguistic survey findings that are a problem. The way the surveys were conducted influ-enced the nature of the findings. In assigning women to a class category, traditional family structure was assumed, with the father as the bread-winner and the whole family taking its social position from him. Wives were assessed on the basis of their husbands' occupation and earnings. As a consequence, women may frequently have been wrongly classified. It seems highly likely that the way women's social class was assigned in terms of the men in their lives could account for some of the results.

The most serious flaw of sociolinguistic surveys, however, lies in the interviews themselves. When confronted with the tables of figures – the neatly processed outcome of the interviews – it is difficult to imagine the face-to-face interaction that must have been involved. The sociolin-guistic interview was the same for all the informants, regardless of their background. For many of the informants it would have been an 'unequal encounter' with the highly educated middle-class interviewer. The status of the informants differed, but they were treated to identical interviews. In Labov's survey work, the interviewers were all men, so that women expe-rienced a different interview context (that is, cross-sex). Empirical research on spoken interaction has shown that differences of this kind are too important to be ignored. They may have played a large part in shaping the survey findings. In particular, it seems highly likely that when the women informants were being interviewed by men they would have been under more pressure to 'talk proper' than their male counterparts; they would have been in a more formal speech situation, warranting greater use of Standard forms.

Another factor which may have had considerable influence on the results is accommodation. People's speech patterns converge or diverge in face-to-face interaction, depending on how cooperative or sympathetically inclined they are towards one another. But as we do not know what the speech of the interviewers was like (did they use any vernacular forms themselves, for instance?), we cannot even begin to assess the possible influence this might have on the interview results. (Trudgill does give some attention to the issue of accommodation in a more recent study (1986), discussing his own accommodation to the speech of his informants.)

In early stratification studies, then, there were a lot of problems with sociolinguists' methods for collecting their material and processing it. They were beset with many of the same problems of bias and stereotype that have troubled other early work on differences between men and women. Alternatives to the social stratification approach to language variation involved attention to people's patterns of interaction, to the speech communities in which they live and work. I will outline some research of this kind next.

Market forces and social networks

This type of study was based on different assumptions about people's reasons for using Standard or vernacular forms of speech. It started with the hypothesis that the most consistent use of the vernacular will be found among people who are most integrated into local social networks. It asked a different question: not why is women's language closer to Standard than men's, but what conditions support people's use of local varieties? Lesley Milroy, a sociolinguist from Northern Ireland, puts it this way: 'Instead of positing a sociolinguistic continuum with a local vernacular at the bottom and a prestige dialect at the top, with linguistic movement of individuals in a generally upward direction, we may view the vernacular as a positive force' (1980: 19).

Group membership was the key issue in these studies: whether or not the informants lived in tight, close-knit communities; what their patterns of work and leisure relations were like. People's speech is influenced by their patterns of interaction in the speech communities in which they live and work. And communities, of course, vary enormously. In some, women are confined to the private sphere and men have wider social contacts. In other communities, the converse situation can be found: it is the women with the wider social contacts and men's contacts that are more restricted.

Some researchers adopted a *market forces* view, identifying economics as the crucial factor influencing use of Standard or vernacular forms. This view looks to work patterns and relations as the determining factor, avoiding the reliance on a notion of pre-existing class structure that characterized the social stratification studies. In Patricia Nichols's research into a black community in Carolina, for instance, she looked to gender differences in employment to account for variations in use of creole forms (Nichols 1983). She found that many women had jobs that took them outside their immediate community and, moreover, required them – forced them – to use more standardized, less localized forms. Men on the other hand tended to work locally and in jobs that did not require Standard English.

Other researchers adopted a similar view, concentrating on the notion of social network strength. Like the market forces account, examining variation in terms of social networks provided an alternative to the social stratificationist view (that Standard or vernacular forms are chosen to secure social status). In the *social networks* view, tightness of community ties is what determines language choices, rather than social status. In other words, you speak the way you do not because you're a social climber but because of the people you are in regular contact with on a daily basis, because of the need to belong in your community, to fit in with the people around you.

These two alternatives to the social stratificationist account – market forces and social networks – are closely related in that the strength of community ties is strongly influenced by market forces. One of the best-known social network studies was conducted in Ulster by Lesley Milroy (1980). Her research took place in three areas of Belfast (Clonard, the Hammer and Ballymacarrett) which each had differing patterns of employment and correspondingly different social networks. Ballymacarrett was the most traditional of the three areas, with the men still working locally in close-knit groups, in the shipyards. The women of Ballymacarrett were in far less dense social networks; many were in daily contact with people outside their own speech community. In this area, Milroy found the expected pattern: men consistently used more local, vernacular forms than women did.

However, the other two areas were rather different. The most striking divergence from the expected pattern was among young women in Clonard, an area with high male unemployment. In Clonard, where the younger women's social networks were denser than those of their male counterparts, *they* were the greater users of some vernacular forms. In this Belfast study, the expected pattern – that is, of women tending towards Standard, and men using fewer Standard and more vernacular forms than women – was only found where the men were in traditional local employment, in tight-knit groups, and the women were more dispersed, in employment outside the area. Other studies, by Susan Gal in Austria (1979) and by Beth Thomas in South Wales (1988), support this account. However, other findings indicate that there is more involved than market forces. Viv Edwards's research among black women in Dudley in the West Midlands indicates that community loyalties can override economic factors (Edwards 1988).

Such studies avoided the 'social climbing' view built into the social stratification studies, like the one I looked at earlier. By using different fieldwork methods, they also avoided the difficulties presented by the sociolinguistic interview. The definition of social network on which this research depended, however, runs into similar problems of male bias (see Cameron and Coates (1988) for discussion). In this chapter, I have focused on early models in variationist sociolinguistics and on the influence of stereotypes, and I have concentrated on research on English. But other languages have been studied too, and research in variationist sociolinguistics continues. As research has covered a range of social contexts, it should not be surprising that findings have differed considerably.

Gender signals

There are, then, perceptible differences in the pronunciation patterns of men and women. While findings have differed, the most consistent has been that women's speech, overall, tends to contain more prestige forms than men's. It has proved unsatisfactory to account for these differences in terms of class and notions of status consciousness, but it is clear that pronunciation is used to signal gender. In addition to norms and expectations about gendered behaviour, this signalling of gender is certainly tied up with community loyalties and work patterns in highly complex ways. In some localities, there are certain local forms that are used markedly more by the men, both working-class and middle-class, than by their female counterparts. For example, in Tyneside – an area in the north-east of England with a strong regional identity – there are two ways of pronouncing the consonant (k) between two vowels in a word such as **local**; there is the Standard variant [k] and the local vernacular variant, a glottal stop [ʔ]. Several small studies carried out in the region indicate that men almost *always* use the local variant, whereas the women's pronunciation of this particular variable is less consistent (Cowhig 1986; Rigg 1987; Turner 1988; all cited in Milroy 1992). It would seem that this single variant [ʔ] contributes in a small way to the establishment of masculine identities in Tyneside. I turn to issues of accent and masculinity in another social context in chapter 9, in a section entitled 'Real men in working-class Catalonia'.

Sex, gender and voice quality

> *As always that deep, slightly husky voice made Annie's spine tingle.*
> Diane Hamilton, *Passionate Awakening*

> *Her voice was ever soft, gentle and low, an excellent thing in woman.*
> William Shakespeare, *King Lear*

When you answer the telephone and the caller speaks, you immediately identify them as either male or female. You are very rarely mistaken. How is this? Clearly there are differences in the voices of women and men. But what are these differences, and are they matters of biology, or are they culturally acquired?

The stereotypes are familiar enough. The hero in a Mills & Boon novel sounds deep and husky, as in the first quotation above. We hear the epitome of masculinity in the hard, gravelly and resonant voice-over in trailers, particularly for films in the action-movie genre. A woman's voice is high-pitched and soft, breathy or squeaky (especially if she's blonde). Men are supposed to have loud voices, while a woman's voice should be 'soft, gentle and low'. These stereotypes are culturally variable, both within and across languages. In American English (at least in a Hollywood variety of it), nasality is another stereotypically masculine trait. This 'nasal twang' is not a feature of masculine-sounding voices in other varieties of English.

The voice is produced physically and a person's voice quality is clearly affected by their anatomy (Laver 1994: 398). But does anatomy alone account for the characteristic differences in voice quality between men and women? To answer this question, I need to consider the physical basis of the voice: the organs of speech. Speech is produced by interference with airflow, virtually always on the out-breath. When we speak, what we do is use our organs of speech to interfere with the passage of air en route from our lungs to the outside world, via our vocal tract. Pitch – how high or deep the voice actually sounds – is determined by the rate of vibration of the vocal cords in the larynx, or 'voice box'. (Put a hand on your larynx and say something; you will feel your vocal cords vibrating.) How voice quality is perceived by others depends on something else, though: namely resonance. Resonance is determined by the dimensions of your vocal tract (from the larynx to the lips). In fact, you have three vocal cavities: in your pharynx (throat), your mouth and your nasal cavity.

The rate of vibration of the vocal cords (technically referred to as *fundamental frequency*) basically depends on their length and thickness, in just the same way as if you were to twang different sizes of rubber band or guitar string. It also depends upon muscle tension. Tensed vocal cords will vibrate more rapidly and so produce a higher pitch than lax ones, something you will be familiar with if you have ever tuned a guitar or some other stringed instrument. A typical male fundamental frequency might lie within the range of 100–150 vibrations a second (Hertz, or Hz), while a typical woman's fundamental frequency might lie in the range 200–250 Hz. The sound produced by the vibrating vocal cords is actually made up of multiples of that frequency (making up its *harmonic structure*). The different dimensions of the resonating chambers of men and women amplify different parts of this frequency spectrum. Compare this with the difference you would get between two instruments with different bodies for resonating chambers that have been fitted with the same strings.

Fundamental frequency, tension of the vocal cords and resonant structure together are heard as voice quality. In speech, people vary their pitch a great deal, in order to produce an intonation pattern. Otherwise speech would be produced in an intolerable monotone. Pitch tends to rise with loudness; for example, when shouting. And, of course, people can 'put on' voices: we can deliberately manipulate our vocal organs to make drastic alterations to our voice quality.

The voice quality of men and women, then, has anatomical determinants: the length and thickness of their vocal cords, frequency of vibration and the resulting impression of pitch, and the capacity of their resonating chambers. Since adult men tend on average to be bigger than adult women, this would appear to explain men's lower-pitched voices. Men have a larger Adam's apple (thyroid cartilage), and since vocal cords are attached to this structure, men's tend to be longer. There is also evidence that men have longer vocal tracts. Experimental work (Fant 1966) shows that men have a pharynx which is an average of 2.3 cm longer than a woman's.

I now need to complicate the picture by considering the voices of children. Male and female children are very similar in size, with boys on average being slightly larger. So we may assume there is not much difference in their vocal anatomy. At birth, boys' fundamental frequency is marginally *higher* than that of girls, a slight difference which is usually attributed to greater muscle tension in boys. It remains either higher or virtually the same as girls' until puberty. Another physical factor affecting perceived pitch is the influence of hormones. Boys reach puberty when their bodies start producing quantities of testosterone/androgen. This is the hormone that brings on sexual maturity: the development of the testicles, the growth of pubic hair. At the same time, they develop their Adam's apple; the larynx and its vocal cord tissue increase in size, causing the voice to drop as much as an octave, sometimes quite spectacularly. In medieval times, boy singers were sometimes castrated before puberty, so that they would not lose their highly valued male soprano voices. Incidentally, castration jokes about men suddenly speaking in high-pitched voices are based on male fears, not facts. The growth of the larynx is irreversible.

Hormones do not come into the picture until puberty, and girls' and boys' fundamental frequency at a particular age is virtually the same. Nevertheless people can recognize the sex of pre-pubertal speakers. We don't just identify small children as girls and bigger ones as boys. In an experimental study with a group of girls and boys aged from four to twelve, listeners were successful in recognizing speaker sex 81 per cent of the time (Sachs, Lieberman and Erickson 1973). They speculated that there were two complementary reasons for this. The listeners were assessing the child's age and size first, before judging its sex; and the children were manipulating their voice quality in order to conform with norms of masculine and feminine speech.

If the second of these is correct – that is, if children are adjusting their voice quality to conform with the appropriate gendered norms of speech – then male and female voice differences are clearly being learned. A study of pitch among adults in the south of England showed that, although there were differences in average pitch between men and women, there was also a good deal of overlap (Graddol and Swann 1983). The men in the study used only the lower part of their pitch range. They did this by using relatively monotonous intonation patterns. Women showed greater variability in intonation; they also varied more from one to another than the men did. A speaker's deployment of pitch range is flexible. Infants, despite their small size, have a huge vocal range, far greater than any of the adults in Graddol and Swann's study. Adults are capable of increasing their range, though, with practice (consider, for example, the vocal agility of impressionists and drag artists).

So it really does seem as though there is some gender display involved in pitch. The differences between the sexes appear to be culturally, as well as anatomically, determined. They are being accentuated or even exaggerated. As Jacqueline Sachs has remarked:

> Adult men and women may modify their articulators, lowering or
> raising their formant frequencies, to produce voices that aim toward

male–female archetypes. Presumably these archetypes are culturally determined. In other words, men may try to talk as if they are bigger than they actually are, and women may talk as if they are smaller than they actually are. (Sachs 1975: 154)

Pitch range may also be providing cues to speaker sex. Greater intonational dynamism seems to be a feature of women's speech. Graddol and Swann's study revealed women in the south of England using a much wider range than their male counterparts. Many women in the United States have an even wider range, its peak being the well-known American women's falsetto shriek. Many American men use a vocal range smaller than that used by British men. Norms for vocal range for both men and women are highly variable. To British ears, for instance, Danish people often sound bored, especially men; conversely, Danes think the British sound over-emotional, and British men somewhat effeminate.

What about the other stereotypes? There is some evidence that women's voices tend to be more breathy than men's (Henton and Bladon 1985). Breathy voice is a phenomenon well known to phoneticians. It involves less vocal cord activity: partial closure and loose vibration, in other words, whispering. It can perhaps be viewed as the speech equivalent of taking up as little space as possible. It is presumably not conscious or deliberate, any more than posture is. Perhaps we can compare it with the unconscious gender display involved in the positioning of legs when seated: men's knees widespread, women's tucked in or even crossed.

We can finish by returning to the husky voice of the Mills & Boon hero quoted at the beginning of the section. Huskiness is a result of mucus in the throat. Sexual stimulation causes increased production by the mucous membranes. So huskiness sometimes has a hormonal cause, but it is not sex-specific. The heroine is aroused by the 'slightly husky voice' of the hero; this just means she is turned on by the fact that she turns *him* on (the desire of Mills & Boon heroines is fundamentally reactive; see Talbot 1997a). And a gravelly voice? That's just too many cigarettes.

Further reading

Men, women and prestige forms

Most sociolinguistics coursebooks contain a little coverage of sociolinguistic surveys and gender (e.g. Mesthrie et al. 2000). Some key readings are Labov (1990) (reprinted in Cheshire and Trudgill 1998); Milroy and Milroy (1993) (reprinted in Trudgill and Cheshire 1998); Eckert (1989) (reprinted in Coupland and Jaworski 1997); and Coates (2004). The last of these also contains detailed criticism of early dialectology. There is a critique of social stratification studies, more detailed than mine, in Cameron and Coates (1988). The collection in which this chapter appears is a good one for quantitative research on sex differentiation (Coates and Cameron 1988). Two recent summaries are chapter 8 of Eckert and McConnell-Ginet (2003) and Romaine (2003).

Anatomical and cultural determination of voice quality

For another account of the physical basis of the voice and discussion of learned behaviour, see chapter 2 of Graddol and Swann (1989). For more detail, with short descriptions of the experiments producing the findings used above, see Smith (1985).

3

'Women's language' and 'man made language'

This chapter examines early feminist claims about language. It presents Robin Lakoff's hypothesis that there is a distinct 'women's language', characterized by excessive politeness, lack of confidence and eagerness to please, and Dale Spender's claim that language is 'man made'.

Within linguistics, there is a long tradition of interest in language change. The eighteenth-century dictionary compilers were concerned by it, being intent on arresting what were perceived as corrupting influences. More recent language scholars have accepted the inevitability of language change and focused their energies instead on uncovering the mechanisms bringing it about. The sociolinguists whose survey work we looked at in chapter 2 were interested in what motivates sound shifts, in which segments of a population start using different pronunciations. One fairly consistent feature has been that, whatever women's contribution to language change is purported to be, it has not been viewed positively.

Early interest

A lot of early writing on the subject was based on little more than speculation, and simply reiterates the stereotypes and prejudices of the period. A classic example is a single chapter on 'The woman' in *Language: Its Nature, Development and Origin* by the Danish grammarian Otto Jespersen, in 1922. His book is subdivided into four parts, each dealing with different aspects; for example, one part is devoted to 'The child'. The chapter entitled 'The woman' appears in the part on 'The individual and the world', along with 'The foreigner', 'Pidgin' and 'Causes of change'. The very presence of this chapter, added in all apparent seriousness in his scholarly book on language, seems to suggest that the language women use deviates from the real thing. There is not, of course, any chapter or part purporting to focus on 'The man'.

Jespersen's claim is that women's contribution to language is to maintain its 'purity', caused by the way they instinctively shrink from coarseness and vulgarity (how does this fit in with your experience?):

> There can be no doubt that women exercise a great and universal influence on linguistic development through their instinctive shrinking from coarse and vulgar expressions and their preference for refined, and (in certain spheres) veiled and indirect expressions. In most cases that influence will be exercised privately and in the bosom of the family . . . the feminine point of view is unassailable, and there is reason to congratulate those nations, the English among them, in which the social position of women has been high enough to secure greater purity and freedom from coarseness in language than would have been the case if men had been the sole arbiters of speech. (Jespersen 1922: 246)

He maintains, however, that it is men's language which is endowed with vigour, imagination and creativity. Without it, 'there is a danger of the language becoming languid and insipid'. He continues with more specific claims about differences in the language used by men and women. These turn out to be indications of male intelligence and importance, and little more than abusive about women (despite the gentlemanly tone of the passage quoted above). He maintains that women have a smaller vocabulary and what vocabulary they do have is not always used properly. For example, women use intensifying adverbs 'with disregard of their proper meaning, as in German riesig klein [gigantically small], English awfully pretty, terribly nice . . . Danish rædsomt morsom [awfully funny]' (1922: 247). Women also suffer, he says, from an inability to complete a sentence, and while there is more volume of talk from women, there is less substance in it.

None of these claims was based on evidence. They were pure conjecture on Jespersen's part. It may very well have been true that the women in Jespersen's experience had smaller vocabularies than their male counterparts; as women were denied the level of education permitted for (some) men, one would expect them to have fewer words at their disposal. However, the claim about women's greater volubility (that is, that they talk more than men) is a familiar folklinguistic claim and there is now a substantial body of evidence to the contrary. It has been suggested (for instance, in Spender (1985)) that the amount of women's talk is not measured against men's, but against silence.

'Women's language'

An early feminist work on language and gender was Robin Lakoff's *Language and Woman's Place*, which first appeared in 1973 and in book form in 1975. In this influential book, Lakoff put forward a hypothesis which was taken up with great interest by other feminists. There is, she claimed, a distinct 'women's language'. She was referring to both language used *by* women and language used *about* them. Women, as she argued, 'experience linguistic discrimination in two ways: in the way they are taught to use language, and in the way general language use treats them' (Lakoff and Bucholtz 2004: 39). I will concentrate on the first of these here.

Careful to stress the cultural reasons behind it, she hypothesized that women use language in a distinctive way, notable for its uncertainty, weakness and excessive politeness. She proposed a range of features – supposed to express uncertainty and lack of confidence – as typical of women's speech. Bear in mind that she was only attempting to describe the language habits of women in what she calls 'Middle America'; she was not claiming to describe those of all women everywhere. Moreover, she appears to shift between claims about actual behaviour and claims about stereotypical expectations. Some of the features that she considers are lexical items:

Vocabulary of women's work A stock of words relating to women's activities and interests, such as **shirr**, **dart**. She says they would only be used tongue-in-cheek by men.

Precise colour terms Words such as **beige**, **ecru**, **aquamarine**. Lakoff reports seeing a man 'helpless with suppressed laughter at a discussion between two other people as to whether a book jacket was to be described as "lavender" or "mauve"' (2004: 43). She concludes from this that from a man's point of view such fine distinctions are trivial and beneath their notice.

Affective adjectives A great many words have affective meaning (to do with expressing feelings), not referential meaning (referring to some object or state of affairs). Lakoff suggests that, out of the wide range of adjectives used in expressing approval or admiration, many are strongly marked as feminine, such as **divine**, **adorable**, **charming**. She refers to such words as 'empty' adjectives.

Superpolite forms Here Lakoff is referring to things like avoidance of swear-words and extensive use of euphemism. Euphemisms are veiled, indirect expressions (saying **passed away** instead of **died**, for instance, or **put down** instead of **killed**). People use swear-words to express strong feelings, but in women they are supposed to be 'unladylike'. Lakoff contrasts these two hypothetical utterances: (a) Oh dear, you've put the peanut butter in the fridge again, and (b) Shit, you've put the peanut butter in the fridge again. She suggests that people would identify speaker (a) as a woman and (b) as a man, acknowledging that some women are becoming capable of uttering (b) 'publicly without flinching' (2004: 44). Oddly, non-swearing seems to be presented as something negative. (Note that swear-words could be called 'empty' words. Like the 'empty' adjectives women are supposed to use, they are used to express feelings, that is, their meaning is of the affective kind and not referential.)

Many of the features Lakoff proposes, however, are discourse particles and patterns of intonation, features which, like swear-words, do not really have any referential function but work affectively. Most of them serve one of two functions: they either weaken or strengthen the force of what a person is saying.

Hedges These are 'filler' items like **you know**, **well**, **kind of**, which reduce the force of an utterance. We often use them to add tentativeness to statements, making them seem less dogmatic. Sometimes they indicate uncertainty, but not always. For instance, **sort of** may be used to weaken the strength of an assertion that might cause offence, as in 'John is sorta short.' Lakoff maintains that women's use of these hedges 'arises out of a fear of seeming too masculine by being assertive and saying things directly' (2004: 79).

The intensifier **so** As in 'I like him so much!' Lakoff puzzlingly calls this a hedge too. It is supposed to weaken a speaker's strength of feeling. It has subsequently been viewed as a boosting device (like **very**).

Tag questions As the name suggests, these are questions tagged on to an utterance, such as **don't you?** or **haven't we?** According to Lakoff, they turn a statement into a question, so that its force is reduced. She takes them as indications of approval-seeking.

Rising intonation In many languages, including many varieties of English, intonation rises at the final point of questions. As with tag questions, this is supposed to turn a statement into a question, thereby weakening the force of it and making the speaker sound uncertain. This is Lakoff's example: (a) When will dinner be ready? (b) Oh . . . around six o'clock . . . ?

Hypercorrect grammar As Lakoff says, 'women are not supposed to talk rough' (2004: 80). What she is referring to here is women's tendency to use Standard forms more than men (see chapter 2). By 'hypercorrect', she seems to imply that they are more correct than they ought to be.

Emphatic stress Lakoff refers to this as speaking in italics, as in 'What a *beautiful* dress!' She suggests that women use over-the-top emphasis because they anticipate not being taken seriously. What she seems to be touching on here is women's greater pitch range (see chapter 2).

Another supposed female characteristic Lakoff mentions is lack of any sense of humour. Women can't tell jokes; not only that, they don't 'get' them either. In her whole account, there is a good deal of confusion as to whether she is intending to describe usage or stereotypes, that is, what women actually do, or what men claim they do. In the matter of sense of humour, she is clearly rearticulating a negative stereotype; presumably one which is, or was, circulated in North America (and among men rather than women, I presume).

The overall effect is a picture of women's language as inferior and deficient. Men's language is, by implication, superior and the norm from which women deviate. In this early speculative book, Lakoff accounted for gender differences in language use in terms of women's deficiencies: how women's language doesn't match up to men's. In doing so, she was unintentionally rearticulating existing prejudices about women's talk. She sometimes seems to echo Jespersen's complaints: compare her point about 'empty' adjectives like **divine** with his about 'improperly used' intensifying adverbs like **awfully**. In retrospect, it seems odd that this first feminist work on gender differences should echo the stereotypes so obviously. But, of course, it's easy to be wise after the event. Subsequent research has sometimes supported Lakoff's claims about women's greater use of particular discourse particles, but not her interpretation of them.

A lot of research triggered by her speculations was marred by a tendency to treat them as though they were set in stone. Very often, the researchers were not linguists and had a very limited understanding of language. For instance, they tended to work with an underlying assumption that a particular linguistic feature, such as a tag question, always has the same function. On the contrary, tag questions can serve different functions, as various linguists have demonstrated. Janet Holmes, a linguist from New Zealand, distinguishes two basic kinds. They may be *referential* (which tend to have rising intonation at the end) or *affective* (which tend to end with falling intonation). The referential tag signals uncertainty about the information content of an utterance; I might end a sentence with one if I need to check on the accuracy of what I am saying. This is the kind of usage Lakoff had in mind. The affective tag is different; it does not signal uncertainty. Holmes distinguishes between two kinds of affective tag: the facilitative tag (expressing solidarity/closeness) which is typically used to encourage a participant to contribute to the talk; the softening tag (softening the threatening nature of a criticism or command). Here are some examples (/ above words indicates terminal rise; \ indicates terminal fall):

Referential   Men use tag questions too, don't they?

Affective – facilitative   It's about your back, isn't it?

Affective – softening   That was silly, wasn't it?

Holmes discovered that, in samples of talk in educational settings, women used more of the facilitative type of tag than men did. Men, on the other hand, used more of the referential type of tag. The distribution of these different kinds of tag question in her data is laid out in table 3.1. Holmes's findings showed that the women in her sample were indeed producing tag questions more often than men. They were not, however, using them to indicate uncertainty. The tags they produced most often were the facilitative kind, used to express solidarity with the other person and encourage them to join in. She found that when men produced tags they tended to be of the referential kind, used to indicate uncertainty or press for agreement.

Holmes also looked at the distribution of tag questions according to role. She distinguished between facilitating and non-facilitating roles (as in teacher and pupil). Her findings are shown in table 3.2. As you can see, when the women in her sample were in facilitating roles they used tag questions more often than men. In non-leadership roles they used marginally fewer tags than the men did.

As it turned out, then, in Holmes's studies of different functions of tag questions, men's usage was closer to Lakoff's account; that is, the men seemed to be using them to express uncertainty more frequently than the women did. She looked at use of tag questions in educational settings. Dunn (1988) collected some examples in student accommodation. The speakers were female friends who were chatting while browsing through a magazine together. She found a few occurrences of the referential kind of meaning in tags, which are reproduced below:

Referential
S: Do you have cream puffs in this country or do you just call them 'profiteroles'?

Table 3.1 Distribution of tag questions according to sex of speaker and function of tag

	Female	Male
Referential	18 (35%)	24 (61%)
Affective		
Facilitative	30 (59%)	10 (25%)
Softening	3 (6%)	5 (13%)
Total	51	39

Source: Holmes 1984: 54.

Table 3.2 Distribution of tag questions according to role and sex of speaker

	Female	Male	Total
Leadership role / facilitator	38 (75%)	23 (59%)	61 (67.8%)
Non-leadership role	13 (25%)	16 (41%)	29 (32.2%)

Source: Holmes 1984: 57.

L:	Profiteroles
C:	Cream puffs are a different thing, aren't they?
	((about a friend with a new baby))
S:	Have you seen him at all?
L:	I haven't
K:	I should imagine for a couple of weeks she'd be sort of out of it, won't she?

But she found a huge number of the affective kind. It appears to be characteristic of friendly interaction between women. Below are just some examples of the affective tags she found in her data.

Affective

C:	Has it got a star sign in it?
S:	No it doesn't
C:	Ahh dear
S:	I know I know
C:	That's no good, is it? ((laughs))

S: I must admit they're fairly new pictures
K: They are, aren't they?
S: Mm

S: Giorgio perfume starts at £28!
L: You like that, don't you?
S: Mmmm it's beautiful

L: We've all got O levels in Maths!
S: God that was quick for you Louise, wasn't it?
L: ((laugh)) Sarcasm! I've been very quick today, haven't I, Clare?

In the last example, the second tag seems to be functioning differently. I think it has referential meaning, despite the falling intonation. Louise is pressing Clare for agreement, as part of her self-defence.

So, returning to Lakoff's hypothesis, empirical studies have backed up some of her speculations. Women do seem to use a lot of tag questions, for example, in some situations. What empirical research has not supported is her characterization of 'women's language' as tentative and uncertain. It's likely that her speculations were heavily influenced by stereotypes of women's speech; it may be, for example, that she interpreted women's tag questions in one way, and men's in another. As Holmes says, one person's feeble hedging is another's perspicacious qualification. Holmes, whose findings on tag questions we have looked at, interprets them differently. She has been building up a body of evidence for supportiveness as characteristic of women's talk – in New Zealand, at least (see Holmes 1995; also chapter 5 below).

Lakoff's early speculations were very valuable. They set the ball rolling. The value of her early exploration of issues in gender and language lies not so much in the identification of particular speech characteristics as in the political argument that she was making, namely that 'women are systematically denied access to power, on the grounds that they are not capable of holding it as demonstrated by their linguistic behavior' (2004: 42). The book as a whole argues that 'the kinds of "politeness" used by and of and to women . . . are, indeed, stifling, exclusive, and oppressive' (2004: 102). Her reflections on linguistic politeness prefigured later research on the subject within the emergent field of pragmatics.

Lakoff's 'hypothesis' now seems far too straightforward and simplistic. The major problems with it were:

1 it rested on identification of a set of linguistic features supposed to be typical of women's language;
2 it reinforced a deficit model of women's language;
3 in accounting for gender differences in language use in terms of women's deficiencies, it was implicitly setting up men's ways of speaking as authentic, neutral language use.

But her book was a landmark; it set the agenda for feminist research into language in the seventies and eighties. In retrospect, two major contributions made by *Language and Woman's Place* are its depiction of what we would now call a potent ideological construct of preferred female behaviour (Eckert 2004; Talbot 2003) and its insight into the damned if you do, damned if you don't aspect of women's language use.

'Man made language'

Dale Spender's *Man Made Language* is another important early work on language and gender. When it first came out in 1980 it attracted a good deal of media interest. It was an influential book and is probably still the best-known book on language and gender. Spender's starting point is that the English language embodies a particular world-view and determines the consciousness of its speakers:

> Language helps form the limits of our reality. It is our means of ordering, classifying and manipulating the world. It is through language that we become members of a human community, that the world becomes comprehensible and meaningful, that we bring into existence the world in which we live. (Spender 1985: 3)

What she is expressing here is a version of the Sapir-Whorf hypothesis (mentioned in chapter 1). Her central claim is that 'the English language has been *literally* man made and that it is still primarily under male control' (1985: 12; my italics). Unfortunately, the book is very muddled; it's impossible to pin down with any precision what she means by 'language', for instance. Before I go on to such problems, however, I need to consider her case.

English, according to Spender, is a 'man's language'. As she says, she does not intend us to understand 'man made' as a figure of speech, but as *literally* true. Women have to use meanings that are not their own. Men have a monopoly on the production of meaning, and therefore on the production of our perception of reality. Women's meanings are not encoded in the language, so that 'reality' is defined by men. Language encodes male versions of events. It reflects male interests and words have a male bias.

Let me consider a few words by way of example: **spinster**, **foreplay**, **motherhood** and **work**. When Spender wrote *Man Made Language* the sociological definition of work did not encompass unpaid childcare and domestic maintenance, so that it effectively excluded what many women did. Housework, by definition, is not work, leading to the frequent self-disparaging comment: 'I don't work. I'm only a housewife.' A spinster is a woman who has never married, with not very flattering connotations, in contrast with **bachelor**. Foreplay, of course, is the disposable element of sexual intercourse that happens before the 'real thing', namely penetration. And motherhood is every woman's goal in life: 'society . . . has a legitimated meaning for *motherhood* which means feminine fulfilment, which represents something beautiful, that leaves women consumed and replete with joy' (Spender 1985: 54).

Spender outlines the problems for women in attempting to articulate other versions of motherhood. Talking about motherhood as something less than totally wonderful is not going to make a woman popular and is liable to get her labelled as neurotic. As a consequence, many women are unprepared, particularly for childbirth. Mothers frequently withhold vital information from their daughters about the potential horror and *agony* of childbirth.

Spender is often quoted for her observations in *Man Made Language* on the subject of women's volubility. Women are perceived as over-garrulous, because preferably they shouldn't be saying anything at all. Women's contributions to talk are measured against silence; any talk is too much. She also observes that when women do speak it must be in 'a form acceptable to men' (1985: 84), or not at all. Women's versions of reality can be dismissed as not legitimate: 'There is a range of clichés that can be called upon to justify male dismissal of women's words, but they are usually variations on the theme of "I think you have a case but why do you have to put it so vehemently / aggressively / irrationally / emotionally?"' (pp. 84–5). That is, what women say can be dismissed, because the way it's expressed is disagreeable to men, regardless of what women are actually talking about. Other ways available to men for silencing women are talking over them or simply not listening. According to Spender, then, men effectively block women's versions of reality. Women's meanings are systematically suppressed.

The points Spender made in *Man Made Language* were very important ones. Her book has reached beyond the women's movement, introducing a wide audience to feminist issues. We should be grateful for her widely publicized challenges to the deep-rooted sexism in the English language. In the new millennium, Spender's understanding of women's dilemma is probably shared, to some extent at least, by millions in the Western world. Her perceptions of motherhood and work are certainly by no means as contentious as they were when she was writing, in the late 1970s. It is perhaps tempting to dismiss her observations as old-fashioned and no longer relevant. That would be a big mistake.

But there are problems with Spender's account. The first of these we need to consider is her monolithic notion of language. This is certainly (and fortunately) overstated. If language were half as monolithic as she claims, she would not have been able to write the book in the first place. The very changes she documents would have been impossible. For instance, in her discussion of the word **work**, she refers to new coinages, like the **double-shift**, which have helped to alter our perception of the nature of work. Similarly, we might consider new 'versions' of reality she discusses, such as the shocking version of motherhood which is 'not an unusual commentary' (p. 55). If such alternative, subversive notions of motherhood are not unusual, then language, and the perception of social reality it provides, is not so irredeemable a constraint as she sometimes claims. In fact, there is not, and never has been, one single, monolithic English language (except perhaps in a dictionary).

A related point is that, in her claim that men have a monopoly on the production of meaning, she has a tendency to condense together the introduction of new words and meanings into language with the codification of them (making dictionaries). Historically, it is men who have compiled dictionaries, and citations used to exemplify words in dictionaries have tended to be from male authors. But a language does not exist primarily in its dictionaries; it exists in the people who use it, both men and women.

Her shifting, sometimes conflicting, usages of key terms weaken the strength of her arguments. This is particularly a problem with 'meaning'. What exactly does she mean when she says women's meanings are blocked? In fact, she uses this expression in three very different ways. There is nothing wrong with this as such, but she doesn't acknowledge doing so, so the points she makes are blurred. As a result her argument is less precise and incisive than it needs to be; all right for preaching to the converted, perhaps, but not to make any new conversions. Given what she says about how women's views are dismissed as irrational, this *is* rather unfortunate.

Let's take these three different ways of using the expression 'blocking women's meanings':

1 The first focuses on semantic content. As we have seen, Spender argues that women have to use words with male-biased meanings. Words reflect male interests. We considered some of her examples: using the word **work** to refer to paid work only, the meanings of **spinster** and **foreplay**. Here what she is talking about are individual words and their semantic content. Women's meanings are blocked because there are no words for them. This way of using the term 'meaning' comes from the branch of linguistics known as semantics.

2 The second focuses on much longer expressions. She also states that women's meanings are blocked because language is used to make male-biased claims and to present male versions of events. Here meaning is not just about individual words and their semantic content, but about statements, propositions, views. For example, statements about motherhood as the source of women's fulfilment articulate society's legitimated meaning. Other versions of motherhood are 'blocked', that is to say, not legitimated. In sociology, masculine bias has led to the exclusion of housework from work as an object of study, so that only 'male meanings of women's existence' have been articulated (Spender 1985: 95). This perspective on 'meaning' is philosophical rather than semantic. One might come across it in sociology, but not in linguistics.

3 The third perspective concentrates on interaction. As we saw earlier, she also says that men block women's meanings by stopping them from speaking: by ignoring women's contributions to talk, silencing them, or permitting them only in 'a form acceptable to men'. To block women's meanings by preventing them from communicating is very different from what I've considered so far. It is not a matter of silencing meanings (either words or claims) that are not male-biased, but of silencing *women*.

The conceptual muddling in *Man Made Language* does not end here. There is also cavalier use of words like 'structure', 'symbol' and 'word' as though they were interchangeable (which they are not) and, with a peculiar short-sightedness, she takes male-biased theoretical observations about language as evidence of male bias within the English language itself. For details of these other conceptual muddles and inconsistencies, see the lengthy review by Maria Black and Rosalind Coward (1990).

I have considered Spender's monolithic view of language. Male power, in her account, is also monolithic. It is assumed that all men are in a position to dominate all women. The direct connection she implies between power and maleness needs to be broken. The way she attributes men with power over women, it is as though it were a biologically acquired characteristic (which we could do nothing about), rather than a culturally and politically bestowed privilege (which can be contested). In talking about men being in positions of power over women, we have to be more specific; I need to consider in what institutions, in what situations and so on. As Lynne Segal, another critic of Spender, says: 'Rather than write, as Spender does, of men's transhistorical and universal control over meanings, I feel we would do better to study how particular groups of people are able to control the specific institutions which construct dominant frameworks of meaning' (Segal 1994: 29).

If we add this perspective to Spender's claim that women's meanings are blocked, then it leads us to consider how ways of speaking in institutional contexts might affect women and men differently. This raises questions like the following: What are the interactional rights in a particular situation? (Who's allowed to tell whom to shut up, for instance?) Do women have restricted access to certain kinds of talk or writing? What about the authoritativeness given to different speakers or writers? Are there practices for downgrading women's talk or writing?

Conclusion and lead-in to part II

In this preliminary section of the book, I have considered some influential early work in the field of language and gender. I have indicated the pervasive influence of existing stereotypes about the sexes. We need to take care to avoid reproducing these stereotypes in studying language and gender. Three of the points established in this section are particularly important. They are worth further comment before we go on to look closely at some empirical research in the next section.

First, we need to attend to gender not sex. This book is not about biology. Its subject is socially acquired behaviour. In the next section, I will go on to show that gender alone is too simplistic. It interacts with age, class / status and, not least, culture. Gender differences come about because of the social roles men and women have. They depend on what spoken and written genres men and women work within, what they have access to, whether they are encouraged, expected or able to participate in public or private discourse.

Second, we cannot expect to find a simple checklist itemizing men's and women's language on the basis of linguistic forms. I gave you an idea of the multifunctionality of linguistic forms in my examination of Robin Lakoff's early attempt to identify 'women's language'. A one-to-one correlation of form and function is impossible. A single linguistic feature can function in different ways, according to the context of interaction it's being used in. We need to shift from itemization of linguistic features to an examination of the dynamics of interaction.

Third, attention to language, and even changing language, will not on its own solve the social iniquities identified by Dale Spender in *Man Made Language*. Language plays an important part in maintaining the status quo, but it is by no means the whole story. The problem is ultimately not 'male language' but unchallenged male power and privilege in our social structures. What attention to language *can* do is denaturalize that male power and privilege, and the system of social relations, sometimes labelled 'patriarchal', that upholds them. Identifying language *per se* as the problem doesn't help. It simply muddies the waters. Feminist interest in language lies in the part it plays, alongside other social practices and institutions, in reflecting, creating and sustaining gender divisions in society.

Further reading

Folklinguistic views / early grammarians

The Jespersen chapter on 'The woman' is reprinted in Cameron (1998). For detail on the early historical background, see ch. 2 in Coates (2004).

Lakoff's women's language

A recent retrospective on *Language and Woman's Place* provides the original text with annotations by the author, plus additional commentaries from numerous other contributors (Lakoff and Bucholtz 2004). One contribution in this volume uses the WL construct to explore the 'ladylike' style of TV 'lifestyle entrepreneur' Martha Stewart (Davies 2004). Elsewhere WL has been applied to account for the exaggerated performances of femininity by drag queens (Barrett 1994, 1999) and phone sex-workers (Hall 1995).

Spender's Man Made Language

I have already referred to Black and Coward's review (1998). Cameron's *Feminism and Linguistic Theory* (1992a) also explores problems with Spender's account. See also Segal (1994: 23–37).

PART II

Interaction among Women and Men

4

Telling stories

This is the first of two chapters focusing on specific genres: verbal activity types, with specific roles assigned for participants. In both chapters I present research that has been conducted, explicitly or implicitly, within a theoretical framework commonly known as 'difference-and-dominance'. This chapter looks at stories and asks: how do women and men engage in storytelling? Drawing on the work of various researchers in the field, I examine how stories are told, and why, as well as what they are about.

Studying stories

Oral narratives come in many forms and in many different kinds of situation. They may be highly formal tale-telling performances, or anecdotes mixed in with informal chat, dinner-table accounts of the day's events, the latest scandal over coffee, part of a horsetrader's sales-pitch . . . There are many ways of going about studying stories. Some researchers have focused principally on story content: what the stories are about in terms of themes, characters and kinds of situation, the way narratives are structured and suchlike. Others, particularly in linguistics, have concentrated on the talk in which stories are produced and interpreted: how stories are produced by the people involved, how many narrators there are, the role of the audience, the nature and extent of audience participation, and so on. Also of interest is what people are doing with stories when they tell them, what they are telling them *for*. One particular function, for example, is 'telling tales', a tactical use of stories that has been studied in children's daily interaction (Goodwin 1993).

This chapter presents a selection of work on everyday storytelling. I will begin with a focus on story content, presenting the findings of two studies. For most of the chapter, however, I will also examine the discourse in which stories are produced, rather than just what they are about. I look closely at a couple's joint production of a single shared-experience narrative, and finish by outlining findings from two separate studies of narrative events at family dinner-tables.

Story content

Barbara Johnstone conducted a study of everyday storytelling in middle America, in which she examined sixty-eight naturally occurring conversational narratives among white middle-class people in Fort Wayne, Indiana (Johnstone 1990). The narratives were not elicited; they arose spontaneously in conversations in people's homes among friends and family, people who knew one another well. Johnstone was not primarily interested in gender differences as such – they formed only a small part of her initial study – but she found consistent differences between the stories told by women and those told by men. These differences are investigated in more detail in later work (Johnstone 1993). In this later work, she focused on the personal experience stories, of which there were fifty-eight: thirty-three told by women, twenty-five by men.

In the stories she looks at, a man is usually the protagonist in his own story; when he is not, then he is telling a story about another man. The men tell about exploits which display their own skill, courage and wit. Johnstone observes that the stories told by Fort Wayne men reflect a local cultural expectation: 'that men are expected to create dangerous situations, or use dangerous situations they encounter, as opportunities for personal display' (1990: 67). Their stories tell of contests, either among one another or with the natural world. Here are Johnstone's summaries of three of them:

> A young man is hassled by another man in a bar but says the right threatening thing to put an end to the situation; he is with others, but no one else is involved in this interchange.
>
> The players on a semiprofessional softball team pour ice water on the club's public relations director, as a sort of initiation ritual; the victim responds in just the right clever way, by breaking into the song 'Stormy Weather'.
>
> By calling on his own willpower, a high school boy enables himself to beat forty or fifty other contestants in a cattle-judging competition. (1993: 70)

As narrators, the Fort Wayne men give attention to descriptive detail, particularly veridical details relating to location in time and place.

By contrast, the women's stories are often about other people, both male and female. They do not deal with individual resourcefulness so much as mutual support of the group, and they are more likely to establish the teller as someone foolish than as heroic. Here are Johnstone's summaries of three of them:

> What could have been an embarrassing mistake (saying 'Good God' instead of 'Good morning' in Spanish) is shrugged off when the Spanish speaker being addressed laughs about it, because he's such a nice fellow.

> A woman trying to rescue her drowning nephew almost drowns too, but her sister borrows a life raft and saves both.

> A woman deals with the aftermath of a frightening skid in the snow with the help of neighbors, who give helpful advice, and the local police officer, who accompanies her back to the scene of the accident to retrieve her license plate and check for damage. (1993: 71)

As narrators, they pay less attention to scene-setting than the men. Details about people (such as their names) are more frequent than details of where and when events take place. Some of the women's stories are full of dialogue. Here is an extract from a story told by a young woman about being stopped by a police officer when she was an inexperienced driver:

> And then I said 'What's the problem here?'
> he says 'Well ma'am . . . ah . . . you didn't stop for that stop sign back there'
> I said 'WHAT?'
> I mean I was mad!
> I said 'WHAT?'
> And he says . . . he says,
> 'It's the In-'
> He just starts off rattling,
> 'It's the Indi- Indiana State Law you must come to a complete stop . . . before the stop sign da da da da'
> I said 'I did!'
> I said 'There's a crosswalk there and the thing's before that'
> I said 'Where were you sitting anyway?' ((laughs))
> He says 'I was right in that parking lot by the church'
> And that parking lot's right back here ((indicating on table))
> you can't even see the stop sign
> I said 'I'm sorry'
> I said 'You didn't see me'
> He said 'It's the Indiana State Law da da da da'
> (Johnstone 1990: 76)

In such constructions of dialogue between people, women are reconstructing the social relations between characters in their narratives. They work the social world into their stories. This attention to social reality is less evident in the men's stories. Johnstone's findings about gender differences in everyday storytelling in Fort Wayne are summarized below:

Men	Women
Protagonist usually teller, always male.	Protagonists often others, male and female.
Individual reality.	Social reality.
Contests among individuals, or with nature.	Community norms and fear of flouting them; joint actions, interdependency.
Skill, resourcefulness, heroism.	Embarrassment and fear, skill abetted by luck.
More detail on place, time, object description.	More detail on characters, named characters, dialogue.

The second study of story content is rather different. Sandra Silberstein examines courtship narratives across three generations and contrasts the characteristics of men's and women's stories (Silberstein 1988). She elicited stories from two North American families, in interviews with each of the fourteen members. One family is Jewish, the other is described as white Anglo-Saxon Protestant. In these elicited stories, she observes differences in the vocabularies of motive used by women and men. The women's courtship narratives centre on having to make a decision: 'the need to decide – to react' (p. 139). As motivation, some of the women cite the opinions of others. In the Jewish women's stories, morality and obligation to family are prominent. There are differences in the women's stories across the generations. Among the younger women, assertions of independence are frequent. Silberstein observes that these mark them as women, since men do not need to make such assertions, indeed would sound odd if they did: 'Imagine a man stressing, "I didn't go to college to meet a wife – I went to get a degree"' (p. 139). The men's courtship narratives, by contrast, are about orchestration and conquest, which may involve a decision at the outset, as in the following: 'I felt that, wow, look at that girl. I'm gonna have this girl' (p. 141). They show far less change from one generation to the next.

Silberstein argues that the courtship narratives the two families told her are not simply historical accounts of what has happened in their lives, but stories they use in creating and maintaining the social categories of gender. The women's stories centre on responding to men by making a decision, while the men's centre on their own active orchestration of events. There is a striking similarity between these non-fictional accounts and what goes on between the highly stereotyped protagonists in popular romances (Talbot 1995a, 1997a).

A couple tell a story

Not all narratives are stories; some are merely reports. In a report the speaker is supposed to deliver the bare facts; in a story, part of the job is to make it interesting, to hold the listener's attention. 'Any parent', as Livia Polanyi says, 'who has ever received a dreary "report" of the day's happenings instead of a "story" in response to a cheery "Well, dear, what happened in school today?" will testify to the difference' (1985: 12–13).

So far I have been looking at some studies of what women and men put into their everyday narratives. Now I need to combine attention to story content with attention to the discourse in which stories come into existence. This section focuses on a single collaboratively produced story about a shared experience. The story was told in the course of informal conversation in my home one evening. The participants are two white, middle-class couples living in Britain. The storytellers are Sylvie, French with virtually native-speaker fluency in English, and her British husband, Chris. The conversation has been about a shared acquaintance who had recently injured a child on the road. This provides the cue for the couple's account of a collision with a dog. I have presented the talk in quite detailed transcription in order to capture some of the quality of the spoken language, which was animated and at times extremely rapid.

In order to examine the story I am going to need some kind of framework. For this I will use a well-known six-part model of story structure (Labov and Waletzky 1967; Labov 1972a):

1 *Abstract* What's it about? A thumbnail sketch of the story.
2 *Orientation* Who, what, when, where? Establishing the characters and the scene.
3 *Complicating action* What happened next? And then? And then . . . ?
4 *Evaluation* So what? How / why is all this interesting?
5 *Resolution* How did it end?
6 *Coda* That's it, story over. Back to the conversation.

With the exception of 'evaluation', these are supposed to occur strictly in the order given. Evaluation involves maintaining the listener's interest and can occur throughout. It is the crucial element that transforms a narrative

from a dreary report into a story. Evaluation takes many forms; it is not
always as overt as introducing an event with 'Listen, this is the good bit!'
The dramatization, repetition, reflection and assessment in the story
below are all evaluative, claims for the story's value. We can see the evaluation right from the start, in Sylvie's part of the abstract in lines 23 to 28. It
contains an intensifying adjective and adverb ('this *bloody* dog just walked
straight into the car') and an evaluative clause ('really upset at the time').
The story begins on line 23:

```
 1  Bryan:    heh a(h)ctually when Sylvie said >>that about him
 2            having knocked down before sounded like that
 3            <<Jasper ⌈Carrott thing about⌉ the guy ⌈('s .)⌉
 4  Chris:           ⌊heheheheheh⌋
 5  Bryan:    car insurance claim-
 6  Sylvie:   ((taking wineglass))                    ⌊th(h)anks⌋
 7  Mary:     ⌈oh heh⌉
 8  Chris:    ⌊heheh⌋
 9  Bryan:    (.) er oh the er (.) >man who was knocked
10            down< said he'd been knocked down three
11            times before
12            ((prolonged general laughter; approx 6 seconds))
13  Sylvie:   pretty frightening when a child walks into your
14            car I can tell you
15  Bryan:    yeah yeah
16  Sylvie:   ouf
17  Bryan:    well I've (told you er) dr driving around these
18            little estates and things quiet estates an' (.)
19            >suddenly turn round a corner< and there's
20            dozens ⌈of kids⌉ playing all over the road
21  Chris:          ⌊mm⌋
22  Bryan:    y'know (.) urh (.) .hh heh
```
Abstract
```
23  Sylvie:   we had a c- a dog walk into the car once and
24            (.) .hh we'd stopped (.) and the dog had stopped
25            (.) started again and as soon as we moved off
26            this bloody dog just walked straight into the car
27            there (was) nothing we could do (..)
28            really upse(h)t at the time y'⌈know⌉
29  Bryan:                                 ⌊yeah⌋
30            ⌈> remember you tell⌉ing me<
```

31	Chris:	⌊yeah >but there wasn't<⌋ (.)
32		we hadn't actually stopped (.)
33		it ⌈almost had one one we⌉
34	Sylvie:	⌊just very slowed down⌋

Orientation

35	Chris:	the one we hit on the Blackpool Road
36	Sylvie:	yeah Blackpool Road on that (.)
37		dual car⌈riageway⌉
38	Chris:	⌊yes (I was) doing a⌋bout sixty
39	Bryan:	mm
40	Chris:	and you could see this dog in the distance
41		on the central reservation (..) and
42		you could see it was halfway it was cross
43		just half crossed the road=
44	Bryan:	=yeah
45	Chris:	an' it was (.) y'know (.)

Complicating action

46		oh shit >so slow down<
47		so I slowed down to about thirty- (.)
48	Bryan:	⌈mm⌉
49	Chris:	⌊made⌋ eye contact with the dog n' was (.)
50		y'know like you do with a person (.)
51		an' it stopped an' it clocked me (.)
52	Bryan:	mm=
53	Chris:	=thought right he's okay y'know
54		it's not (.) didn't look a stupid dog
55	Bryan:	yea(h)h
56	Chris:	yeah so I started to accelerate again (.)
57		and bugger me suddenly he just (.) leaps
58		in front of the car
59	Bryan:	heheh
60	Chris:	((claps hands loudly))
61	Bryan:	mm
62	Chris:	and I saw it came out the back of the car
63		in the mirror
64	Bryan:	hhhh shw
65	Chris:	y'know 'nd er (.) he was sorta limping off
		n' (.) just y'know it just sorta lay down
66		on the ⌈side of the road⌉
67	Sylvie:	⌊and we could⌋

```
                                        n't even stop because
                        there there were roadworks and ⌈there were⌉
 68  Bryan:                                            ⌊mm⌋
 69  Sylvie:   cars behind as well
 70           there was no way ⌈(we could stop)⌉
 71  Chris:                    ⌊when it came out –⌋
 72  Bryan:                    ⌈( xxxxxxxxxxxx)⌉
```

(Candidate resolution)
```
 73  Sylvie:                    ⌊so we went to the⌋police station
```

Complicating action
```
 74  Chris:    when it reappeared from underneath
              the back of the car
 75  Sylvie:  oh
 76  Bryan:   mm
 77  Chris:   in the mirror (.) it was bouncing y'know
 78  Bryan:   hhhhh yeah
 79  Chris:   and there's a heavy (xx) (.) you felt it go
 80           underneath
 81  Bryan:   yeah yeah
 82  Sylvie:  mm
 83  Chris:   s'a crump at the front and (.)
 84           bang under the driver's seat and bang again
 85           by the back axle (.) then it sorta ro (.)
 86           it sorta bounced down the road for about (.) sh
 87  Mary:    and it got up after that?=
 88  Bryan:   =it got up and limped off?
 89  Chris:   got up got got up and crawled off y'know
 90  Sylvie:  crawled oh ⌈god⌉
```

Resolution
```
 91  Chris:              ⌊I felt⌋ really sick (.)
 92            and Sylvie was crying
 93  Bryan:   mm
 94  Sylvie:  I was really quite upset
 95  Bryan:   well I was ⌈(I was)-⌉
 96  Chris:              ⌊I was⌋ f I was sick for the dog
 97            and I was also bloody annoyed because it'd
 98            (.) bashed a big dent in the front of the car
 99                 ⌈heh heh⌉
100  Bryan:        ⌊heheheh⌋
101  Chris:   heheheh and Sylvie nev(h)er forgave me for that
```

102		(she said said)
103		[she > th(h)ought I was rea(h)lly callous< heh
104		((general laughter))]
105	Sylvie:	[(of course you were you)] stupid pillock
106		[heheheheh]
107	Chris:	[heheheheh]
108		((laughter subsiding: 2 to 3 seconds))
109	Bryan:	yeah I was going t'Tuson once . . .
		((continues with new story))

The narrative that Chris and Sylvie produce between them is no mere report. It is clearly a story, with a lot of effort put into dramatizing the sequence of events, as well as reflection on and assessment of them.

This model of story structure was designed for the study of elicited oral narratives. Since they were elicited, the narratives were in a sense artificially produced. Compared with the story in the conversation above, they were all rather 'tidy'. They had single narrators and concluded with a coda: an explicit linking device back into the main flow of talk ('So that was my story', for instance). The couple's story was not elicited; it occurred naturally in the course of the evening's conversation. There are, as we have seen, two narrators. There is no coda: the conversation goes straight into another story on a related theme (Bryan is trying to start it on line 95, and succeeds on line 109).

The story begins in lines 23–8, as Sylvie provides a small, self-contained narrative, which may not have been intended as an abstract to a fuller story at all. Chris amends her micronarrative in line 31, an amendment endorsed by Sylvie in her offer of an utterance completion in line 34:

31	Chris:	[yeah >but there wasn't<] (.)
32		we hadn't actually stopped (.)
33		it [almost had one one we]
34	Sylvie:	[just very slowed down]

He then takes over as main teller; treating her micronarrative as an abstract as he launches into the orientation and complicating action. At the onset of his orientation, Sylvie offers another endorsement, underlining the shared nature of what is being related:

35	Chris:	the one we hit on the Blackpool Road
36	Sylvie:	yeah Blackpool Road on that (.)
37		dual car[riageway]

There are two storytellers, and there are two different resolutions.

Chris's sequence of twelve distinct complicating actions is completed on lines 65–6. Sylvie then provides some more evaluative elements (lines 67, 69), and offers a resolution: the last action on their part (line 73):

67	Sylvie:	⌊and we couldⱼn't even stop because
		there there were roadworks and ⌈there were⌉
68	Bryan:	⌊mm⌋
69	Sylvie:	cars behind as well
70		there was no way ⌈(we could stop)⌉
71	Chris:	⌊when it came out – ⌋
72	Bryan:	⌈(xxxxxxxxxxxx)⌉
73	Sylvie:	⌊so we went to the⌋ police station

Chris begins to evaluate by repetition, providing somewhat grisly 'edited highlights' from lines 71 to 89 before offering a different resolution: how their distress manifested itself.

The couple both produce a great many evaluative elements. The listeners contribute to story evaluation too, particularly in lines 87–8 where Chris's repetition succeeds in extracting vocal responses from his audience:

87	Mary:	and it got up after that?=
88	Bryan:	=it got up and limped off?
89	Chris:	got up got got up and crawled off y'know
90	Sylvie:	crawled oh ⌈god⌉

These expressions of incredulity prompt yet more evaluation from the tellers: an intensifier in Chris's rewording of 'limped' as 'crawled', and two more in Sylvie's echoing and expletive. The couple tend to evaluate differently. Chris's relish in the grisly nature of the story is evident in his dramatic use of sound effects, and in his repetition. Sylvie is concerned to establish her distress and their responsible behaviour.

The couple's collaboratively produced shared-experience story functions as a presentation or enactment of their 'couplehood'. I have said there is no coda, but the final little name-calling episode could be viewed as such. It advances beyond the story setting, framing them as a couple:

101	Chris:	heheheh and Sylvie nev(h)er forgave me for that
102		(she said said)
103		⌈she > th(h)ought I was rea(h)lly callous< heh

104   ((general laughter))⌉
105   Sylvie: ⌊(of course you were you)⌋ stupid pillock
106   ⌈hehehehe⌉
107   Chris: ⌊hehehehe⌋

They produce divergent sequencing, different uses of, and types of, evaluation. Chris produces an 'action' story, Sylvie a 'feelings' story. But they tell it (them?) together, and Chris concludes with their shared distress. Crucially, their stories converge. This collaboration breaks down with another story on the same evening, and Chris ends up delivering it as a monologue (see Talbot 1992a, an article called 'I wish you'd stop interrupting me!').

At the family dinner-table

This section deals with particular social roles taken up by women and men in the institution of the family. What contributions do mothers and fathers make in dinner-table narratives? What follows are short accounts of two studies of everyday storytelling at the dinner-table in two-parent families. Both studies examine child socialization within the family.

Comparing two cultures

The first is a comparative study of dinner-table narratives in middle-class Jewish-American and Israeli households (Blum-Kulka 1993). Shoshana Blum-Kulka investigated the production of stories in the dinner-table conversations of eight families in Boston and eight in Jerusalem. Her database was collected for a larger project run by a team of researchers. On each occasion a member of the research team, who was from the same cultural background as the family, was present as an observer. This person was a guest at the family dinner-table, and the family's self-presentation in interaction with the outsider is the subject of the study (thus providing an interesting, and rather elegant, way of overcoming the problem of observing naturalistic talk). The main interest in the study for us here is in the contributions of the parents in their roles as father and mother. To see these in the context of the dinner-table talk, however, we will need to take into account what the others present are doing as well.

The American and Israeli dinner-table narrative events have a good deal in common. Eating at the dinner-table is used as the prime occasion for developing the children's narrative abilities in both cultural environments. The children are active participants, although the way they participate differs, as we shall see. At both the Boston and Jerusalem dinner-tables, stories are frequently produced collaboratively in the interaction, even though they tend to be about one person's own experience. In other words, like the couple's story we looked at in the last section, they aren't simply monologues.

There are, however, many differences. The American families in the study engage in ritualized 'how was your day?' sessions while at the table. They focus on the act of telling and there is a lot of talk about the talk (metadiscourse), for example about whose turn it is next. In the following, four-year-old Sandra wants to participate:

Sandra: Mommy to who will I tell how my day goes?
Mother: OK let's hear your day.
Sandra: Well (.) I played puzzles . . .

(Blum-Kulka 1993: 377)

The children are the main tellers of two-thirds of the stories and introduce half of them themselves. Of the parents, fathers introduce more. Outsiders initiate few (see figures 4.1 and 4.2 for the distribution of the main teller and the narrative introduction respectively). What this means is that the children are very much in the spotlight. They frequently give accounts of their activities that day and, when they do not, the parents, especially the father, prompt them to do so. The American dinner-tables are formal, the talk being structured around the 'Today' ritual and its correct performance by the children. The observers are present as interested listeners. The children participate by producing their own personal narratives, but very little as interested listeners. Fathers appear to take on the entertainment of the observer as their responsibility. Responsibility for the food is left to the mother.

In contrast with the American dinner-tables in the study, the Israeli ones seem informal to the point of chaos. There are often accounts of the events of the day in the narratives at the Israeli dinner-tables, but not with the same ritual character or spotlight on the children. The main telling of stories is distributed more equally between adults and children than at the American dinner-tables, with the adults producing slightly more (see figure 4.1). Story introduction is also distributed more equally, with the fathers introducing fewest (see figure 4.2). Where the American families focused on the telling of stories, the Israelis focus on the stories themselves. Listeners express interest and concern for the tale throughout, frequently producing cooperative promptings, pre-emptive interpretations of story

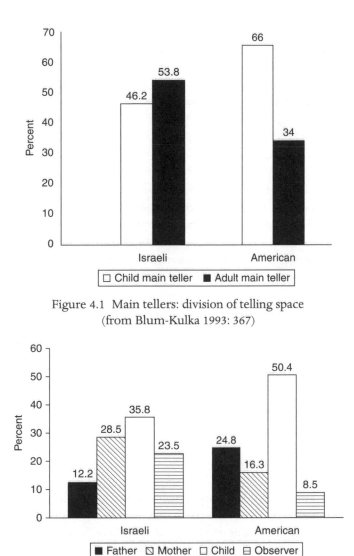

Figure 4.1 Main tellers: division of telling space
(from Blum-Kulka 1993: 367)

Figure 4.2 Narrative initiation at Israeli and American dinner-tables
(from Blum-Kulka 1993: 368)

information and suchlike. Below is an example of collaborative entry into a story. Notice the mother's completion in line 4 of the observer's utterance in line 3, and her prompting in line 6:

1	Observer:	Etmol hayinu,	Yesterday we were
2		hayiti ecel	I was at the home

3		pnina ve=	of Pnina and=
4	Mother:	=ve-cvika?	=And Cvika?
5	Observer:	ve-cvika ken.	And Cvika, yes.
6	Mother:	nu(.)ve-ex halax?	So how did it go?
7	Observer:	haya meod nexmad.	It was very nice.
			((Story proceeds))

(Adapted from Blum-Kulka 1993: 371)

A striking feature of the Israeli stories is their 'polyphonic' narration. That is, everyone seems to chip in with the construction of the story. One such story is a comic tale about the father rescuing a runaway watermelon. It follows an account of a car accident, which the mother was involved in on the same day, and is offered as a humorous counterpart to it. He introduces it himself like this (Naomi and Ruti are daughters, aged eight and eleven):

1	Father:	ani etmol ani	I yesterday I saved
2		etmol hicalti	a watermelon
3		avatiax	yesterday
4	Observer:	oh heheh	oh heheh
5	Naomi:	ex ex?	how? how?
6	Ruti:	ex hu hicil?	how did you save it?
7	Father:	atem lo ta'aminu . . .	you won't believe it . . .
			((continues))

(Adapted from Blum-Kulka 1993: 393)

This kind of very active listening is sometimes called 'high-involvement style' (Tannen 1984). Everyone participates in it, including the children. Even though only the father experienced this event, everyone at the table joins in its telling as a tale (with the exception of a four-year-old son). The most intensive collaboration from the audience begins when he has completed the complicating action stage: once the story's happy outcome is clear. This is where the following extract begins:

1	Father:	bari ve-shelem	I returned it safe and
2		hexzarti oto	sound into the arms
3		le-zro'ot ha-yalda	of the little girl
4	Ruti:	⌈ha-yalda ha-	⌈the sobbing child⌉
5		mityapaxat⌉	

6	Mother:	⌊acarta et ha-	⌊you stopped the car⌋
7		mexonit⌋	
8		acarta et ha-me-	you stopped the-
9	Father:	avarti oto. acartii	I passed it.
10		et ha-mexonit-	I stopped the car-
11	Mother:	acarta ve-yaradta	you braked, got out
12		me-ha mexonit	of the car and saved
13		ve-hicalta et	the watermelon?
14		ha-avatiax?	
15	Father:	natati la avatiax	I gave her a watermelon
16		ve-hicalti et xaye	and saved the life
17		ha-mishpaxa sham	of the family there
18	Mother:	ve-ma amrulexa	and what did they say
19		ha-mishpaxa	to you, this family?
20		ha-zot?	
21	Observer:	oh heheh	oh heheh
22	Father:	ʻtoda raba beʼemet	ʻthank you very much
23		toda ve-shuv todaʼ	really and thanks againʼ
24	Mother:	be-amerika ish lo	in the States nobody
25		haya ose et ze	would have done it
26	Father:	be-amerika	in the States there is
27		avatixim ze	a tradition to save
28		masoret lehacil	watermelons
29	Mother:	ze rak ba-arec	it's only here that
30		⌈mishehu yored	somebody ⌈would get
31		me-ha-mexonit⌉	out of the car⌉
32	Father:	⌊ma at medaberetxx⌋	⌊what are you saying⌋
33		⌈dvarim kaele-⌉	⌈things like this-⌉ ((trailing off))
34	Ruti:	⌊be-amerika yesh	⌊you have in the States
35		hehheh⌋	hehheh⌋
36	Father:	hem meod adivim	they are very polite
37		ba-dvarim he-ele	in these things
38	Observer:	aval avatiax, im	but a watermelon
39		ha-yalda hayta raca	if the child had chased
40		la-avatiax az haya	the watermelon things
41		yaxol lihyot nora	might have become
42		mesukan	very dangerous
43	Father:	lo. hayta sham	no. there was a
44		beaya.	problem.
45		zot omeret	I mean the woman's

46		ha-ba'aya shel	problem was either
47		ha-isha hayta	the watermelon
48		o ha-avatiax	or the child
49		o ha-yalda	
50	Mother:	ve-hi hexlita	and she decided
51		ha-yalda [be-shlav	for the child
52		dey mukdam]	[quite early on]
53	Father:	[hi hexlita	[she decided for
54		ha-yalda] aval	the child] but
55		ha-yalda hexlita	the child decided
56		avatiax	for the watermelon

(Adapted from Blum-Kulka 1993: 393–4)

In this extract, the husband and wife collaborate in shifting the story's topic from 'saving a watermelon' to 'saving a family'. After the woman's question asking for clarification in lines 11–14, her husband reformulates the story's point ('I gave her a watermelon and saved the life of the family there'). The observer reinforces this transformation in lines 38–42, by changing the comic tone to a serious one ('things might have become very dangerous'). The parents wind up the story with a collaborative shift in perspective to the mother and her concern for the child.

'Father knows best'

The second study of narrative events just looks at American families (described as middle-class, European-American). It examines the functioning of everyday storytelling in the assertion and maintenance of the father's position of authority (Ochs and Taylor 1992a, 1992b, 1995). Elinor Ochs and Carolyn Taylor taped seven Californian two-parent families on two evenings, for part of which time the families sat at the dinner-table. Unlike the researchers in the previous study, they did not join in the meal, so they were not present as observers. They did, however, video- and audio-tape on each evening, leaving the video camera to run when the families sat down to eat. Like Blum-Kulka, their interest is in child socialization. Rather than looking at cultural differences, however, they concentrated on how it is children learn gendered behaviour within a single culture. Their focus was 'gender instantiation' in narrative practices. As it turned out, they found that the father in each family is set up as the primary audience, judge and critic of the other family members. They refer to this as the 'Father knows best' dynamic.

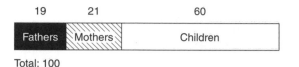

Total: 100

Figure 4.3 Story protagonists at seven Californian dinner-tables
(data from Ochs and Taylor 1995: 102)

As in Blum-Kulka's everyday narratives, the stories and reports that Ochs and Taylor studied dealt with the narrators' own experiences during the day. Firstly, like Blum-Kulka, they look at who the protagonist / main teller is in the narrative and at who introduces it. They also look for its primary recipient – that is, the person it is directly addressed to – and for the 'problematizing' of narratives. Problematization refers to taking issue with elements of the story, querying the teller (for example, questioning the teller's competence). What is of interest here is whose narratives receive this treatment and by whom it is meted out.

When someone is the protagonist in an everyday narrative, their experiences and concerns are placed in the spotlight. There are positive and negative aspects to this. It means being the centre of attention, to be sure. But this might not be such a good thing. It is not just a matter of receiving praise; some of the attention they receive may be rather less welcome. As Ochs and Taylor point out, 'this attention is not always a plus, given that protagonists' actions, thoughts, and feelings are not only open to praise but also exposed to familial scrutiny, irony, challenge, and critique' (1995: 101). Being the protagonist puts the teller in a vulnerable position, open to family scrutiny. In their study, Ochs and Taylor found that children were most often the protagonists; fathers were protagonists least often (see figure 4.3).

Given this vulnerability of protagonists, who introduces a narrative is highly significant. It is the introducer who determines who is going to be the focus of attention (and potential target for criticism). In the study, the parents were most often introducers, especially the mother (see figure 4.4). Thus parents, most often mothers, were largely responsible for setting up their children as protagonists.

The introducer also selects the primary recipient. This may be explicit (as in 'Tell your father about X') or implicit. The role of primary recipient is a powerful one. Whoever takes it up is entitled to criticize, assess other members of the family, as protagonists and as narrators. Someone who has this position a lot is set up as the family judge. Ochs and Taylor found that, as you would expect, the parents most often have this privileged position

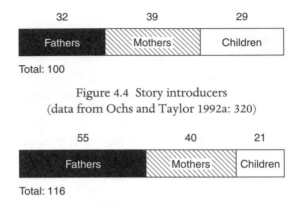

Figure 4.4 Story introducers
(data from Ochs and Taylor 1992a: 320)

Figure 4.5 Primary recipients
(data from Ochs and Taylor 1992a: 323)

of recipient–judge (see figure 4.5). Fathers often initiate narratives from their children with themselves as primary recipient, as in the following extract:

Dad: (Your) mother said you were thinking of uh
         (.) getting on the swim team?
Lucy: ((nods yes once emphatically))
         (1.00)
Dad: ((nods yes)) (.) (good)
         ((report continues))

(Ochs and Taylor 1995: 105)

In some of the families, mothers frequently nominate fathers, initiating narratives with an introduction such as 'You wanna tell Daddy what happened to you today?' In most of the households, the women know more about the children's daily lives than the men, since they very often finish work earlier and have already heard their children's accounts before dinner. But, for various reasons, this is not enough on its own to explain why fathers are primary recipients of the children's narratives so often. For one thing, in two households the fathers know more about the children's day by dinner-time than the mothers do, but the situation is not thereby reversed (that is, there are no examples of 'Tell your mother about X'). For another thing, when children do volunteer narratives themselves, it is their mothers, who generally know more about their day, that they tend to address them to, not their fathers. Moreover, the one person whose day

The Parental Panopticon

the family as a whole knows *least* about is the father, but he is not called on to give an account of it. And neither parent selects the children as primary recipient (there are no examples of 'Tell the children about X').

Altogether, the way talk is distributed at these family dinner-tables shows a one-way, non-reciprocal state of affairs: 'the overall pattern suggests a fundamental asymmetry in family narrative activity, whereby children's lives were told to parents but, by and large, parents did not narrate their lives to their children' (Ochs and Taylor 1995: 105). Ochs and Taylor liken it to a *panopticon* (Bentham 1791; Foucault 1979). The term refers to a construction (such as a prison with a watchtower) which enables one person to monitor a group of other people without that person being observed. Panopticon-like structures bestow on the watcher a position of power over those scrutinized. Similarly, the role of primary recipient, bestowed most often upon fathers in Ochs and Taylor's data, exposes the other family members to his surveillance. The women play a significant part in setting up their husbands in this role.

As well as noting the surveillance-like aspect of dinner-table talk in these families, Ochs and Taylor also examined the problematization of stories and reports. Problematizing involves taking issue with elements of the narrative, or with the teller as narrator. They found it in exactly half of

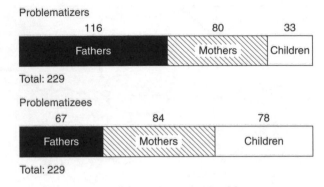

Figure 4.6 Problematizers and Problematizees
(data from Ochs and Taylor 1992a: 325)

the narratives, most of it between the parents. Only 10 per cent was 'self-inflicted'. Fathers most often took on the role of *problematizer* (that is, the one who identifies problems), children least often. Mothers were most often the *problematizee* (that is, the one who is targeted *as* the problem), fathers least often (see figure 4.6).

Women's narratives were most often problematized by their husbands. Here is one example. The woman has just taken on an assistant at work. Her husband has already quizzed her about it at some length:

1	Father:	((eating dessert)) well (.) I certainly
2		think that (.) you're a- you know
3		you're a fair boss (.) you've been
4		working there how long?
5	Mother:	((as she scrapes dishes at sink))
6		fifteen years in June
7	Father:	fifteen *years* (.) and you got a guy
8		((turns to look at her directly))
9		that's been workin there a few *weeks*
10		and you do (it what) the way *he* wants
11	Mother:	hh heh ((father smiles slightly (?)
12		then turns back to eating dessert))
13		(..) it's not a matter of my doin it
14		the way *he want* (.) it *does* help
15		in that I'm getting more *work* done
16		It's just that I'm working too *hard*
17		I don't wanta *work* so hard
18	Father:	((turns chair around to half-face mother))

| 19 | well (.) you're the boss It's up to you |
| 20 | to set the standards ((continues)) |

(Adapted from Ochs and Taylor 1995: 108)

He is implicitly putting her competence at work into question in lines 7–10 and lines 18–20. Husbands tend to make problems of wives as protagonists, often implying incompetence. The women, for their part, engage in problematization too, of their husbands. Rather than criticizing them as protagonists, however, the women make problems of husbands' understanding of narratives, as in lines 11–15. They do so mostly in self-defence, or in defence of the children. In two of the families, women airing self-doubt in their narratives elicit 'dumping', that is, a barrage of criticism from their husbands.

The children are mostly on the receiving end. They problematize very rarely, but when they do, the father is most often their target. (Full statistical details can be found in Ochs and Taylor (1992a, 1992b).) Here is an example of a father's story being challenged by his son:

Father: and I commanded the earthquake to
         stop (.) and [it did]
Son: ((making a face)) [*hah*] heheh liar liar pants on
         [fire]
Father: [I said] '*Earthquake* you *stop* at once
         You are *fright*ening my children
         and we will not tolerate this'
Son: no you di(h)dn't
Father: no?
Son: no
Father: well (.) I was *think*ing that
Son: hun uh?

(Adapted from Ochs and Taylor 1992a: 312)

The boys do 50 per cent more of this than the girls. One particularly striking example follows on from a mother's self-targeting in a narrative about her seven-year-old son eating a chilli by mistake in a restaurant. The child frames it as a funny experience at first, but after she puts his stance as narrator into question (insisting that it was serious) he changes tack, ending with:

Son:	((pointing and reaching over until touching mother's cheek with index finger)) YOUR FAULT (.) YOUR FAULT=
Mother:	((nodding))=it was my fault
Daughter:	hhh ((softly))heh
Mother:	I thought it was ((son pinching her cheeks as she talks)) a um (.) green pepper (.) .HHHHHH ((pulling his hands away)) OW that really hurts honey
Son:	your fault (.) I get to do whatever I want to do once

(Adapted from Ochs and Taylor 1992a: 315)

This particular small child not only identifies a problem (actually his mother identified it for him), but also metes out punishment. Ochs and Taylor liken the women's self-targeting to shooting themselves in the foot.

The men are the family judges. It is not just because men are most often designated as the primary recipient of narratives, although this is one important reason. They exploit the role more fully, problematizing more often for each narrative than the other family members do. Also, when men are primary recipient, the level of problem-finding goes up overall. This is largely because of the women taking issue with their husbands: 'counterproblematizing' in their own, and their children's, defence. Moreover, men elbow in, finding problems in narratives for which women are primary recipients, not themselves. All in all, they take on problem-finding as their right, as part of the paternal/husband role: 'The role of problematizer seems to be a particular prerogative of the family role of father/husband, manifesting the ideology that "Father knows best", socializing and (re)constituting paternal prerogative and point of view in and through narrative activity' (Ochs and Taylor 1995: 112). In so far as women regularly set men up in the primary recipient role, they contribute to establishing their husbands as the family judge.

Family narrative productions at dinner contribute to the socialization of children. At the same time as establishing fathers as authority figures, they position mothers as people who may be legitimately criticized (in contrast with a mother's powerful position, in relation to her children, as the person in immediate control over goods and services: chocolate, crisps, pocket money . . .). Judging by the boys' greater tendency to engage in problem-finding, it seems they are already learning how to be husbands and fathers. The girls are presumably learning to be the problem.

What I have just been looking at are the findings from a study of two evenings with seven American families, and we must not forget this and generalize to the whole of humanity. There was variation even in Ochs and Taylor's small sample. To some extent, Blum-Kulka's research backs it up, however. From what we have seen, American children are expected to perform; they are put under a good deal of pressure to speak. The ritual nature in Blum-Kulka's study may have been a result of the observer's presence as a guest; or it may have been something specifically Jewish-American, or Bostonian. It may even have been just those households. Nevertheless, it stands in marked contrast with dinner-table talk in the other culture. In the Israeli households, children do not appear to be in the spotlight as their American counterparts are.

Generalizing from research findings

Everyday storytelling is a rich area for research. I have barely scraped the surface in this chapter, looking at some studies of story content and the discourse in which stories are produced: at a couple's joint production of a single shared-experience narrative and at narrative events at family dinner-tables. This is only a small sample of research on stories; references for others are given at the end of this chapter.

Let me conclude with a couple of points about generalizing from research findings. The things we have been looking at are highly culturally specific and we cannot expect to find the same patterns of interaction across cultures. In the case of my study, for example, where I examine closely a single collaboratively produced story, I used a model of narrative based on temporal sequencing. I do not claim that this model is universally applicable: what counts as 'proper' narrative construction is culturally variable. There is also, as I have already indicated, a limit to the extent that we can generalize from findings within particular groups to the broader culture the groups belong in. It would be absurd, for example, to generalize from the findings of my study to all couples everywhere. Cultural specificity and small size of sample are both limits on the generalizability of research findings.

Further reading

Women and men as storytellers

Aspects of women's and men's storytelling are explored in Coates (1996, 2003, 2005). The last of these is one of the chapters in a collection on *The*

Sociolinguistics of Narrative (Thornborrow and Coates 2005). On conversational storytelling as a genre, see ch. 6 of Eggins and Slade (2005). For a book-length study of everyday storytelling, see Ochs and Capps (2001).

Dinner-table talk

Two recent studies of dinner-table talk and child socialization are Kendall (2006a) and Paugh (2005). Blum-Kulka (1997) is a book-length account of cross-cultural research on dinner-table narratives.

5

Conversation

This is the second of two chapters dealing with specific genres. Conversation – an informal, private genre of talk – is its focus. It presents research into the conversational division of labour, male–female miscommunication and distinct 'interactional styles', and politeness strategies used by women and men.

Conversation as a genre

In the last chapter, I concentrated on storytelling going on in everyday conversation. Now I want to turn your attention to conversation itself. The term 'conversation' is sometimes used, very loosely, to refer to spoken language, talk in general. By identifying a conversational *genre* I am focusing more specifically on a kind of talk. As a genre it is still very broad, but it is characterized by a friendly and informal relationship between participants. At its most informal and relaxed we would call it chatting or gossiping. The most important thing about chatting is not so much what is being talked about as the fact that talk is taking place at all. Chatting is friendly talk, talk for its own sake (in Britain, the mainstay of such talk is the weather). What all conversation is about is keeping the channel of communication open (known as the *phatic* function of language). It is the vital social glue that keeps relationships going.

When people engage in conversation they do so in a fairly symmetrical way. The ebb and flow of talk from one person to another is one of its defining characteristics, even between people with very different social positions, such as teacher and pupil. If they are in *conversation*, they each have a share of the talk. And their turns at talk are likely to be very short. In contrast with other genres, such as a lecture, or the interview genre, it's not a matter of one person doing all the talking, or one person asking a lot of questions and the other answering them. If that were to happen in what we thought was a conversation, we'd probably say, 'What's with all the questions? Is this an interview or what?'

We tend to think of conversation as private, but it occurs in public places as well. We may engage in conversations in shops, which are public places, with shop assistants, who are probably strangers to us. For most people, conversation is an important part of relationships at work. So, all in all, the public–private distinction is a difficult one to sustain. It is not a clear-cut thing, but a matter of degree. However, conversation *is* distinct from public kinds of talk in important ways. Imagine two speakers on a podium, chatting among themselves in between speeches. Their speeches are for public consumption, their chat is not.

I have established the phatic function of conversation as its most important feature. This does not mean that what's talked about is entirely irrelevant. An American feminist, Deborah Jones, identifies four distinct kinds of conversation among women, which she views as different varieties of gossip. These are 'house-talk', occupational talk which is the housewife's equivalent of 'talking shop'; 'scandal', which involves the verbal policing of other women's behaviour; 'bitching', a form of troubles-talk involving complaints about men to other women; and finally 'chatting', which is purely phatic (Jones 1990). What they have in common is a sharing of personal experience in conversation (sometimes, incidentally, in narrative form). Gossip is a type of conversation stereotypically associated with women. According to Jones, women's gossip is 'a "language of intimacy" . . . arising from the solidarity and identity of women as members of a social group with a pool of common experience' (1990: 244). One contribution to feminist linguistics by the British linguist Jennifer Coates has been a positive reappraisal of kinds of talk that women are supposed to engage in, especially gossip, which has traditionally been viewed negatively (Coates 1988, 1996). Other researchers have demonstrated that men engage in it too (Johnson and Finlay (1997) – and, taking a narrower definition of gossip as malicious talk about other people in their absence, Cameron (1997)).

The conversational division of labour

In an investigation of gender roles in private conversations, Pamela Fishman examined talk between intimates. These were conversations of three couples, taped separately, in their homes (Fishman 1983, 1998). They were all white, middle-class, heterosexual Americans. They lived in small apartments so most of their conversation could be picked up, including loud talk from bathroom and bedroom. Fishman left them in control of the tape-recorder; most often it was the men who took care of the taping, often turning the machines on without the women's knowledge. They were left to run for periods of from one to four hours; twelve and a half hours' worth in all.

To put it bluntly, what Fishman found in these conversations was that the women were doing the donkey-work in conversation with their husbands: 'As with work in its usual sense, there appears to be a division of labor in conversation. The people who do the routine maintenance work, the women, are not the same people who either control or benefit from the process' (1983: 99). In her analysis of the conversations, she attended to the distribution of questions, minimal responses, attention-getters, topic initiation and topic uptake. This is what she found:

Questions women 3x men
The women asked three times as many questions as the men. As Fishman sees it, they need to elicit responses from men and are asking interested questions to engage in interaction at all.

Minimal responses
These are 'interested listener' noises (such as **mm**, **yeah**). They are sometimes called supportive feedback or backchannel feedback. They are an essential part of cooperative talk (we have seen a lot of them in the chapter on stories). Fishman found that the women used them supportively to develop the topic. The men withheld or delayed minimal responses to curtail the topic, which Fishman interpreted as uncooperative.

Attention-getters
Women used 'D'ya know what?' to engage their husbands' attention. To make sense of this, we need to consider the context in which this kind of question appears. It is often used as the first part of a pre-sequence:

A: 'D'ya know what?'
B: 'What?'

This is a kind of preamble that is used to attract attention before introducing a topic. It is typical of children trying to claim the attention of adults. The women in Fishman's data used it. They also used 'y'know' as an attention-getter after a delayed or withheld minimal response.

Topic initiation and uptake
The 'success' of topics is what is of interest here. In brief, men's topics always succeeded, women's were often not taken up. According to

Fishman, the success of men's topics is due to the supportive efforts of women. She reports that women used minimal responses (such as 'interested listener' noises) supportively to develop the topic, while men withheld or delayed minimal responses to curtail topics.

Fishman concludes with the observation that women are pushed into low-status interactional work, just as they are pushed into low-status jobs. She saw the differences in language used by husbands and wives in conversation as manifestations of the larger social order in everyday interaction. Just as there is an unequal division of labour on grounds of sex, so conversational 'labour' is divided unequally. The original version of her paper had the rather expressive title of 'Interactional shitwork'.

Her study was very small, of course, just three couples. But it is not the only one showing men behaving like strong, silent types at home. Victoria DeFrancisco looked at the interaction of seven couples and her findings were much the same. She extended Fishman's methods by incorporating the views of the people involved by means of individual interviews in which she played back extracts from the taped conversations. The women all had similar complaints about their husbands:

> All the women expressed concern about getting their husband's attention and mentioned the extra efforts they made to try to do so. One woman, Sandy, said: 'He doesn't talk to me! If it were up to him, we wouldn't talk.' She described various attention-getting strategies: she quizzed him if she suspected he had not been listening; she used guilt and jealousy strategies, and she purposefully raised topics he enjoyed. (DeFrancisco 1991: 418)

DeFrancisco gives two fragments of a conversation between one couple:

```
1   Mary:   I went to Diana's today for lunch
2           got a salad you know? (.)
3   Bud:    ahha=
4   Mary:   =ran into your mom=
5   Bud:    =ran into who?
6   Mary:   (.) your mom (.)
7           she didn't even know who I was
8   Bud:    (.) ahh
9   Mary:   (.) she was at the she was at the meat case
10          and and I was looking at you know
11          I was gettin my salad and I come around
12          and she was at the meat case and then
```

13		she took off and then- (.)
14	Bud:	be right back ((goes outside))
15		ouch my elbow! (4.5)
16		((door bangs; he returns)) (..) emm (.)
17	Mary:	so I followed her all the way up through
18		the store (.) and she was (xx-)
19	Bud:	well you have to remember my mom
20		my mom has tunnel vision too I mean
21		she don' see nothin but straight ahead

...

22	Mary:	I've got this all figured out (.) I talked
23		to Doyle today? (.) and (.) you know
24		explained to him the fact that you know
25		come April I'll probably have to (.) ahm
26	Bud:	(.) excuse me open the back door
27		I'm gonna give this to (the dogs) (..)
28		((he returns))
29	Mary:	I'll probably have to terminate
30		my appointment

(Adapted from DeFrancisco 1991: 417–18)

During the husband's interview, he said 'he did not feel like talking at the time of the conversation and that he had "heard it all before"' (1991: 418). He certainly gives the impression of someone who does not feel like talking: he only produces two 'interested listener' noises (lines 3 and 8), he cuts her off three times (lines 14, 19 and 26) and even leaves the room twice. He seems to flatten the 'punchline' in line 19, abruptly cutting off her narrative.

In some work that I did on interruptions (Talbot 1992a), my findings also suggest that husband and wife may have different speaker-rights. The partners in my study are not home alone, but socializing with friends. We have met them already in the last chapter, when I presented a couple's collaborative production of a narrative. During the course of the evening's conversation, the same couple engaged in joint telling of another story. In this one, however, the collaboration breaks down: the husband effectively silences his wife (and everyone else) with the words: 'I wish you'd stop interrupting me!' Was she, though, I wondered? It didn't look like it to me.

Whatever I thought, the husband clearly *felt* that he was being interrupted.

I did not follow up the taping with interviews, as DeFrancisco did, but I did ask the couple for their impression of the evening's conversation immediately afterwards. He remarked on how his wife interrupted him all the time. She agreed with him. What his complaint did was cut off his wife's contribution to the narrative development, a contribution which consisted of answering interested questions from their audience and correcting some of his details. The husband seemed to be objecting to sharing the narration with her. The complaint also put an end to the supportive work of his audience. He ended up delivering the rest of it as a monologue, which I very much doubt was the effect he wanted. At the point of his complaint, he was probably irritated at losing the thread of (his version of) the story because of others' contributions, not just his wife's.

But was she interrupting? Only if she should not have been contributing in the first place. The trouble is, identifying interruptions is a problem (see Talbot 1992a). They cannot be identified solely by mechanical means, such as by looking for where people are speaking at the same time. Some early work on interruptions as ways of 'doing power' in conversation now seems simplistic, because they tried to do just that (West and Zimmerman 1983; Zimmerman and West 1975). If there are two or more people speaking at the same time, it does not necessarily mean there is interruption going on, as Jennifer Coates's research into all-women conversation has demonstrated (Coates 1988). Deborah Tannen's work on high-involvement style, too, has shown that simultaneous speech can be quite the opposite of disruptive (Tannen 1984). In the various samples of everyday narratives we examined in the last chapter, we saw a good deal of butting-in which was cooperative rather than turn-violating. Conversely, when there is no simultaneous talk at all, a speaker may interrupt by cutting someone off mid-turn (as in lines 14, 19 and 26 of DeFrancisco's data above). Interruptions are turn-taking violations, one person taking another person's speaking turn away from them. They are very much in the eye of the beholder (or the ear of the interruptee, perhaps).

Miscommunication

As they are growing up, children very often spend their time playing in single-sex groups. Boys' and girls' play groups tend to be rather different, so that children grow up, to an extent, in gender-specific cultures; they learn about such things as how to interact in friendly ways from their peers rather than from adults. Consequently, learning cross-sex talk can be a big problem in adulthood.

At least, that is a claim that has been made by various American linguists. The first to do so were Daniel Maltz and Ruth Borker (1982). What they did was re-examine some of the language and gender research to date (that is, up to the beginning of the 1980s), rethinking the findings in terms of miscommunication between adult women and men. Among the existing findings they reconsidered were Pamela Fishman's on the conversational division of labour, which we looked at in the last section.

Maltz and Borker's approach has two major influences. Its origins lie in the sociolinguistic work of John Gumperz and associates on cross-cultural miscommunication. This body of work examined how differences in cultural background lead to misunderstandings: for example, between British and Indian speakers of English. Mismatches in expectations about talk cause problems for minority groups in the host culture; intonation patterns used by Indian speakers, for instance, may be perceived as abrupt and rude by prospective British employers. Maltz and Borker's other major influence was extensive research on African-American children at play by Marjorie Harness Goodwin (1980). The boys and girls often played in single-sex groups and Goodwin found some very striking differences between these groups (she also found a great many similarities, which Maltz and Borker ignored, incidentally). I will look at some of her findings before going on to consider miscommunication among adults.

Goodwin became a part of the scenery in the children's neighbourhood in Philadelphia, following them around with a video camera as they played. She looked at the way these children organized themselves socially as they played in the street: at their group dynamics and language strategies. An important part of play is planning what to do and getting others to go along with you. Play involves deciding and agreeing on courses of action. All this requires issuing *directives* of some kind.

The girls played in twos and threes, in small non-hierarchical groups. There was joint participation in decisions and minimal status negotiation; in other words, nobody had to be the leader. Proposals about what to do were made by all the participants; and they were generally agreed with. In issuing directives they tended to use forms like **let's**, the inclusive **we** and conditionals like **could** (in the play from which all the extracts are taken, the girls were hunting around for glass bottles so that they could cut their tops off and make rings with them):

> Let's move *these* out *first*
> we gonna make a *whole* display of rings
> uh we could um (2.4) shel*lac* em
> (Goodwin 1980: 166)

Less frequently, they used the form **gotta**, which has more of the imperative force of a command. But when they did, what they were proposing was some joint action or obligation:

1	Sharon:	Pam you know what we could do
2		(.) we gotta *clean* em first
3		we gotta *clean* em
4	Pam:	huh
5	Sharon:	we gotta clean em first you know
6	Pam:	I know ⌈cuz they got germs⌉
7	Sharon:	⌊wash em and stuff⌋ cuz
8		just in case they got germs on em
9		⌈and then you clean em⌉
10	Pam:	⌊I got some pictures⌋
		(3.5)
11	Sharon:	clean em and then we *clean* em
12		and we gotta be careful with em
13		before we get the glass cutters
14		you know we gotta be careful with em
15		cuz it cuts easy

(1980: 167)

When the girls did not agree, they tended to have little difficulty negotiating differences. For example, on reaching an urban (hence dirty) stream in their search for bottles, the following ensues:

1	Pam:	y'all gonna walk in it?
2	Nettie:	walk in it you know where that water
3		come from? the toilet
4	Pam:	so I'ma walk in it in my dirty feet
		I'ma walk in it and I don't care
5		if it do come-
6		you could easy wash your feet
7	Nettie:	((to investigator)) gonna walk us across?
8		yeah I'll show y'all where you can come

(1980: 169)

Goodwin is not claiming that girls *cannot* use direct forms, but that they *do* not in friendly interaction among themselves. They do use them when they are playing house or school, in the roles of parent or teacher. They also use them when telling younger children what to do and when they are in very hostile encounters, including with boys.

Now let's look at the boys. They were grouped in hierarchical teams or 'gangs'. On one occasion, two teams of boys were making slingshots out of coathangers, preliminary to a battle. Making the slingshots itself became highly competitive between the two teams. The boys engaged in status negotiation; in other words, they were competing over who was the leader. Their choice of language strategies played a key part in this. Their directives typically took the form of explicit commands. These are often in highly aggravated forms, such as simply in terms of the speaker's desires:

> GIMME THE WIRE . . . *Look* man, I want the wire cutters right *now*
> PLIERS I WANT THE PLIERS!
> Man I told you it kinda crowded around here now I can't *stand* it
> (1980: 160)

Only the leader uses such commands successfully. Huey, below, tries and fails:

Huey: Gimme the *things*
Chopper: you shut up you big lips

(1980: 159)

The behaviour that the boys engage in would be deplored among the girls (similarly, throughout my schooling in Britain, I recall that 'being bossy and showing off' were the two cardinal sins in girls' groups). The contrasting group dynamics and language strategies in the boys' and girls' groups can be summarized as follows:

GIRLS	BOYS
Social organization	
Mostly in pairs	Large groups
'Best friends'	'Gangs'
Non-hierarchical	Hierarchical
Directives	
'Hey y'all let's use these first and then come back and get the rest cuz, it's too *many* of em.'	'Gimme the pliers.' 'Get off my steps.' 'Man, don't come down

'We gonna paint em and stuff.'   *in* here where I *am.*'
'We could go around looking
for bottles.'

Maltz and Borker (1982) use the evidence of these subcultural differences among children to account for miscommunication among adults. Their claim is that women and men are socialized in distinct subcultures. They grow up with different expectations about friendly, conversational behaviour. There is an analogy between gender and ethnicity here, with gender segregation in childhood leading to differing patterns of interaction, hence fuel for misunderstanding. Like people from different cultures, men and women miscommunicate because their expectations of the discourse differ. With this in mind, Maltz and Borker looked afresh at Fishman's findings and interpreted them differently. For example, they saw mismatches of expectations in the use of minimal responses (**mm**, **yeh** and suchlike) by women and men. Women have learned to use them as interested-listener noises. Men have not. So women think: Why do men never listen? And men think: Why do women always agree with you?

This work on miscommunication between men and women has since developed into a view of fully fledged, distinct male and female styles of interaction. I present this view in the last section of this chapter. First, though, I need to look at another, very substantial body of work on women, men and politeness, which has fed into it.

Politeness

People establish friendship partly by signalling closeness with, and mutual interest in, one another. This kind of friendly behaviour is sometimes called being 'positively polite' (Brown and Levinson 1987). Positive politeness involves people in attention to one another's 'positive face': their need to be liked, to be approved of. The term is not an evaluative one. It is called positive politeness to distinguish it from the kind of politeness common both among strangers and from subordinates, that attends to 'negative face': people's need for freedom from being harassed and imposed upon. The distinction is between friendly behaviour and respectful behaviour. The latter – the negative kind – is probably more familiar as 'being polite', being closer to our everyday-language notion of politeness. In fact, though, both positive and negative kinds of politeness make up the vital social lubricants that keep people talking. After all, signalling friendship is every bit as important as signalling respect.

There is research to suggest that men and women have different ways of going about being friendly. Women have been found to use a lot of politeness strategies, including in friendly conversation. Janet Holmes presents a detailed picture of women's extensive use of politeness strategies in New Zealand (Holmes 1995). They are mostly of the positive variety: hedges, boosters and compliments (Holmes also found that women apologize a lot: a negative politeness strategy). Hedging and boosting devices are modal elements; that is, elements that modify the force of a statement, either weakening it or intensifying it. We use hedges to avoid stating things categorically, to avoid sounding too dogmatic and sure of ourselves. Examples are **sort of, rather, a bit, kind of, about**. Tag questions (**isn't it?, can't we?**, etc.) are sometimes used as hedges. Boosters are ways of adding friendly enthusiasm, expressing intense interest. Examples are **really** and **so**. Compliments between women consolidate solidarity between speaker and addressee. They function as social lubricants, creating or maintaining rapport, as in the example below. Two female co-workers, meeting after the weekend, exchange complimentary remarks about the beneficial effect of a little, long-overdue English sunshine on their pale English faces:

Sarah: Hi Sallie (.) how's things? ok?
Sallie: HI: Sarah (..) .hhh oh not so bad (1.5)
        you look as if you had a good weekend!
Sarah: Oh yeah, you bet! been out in the sun all
        weekend (..) my nose was all red yesterda(h)y
        though
Sallie: Well it's not now (.) you look great
Sarah: Mm thanks I needed a bit of colour all
        winter in this place (.) you're lo- you're
        looking good (.) can see you been in the sun
Sallie: Really? Go(h)d (.) was only in it for about an hour
Sarah: Oh yeah can see it in your face (.) it suits you.

This exchange bears some resemblance to a complimenting ritual discussed in Tannen (1994: 209–11).

In chapter 3, I looked at some of Holmes's work on one particular item used as a hedge: namely tag questions. As we saw in chapter 3, she found that men and women tend to use tag questions as hedges in different ways. Men more often used the referential tag, which is used to check on the accuracy of what is being said. The referential kind of tag signals uncertainty about the information content of an utterance (that is, its *referential* content). Women more often used affective tags. This is the kind of tag that does not signal uncertainty, but is typically used to encourage a participant to contribute to the talk, or to soften the potential threat of a criticism or a request. Holmes found this overall pattern – men focusing on the referential function of language (information), women on the affective function (feelings) – with a range of hedging and boosting devices.

In a lot of empirical studies, men have been found to use politeness strategies a great deal less than women, in a range of situations and in many different cultures and languages. Brown and Levinson (1987) examine politeness strategies in a language of the Indian subcontinent (Tamil) and one of Mexico (Tzeltal, a Mayan language), as well as in English. What are we to make of this gender difference? Are men less polite, or is it that they express politeness differently?

We can explore this issue by attending to one politeness strategy in some detail. For this I have selected a positively polite type of utterance: giving compliments. The giving of compliments is one of the most interesting, and perhaps most obvious, ways of being positively polite. Complimenting is a way of making the recipient feel interesting, valued, approved of. Holmes defines a compliment in the following way: 'A compliment is a speech act which explicitly or implicitly attributes credit to someone other than the speaker, usually the person addressed, for some "good" (possession, characteristic, skill, etc.) which is positively valued by the speaker and the hearer' (1986: 485).

With a positive critical remark such as **That's a nice jacket**, the speaker may be primarily being friendly and sociable. This does not mean the remark is insincere, but that the opinion (that the jacket is nice) may not be the speaker's main concern when she opens her mouth to express it. As such, the speaker's focus is on the affective rather than the referential function of language. She is establishing or maintaining closeness with the wearer of the jacket, rather than imparting information about the jacket itself. This does not mean compliments are empty of referential meaning, however. They have to have a topic, a particular 'good' selected for praise.

The way compliments function and the way they are perceived by their recipients are affected by the power relationship between complimenter and recipient, and also by what genre of interaction they are engaging in. For example, between teacher and pupil in a classroom, a compliment will not be functioning in the same way as in a conversation between equals. So, for instance, the function of **That's really good**, as a remark about someone's work, depends on who utters it, to whom, and in what situation. Such a compliment from a teacher to a pupil in class functions differently from the same remark in a chat between friends. It functions as praise from a superior rather than simply as an expression of friendship. In conversation, power asymmetry between the people involved may influence the recipient's perception of a compliment. So the same pupil, let's say, in conversation with the teacher outside the classroom, may be unsure how to construe a compliment from the same teacher, even if the wording is identical. Is it still functioning as praise from a superior (in which case the teacher is reasserting the hierarchy of the classroom)? Is the teacher trying to establish rapport as a friend? Or is the compliment somehow doing both at the same time?

Speech acts like compliments always have an element of ambivalence. They are used in hierarchical situations, as in the classroom example (or from manager to secretary in a work setting, or from parent to child). Since this is the case, they can be a bit tricky. Power relationships are important in how compliments are perceived. It is possible to use the act of complimenting not just in a friendly way, but as a way of asserting power over the recipient. Compliments are always open to being interpreted as assertions of hierarchical relationships, even if that is not the way the complimenter intends them to sound. It is possible to interpret a compliment as a patronizing 'put-down'.

These observations about the single positive politeness strategy of complimenting may help us to account for the more general finding that men use fewer politeness strategies than women do. Bearing in mind the research we looked at in the last section, on boys' socialization in hierarchical groups, it may be that men are sensitive to power differences and interpret people's use of speech acts such as compliments as attempts to assert power-over, as claims to top-dog position in a hierarchy. If the recipient thinks the complimenter is doing this, then the compliment will be perceived as a threat. Mind you, it is not *only* men who can interpret compliments as threatening or patronizing, as any woman will attest who has been congratulated for successfully parking her car.

Power is not the only social variable influencing the way compliments are interpreted. How well giver and receiver know one another is also important; they tend to be exchanged between friends and acquaintances. In complimenting somebody, we are assuming some degree of intimacy. A compliment may be seen as a threat if the person on the receiving end does not think the assumed intimacy is warranted; if, for example, it is from a total stranger. A young woman receiving a favourable critical remark from a man on a building site may not receive it as a compliment. Both power

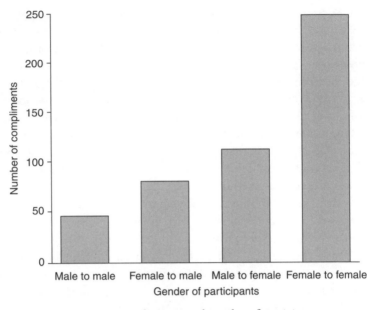

Figure 5.1 Compliments and gender of participants
(Holmes 1995: 123)

and social distance, then, influence complimenting. Like other politeness strategies, compliments are likely to be hugely variable across cultures.

Holmes conducted a study of compliments and compliment responses among New Zealanders, mostly Pakeha (that is, of European origin). With the help of data collectors, she gathered 484 noted-down compliments and responses that occurred naturally. She found that the biggest proportion of them were between women. We can see from figure 5.1 how the compliments were distributed by gender. Compliments were far less frequent from men, especially *between* men. Are men more likely to perceive them as threatening? Are they uncomfortable with the frequency of solidary complimenting that women engage in, perceiving them as attempts to assert power-over, rather than closeness? One thing that comes across unequivocally in Holmes's research findings is that people are *highly* sensitive to status in complimenting behaviour, not only men but women as well. Holmes found that by far the largest proportion of compliments were between people of equal status. In hierarchical situations where there were unequal power relations, compliments were infrequent. When they did occur, they were more likely to be given by the person in the more powerful position.

Holmes also examined the choice of compliment topic. She found that people complimented on either appearance, ability, possessions or

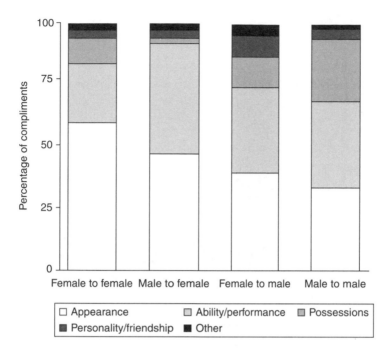

Figure 5.2 Compliment topic and gender of participants
(Holmes 1995: 132)

personality. Here the difference in distribution by gender was less striking, but still quite distinct. More than half of the compliments between women were about appearance. Between men, appearance was the topic of about a third (see figure 5.2).

Compliment responses were of three broad types: acceptance, rejection or deflection. Their overall distribution between women and men was very similar in Holmes's New Zealand study (figure 5.3). Both men and women were most likely to accept, usually with an agreement token (**thanks**; **yes**) and agreeing utterance (**I think so too**). There were, however, some gender differences in the choice of strategy used for rejecting and deflecting compliments. Women were more likely than men to reject compliments by disagreeing with them (**I'm afraid I don't like it much**), other possibilities being to question the accuracy of an utterance (**Is beautiful the right word?**) or challenge the speaker's sincerity (**Oh, you don't really mean that!**). Men were marginally more likely to deflect a compliment by ignoring it and changing the subject (**Gosh, is that the time?**), or some other evasive action.

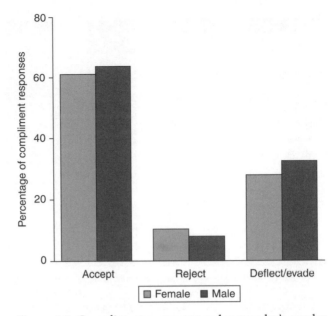

Figure 5.3 Compliment responses and responder's gender
(Holmes 1995: 140)

The overall tendency to accept compliments in the New Zealand study contrasts with findings elsewhere and points to possible cultural differences. In some Malaysian research on compliment responses, rejection was more frequent than acceptance, especially from women (Azman 1986). This finding can be readily accounted for by Malaysian pressure for modesty and avoidance of self-praise, particularly among women.

I have been examining a single positive politeness strategy very closely and have come up with a partial answer to the question: do women and men have different ideas about how to be friendly? The answer tells us more about women than men, though, since we have looked at compliments as expressions of solidarity among women. In terms of men's friendliness, it has not been very informative. We have found out what they do *not* do. Is there more substance?

Some men's idea of signalling friendliness involves sparring and they often seem to be amused by carping criticism. In a less intense fashion, I have noticed some male friends of mine maintaining a continual low-level grumbling with one another, as part of their friendly interaction. An example is the following petty complaint, uttered quite quietly, and not sounding particularly annoyed at all (the recipient paid little attention). They were with a group of people attending a talk to be given by a novelist. The speaker and his addressee have both bought a copy of the author's novel that evening:

Dave: ey! get off that! read your own book. know a bloke for years, think
         you trust him. and then what does he do? comes along and starts
         reading your book
Keith: ((absently)) (I) put mine away in my bag
Dave: never mind that. bend the spine of your own book

Competitive verbal abuse and mock insults seem to be popular too. In some cultural contexts these may be highly ritualized. There has been some research on ritual insults among boys and men: in black teenage gangs in New York (Labov 1972b), among Turkish boys (Dundes, Leach and Özkök 1972), in a New Zealand rugby locker room (Kuiper 1991). It seems distinctly odd to call this kind of behaviour polite, but if the insults produced are functioning as expressions of solidarity, as they seem to be, then they are functioning as 'friendly signals', just as positively polite compliments are for women. This presents an intriguing mirror image of the pattern Holmes found about women, as she herself notes. Men are threatened by compliments, but use insults to cement friendship.

It is not just men who do this, though. In the jointly produced narrative we looked at in chapter 4, you may recall the wife calling her husband a 'stupid pillock'. To my knowledge, she never uses terms of abuse for anyone else (except sometimes herself). You could perhaps say she adopts a masculine way of showing affection to her husband. There is some evidence of insults being used as expressions of solidarity among women in the United States. Laurel Sutton has recorded the use of bitch and ho as terms of affection among women (Sutton 1995). Donna Eder has investigated insults in playful disputes among groups of girls (Eder 1990, cited in Goodwin 2003: 239).

Men's and women's interactional styles

Consider this fragment of conversation between husband and wife at dinner:

Wife: That meeting I had to go to today was just awful.
Husband: Where was it?
W: In the NLC building. People were just so aggressive.
H: Mm. Who was there?

W: Oh the usual representatives of all the government depart-
            ments. I felt really put down at one point, you know, just so
            humiliated.
H: You should be more assertive dear. Don't let people trample
            all over you and ignore what you say.

(Holmes 1992)

The wife was a bit put out by this exchange. She felt her husband had
missed the point. What did he do? He gave her advice. What did she want?
A bit of sympathy.

   Advice and sympathy; or to put it another way, problem-solving and
problem-sharing. This is one of the contrasts between men's and women's
expectations in conversation that are talked about in a recent presentation
of the two-cultures view of differences in men's and women's talk (Tannen
1991). American linguist Deborah Tannen has brought the notion of men
and women having distinct styles of interaction to a wide audience in a
series of books in the self-help genre (Tannen 1986, 1991, 1995). These
popularizing books have had a hostile reception from feminist linguists (I
will consider why in chapter 6). She makes use of a variety of binary oppo-
sitions to characterize women's and men's different styles of talk:

sympathy   problem-solving
rapport   report
listening   lecturing
private   public
connection   status
supportive   oppositional
intimacy   independence

These overlap a good deal, but they are quite revealing and may strike a
chord for many people. Her distinction between rapport talk and report
talk is an interesting one. We can liken this dichotomy to the distinction
Holmes makes between affective and referential functions of language.
For most women, says Tannen, conversations are about rapport: they are
about establishing friendship, consolidating relationships. A lot of energy
in women's talk goes into emphasizing what they have in common.
Interaction is non-hierarchical; they are striving for solidarity. I looked at
compliments in the previous section and saw women using them as a way
of being friendly, establishing solidarity. Women have also been found to

agree with their interlocutor a lot, at least among the white middle-class in the United States. As a way of engaging in friendly conversation, though, this is culturally variable. Tannen recalls her own conversational difficulties with Greek women, who would not accept her 'relentless agreement' and strove to find something to disagree with (1995: 238–9).

For most men, continues Tannen, conversations can be rather different. They can be highly competitive. Men tend to use conversations as arenas for negotiating and maintaining status, so that they tend to involve exhibitions of knowledge and skill, performances intended to get attention and keep it. Jokes, storytelling and the imparting of information are important. Men are focused on report rather than rapport. Conversations are about imparting information, talking for a purpose, demonstrating expertise. This concern to provide information and demonstrate expertise crosses into other spoken genres, as some research on Greek men giving directions has shown (Dendrinos and Pedro 1994). They found that, having been asked for information, Greek men *insisted* on supplying some, at length, whether it was right or wrong. They gave bad directions rather than none at all! The request for directions was taken as a request, or licence, for public self-display.

Tannen observes that the same men who are outspoken and talkative in groups become quiet and uncommunicative at home, or so their wives complain. She refers to the familiar North American stereotype of the silent husband behind the newspaper at breakfast, suggesting that men are not interested in engaging in conversations with wives because they see nothing to be gained from it. Ever conciliatory, she simply observes that this shows that husbands and wives have different ideas about talk at home. For men, conversational talk is a forum for self-display. They are operating in a competitive framework, either winning or losing. Home is a haven where the pressure is off: 'the comfort of home means the freedom from having to prove themselves and impress through verbal display' (1991: 86). This is certainly one way of accounting for the taciturn husbands we met in the section on the conversational division of labour. My own view is rather less charitable, and more in line with Fishman's and DeFrancisco's interpretations of their findings (see earlier in this chapter).

In Tannen's account of the contrasting conversational styles of women and men, differences in style lead to minor, but regular, difficulties among couples. Many couples find one another irritating; Tannen accounts for this irritation in terms of unsatisfactory conversational interaction. Here is one of her many examples. A woman repeats to her husband what someone has said to her. She does so because it was very similar to a point he had made previously and she thought this would please him. She is, in effect, agreeing with her husband, being 'agreeable' by offering support for his position. To her dismay, he challenges it with an opposing view:

> Even when she was sure she was sowing agreement, she reaped a harvest of disagreement. To John, raising a different point of view is a more interesting contribution to make than agreeing. But Marge finds his disagreeing disagreeable . . . For Marge, disagreement carries a metamessage of threat to intimacy. John does not see disagreement as a threat. Quite the opposite, he regards being able to express disagreement as a sign of intimacy. (Tannen 1991: 168)

Tannen informs us that the husband felt he was being supportive, but his idea of support is 'modeled on an adversarial stance – a stance that is more expected and appreciated by men than by women' (1991: 168).

Tannen's popularizing work on gender differences is anecdotal and highly speculative. This cannot be said of the following, however: an interesting study of videoed talk between pairs of friends in four age groups, ranging from small children to adults (Tannen 1990, 1991). She looked at how they aligned themselves physically, including with their eyes, and at their introduction and development of topics. There were striking differences between the male and female pairs of friends in conversation at every age. She found that the second-grade girls had more in common with the women in their mid-twenties than they had with the boys of their own age. These pairs of friends were placed in an experimental situation, so that it was a bit artificial. They were placed in an office in front of a video camera and given a broad conversational task. The female friends physically aligned themselves with one another and frequently looked at one another directly. They rapidly established topics for talk and sustained them for some time. The male friends, especially the younger boys, aligned their bodies and eyes very much less, and produced small fragments of talk about a wide range of topics.

Here is some detail on the youngest children, the six-year-olds. The girls were very composed. They sat close together, looking steadily into each other's faces. The two boys did not keep still; they sat apart, fidgeting and casting their eyes about the room, everywhere but towards each other. Both pairs of friends had been asked to talk about 'something serious'. The boys' response was to make faces at the camera, practise some rude words, tease each other, tell jokes and above all to cast around for *something to do* (other than the conversational task asked of them). The girls set about the task earnestly, finding topics to talk about which would comply with the instructions they had been given: talking about something serious.

Jane: One time, my uncle, he was, uh, he has like this bull ranch? in
         Millworth? And the bull's horns went right through his head
Ellen: That's serious

(Tannen 1990: 185)

While the boys seemed to be working hard at being 'naughty', the girls
were as perfect a pair of goody-two-shoes as you could imagine.

According to this body of research on male and female conversational
styles, women tend to focus on rapport and the affective, supportive
function of conversation; broadly speaking, to be oriented towards the
interpersonal. Men on the other hand tend to focus on report and the informational function of conversation. But these are problematic dichotomies.
Impressing your talking partner that you are brilliant involves just as much
focus on the interpersonal as impressing on them what a caring person you
are. The six-year-old girls talking about 'something serious' were evidently
concerned about the informational content of their talk, as part of being
concerned about pleasing the experimenter. Dichotomies are easy ways of
remembering, but they can lead to oversimplification. They are convenient,
but we must not forget that it is only a matter of degree or focus. When we
talk about the function of a particular stretch of talk, we have to bear in
mind that language is multifunctional. People never do just one thing at a
time with it. Even the biggest show-off has to show off about *something*.

Equal but different?

The research presented in this chapter has painted a picture of male and
female conversational differences in very broad strokes; notably absent
in it are the important social factors of class and ethnicity. I have looked
at work on the division of conversational 'labour', miscommunication
between men and women as 'cross-cultural', gender differences in politeness strategies in conversation and work on distinct male and female
conversational styles.

Is it just a matter of women and men being equal but different, then,
in their conversational interaction? That is the overall impression you get
from reading a lot of work in the field, especially Tannen's books (not the
work we looked at in the section on the conversational division of labour,
however). We need to consider the consequences of using these different
styles of talk, particularly in work settings (in fact, to be fair to Tannen, she
does this on occasion; a more recent book of hers (Tannen 1995) explores

the consequences of the alleged male and female styles at work). As Coates observes, women are disadvantaged in many public contexts: 'Women are linguistically at a double disadvantage when entering the public domain: first, they are (normally) less skilful at using the adversarial, information-focused style expected in such contexts; second, the (more cooperative) discourse styles which they *are* fluent in are negatively valued in such contexts' (1995: 14). They tend to avoid the dreaded 'being bossy and showing off', for example. But how is this interpreted in a mixed group, in a professional setting? A woman in charge of a workforce who cannot, or will not, behave in 'bossy' and self-assertive ways risks being perceived as incompetent.

A possible alternative is for women to start using the kinds of linguistic strategy associated with men; but aren't these interpreted differently when used by women? Women are in an awkward double-bind here: being encouraged to adopt 'masculine' assertiveness in their professional lives, but perceived as confrontational and aggressive if they do. Margaret Thatcher, whatever one may think of her political career, was on the receiving end of some viciously vituperative attacks when she was prime minister which were nothing to do with her politics and everything to do with her sex. Just adopting a different way of interacting is not necessarily a good thing anyway. It has been claimed that typical characteristics of women's interaction are features that generate more exploratory kinds of talk, of a kind useful for examining ideas and issues. If this is the case, why suppress them?

I return to many of the issues raised here in chapter 6, where I critically examine the 'difference' and 'dominance' models underpinning the research on conversation we have looked at. In particular, I examine the criticisms which Tannen's popularizing books on male and female conversational styles have provoked and the major problems with the overriding preoccupation with 'difference'.

Further reading

Two useful readings for problems with 'competitiveness' and 'cooperativeness' as bipolar categories are Hewitt (1997) and Cameron (1997). I will indicate readings exploring problems with other issues presented in this chapter in the further reading for ch. 6.

Gossip

There is a group of articles on gossip reprinted in part IV of Coates (1998). See also Guendouzi (2001) and Pilkington (1998). For analysis of gossip as a genre, go to ch. 7 of Eggins and Slade (2005). Gossip activity in girls' friendship groups is examined in Goodwin (2007), especially ch. 6. Three chapters in Johnson and Meinhoff (1997) deal with men and gossip. Talbot (2003) examines stereotyping and contains discussion of one particularly resilient stereotype: the gossipy woman.

Women, men and politeness

I've already referred to Holmes (1995), a book-length account of research conducted in New Zealand. Her more recent work explores politeness in workplace talk (Holmes 2000; Holmes and Schnurr 2005). Other recent readings are Mills (2002, 2003, 2005). Eckert and McConnell-Ginet (2003: 144–56) covers the speech act of compliments in some detail. Compliment-responses in Jordanian Arabic are the topic of Farghal and Al-Khatib (2001), and a contrastive study of them in Spanish and English is found in Lorenzo-Dus (2001).

6

Difference-and-dominance and beyond

This final chapter in part II considers some of the theoretical underpinnings underlying research presented so far and the problems they pose for researchers in language and gender. It focuses chiefly on the preoccupation with 'difference' and includes discussion of the reception among feminist linguists of Deborah Tannen's popularizing work on male and female 'interactional styles'.

Deficit, dominance and difference

I need to start by considering once again what the early concerns of language and gender were and how they shaped feminist research. At the risk of oversimplification, it is possible to identify three frameworks: 'deficit', 'dominance' and 'difference'. In chapter 3, I discussed the influence of the deficit and dominance frameworks on early research into language and gender. In part II I presented research operating within the dominance and difference frameworks, most explicitly in the chapter focusing on research into conversation (chapter 5).

According to the deficit framework, women are disadvantaged as language users. They present themselves as uncertain, as lacking in authority. The best-known text (and in that sense, the key text) putting forward this view is Robin Lakoff's *Language and Woman's Place* (1975), which I looked at in chapter 3. This book gives the impression that women's language is inferior and deficient. The language men use is, by implication, the norm that women don't match up to. This early book accounted for gender differences in language use in terms of women's deficiencies, how women's language deviates from an implicit male norm. This deficit model is widely used in assertiveness training, and has been since the 1970s, if not earlier (Crawford 1995).

In the dominance framework, language patterns are interpreted as manifestations of a patriarchal social order. Hence asymmetries in the language use of men and women are interpreted as enactments of male privilege;

for example, interruptions are viewed as 'a way of "doing" power in face-to-face interaction' (West and Zimmerman 1983: 111). The best-known book working firmly within the dominance framework is Dale Spender's *Man Made Language* (1985), which I examined critically in chapter 3. As I observed there, she has a monolithic view of male power. It is as though all men were in a position to dominate all women, which is patently not the case. Other well-known research using the dominance model is Pamela Fishman's work on the conversational division of labour, which we examined in chapter 5. In her study of three couples at home, she found that the wives worked hard to keep conversations going with their husbands, doing a lot of support work to develop the men's topics, and so on. Fishman saw the differences she found in these conversations as manifestations of the larger social order in everyday interaction. Just as there is an unequal division of labour in the workplace on sexual grounds, so the 'labour' in private conversations is divided unequally.

The difference framework for accounting for patterns of language use has its origins in the sociolinguistic work of John Gumperz and associates on cross-cultural miscommunication. I introduced it in chapter 5. As people are growing up, so the story goes, girls and boys spend their time in subcultures with different social organizations. Children learn the rules for friendly interaction from their peers, not from adults. They grow up in gender-specific cultures. The difference model, then, depends on a 'two cultures' account of male and female socialization. It is often offered as an alternative to the dominance model as an explanation for patterns of language use. Behaviour that had previously been perceived as men's efforts to dominate women in interaction is reinterpreted as a 'cross-cultural' phenomenon, a result of mismatches in what men and women expect interaction to be like. The difference model is put forward to explain misunderstandings between women and men.

As Cameron observes, dominance and difference represented, historically speaking, particular moments in feminism: 'dominance was the moment of feminist outrage, of bearing witness to oppression in all aspects of women's lives, while difference was the moment of feminist celebration, reclaiming and revaluing women's distinctive cultural traditions' (1996: 41). What I have presented above is a somewhat simplified picture of the three frameworks: deficit, dominance and difference. In practice there is a good deal of overlap between them and they are chronologically not as straightforward as I have implied. There is still some research conducted in the dominance framework; one example is Victoria DeFrancisco's recent study of the conversational division of labour, which we saw in chapter 5.

The difference and dominance models can be used together, so that they complement one another. On the one hand, men and women are socialized into male and female subcultures. On the other hand, social relations, being patriarchal, affect men and women differently and in men's favour.

Difference-and-dominance provided an early model for the analysis of language and gender in the social sciences, specifically sociolinguistics and sociology (for example, see Thorne and Henley's 1975 collection entitled *Language and Sex: Difference and Dominance*). One of the best-known proponents of the difference framework is the linguist Deborah Tannen; we saw her work on male and female conversational styles in chapter 5. In both her popularizing books and her work for a more scholarly readership, Tannen maintains a carefully neutral position regarding these two styles. She avoids making value judgements, insisting that the distinct conversational styles of women and men she describes are equally valid. Similarly, sociolinguists do not make value judgements in describing varieties of language, such as social and regional dialects; from a sociolinguistic point of view, all varieties are equally valid. This is a stance often taken in defence of language varieties which are stigmatized (such as social dialects, for example, which for a sociolinguist are neither better nor worse than the prestige 'Standard' variety of a language; just different). So Tannen's position is in line with the neutrality and relativism of sociolinguistics.

The difference model also has wide currency in the world at large; that is to say, in institutions other than academia. It continues to be popular with journalists and other writers for mass media, including advertisers (Talbot 2008). In Britain in the mid-1990s, a telephone company was using it to stimulate social use of the telephone. Some British Telecom advertising contrasted men's and women's use of the phone, setting up women as good communicators who know the importance of phatic talk (well, they would, wouldn't they?). Tannen's popularizing books are bestsellers, available from book clubs. They are sold as self-help books. These books, and digests of them appearing in women's magazines, build on and fuel the burgeoning market for self-help merchandise: books and courses, management training manuals and suchlike. Books on relationships – a large part of the self-help genre – are read almost exclusively by women. The latter-day Professor Higginses who write them are highly prescriptive. They tend to consist of laundry lists of dos and don'ts, often mixing together difference and deficit models, or rather reducing difference to deficit. Some of them contain some pretty gross examples of victim-blaming, like this one from a book called *Leadership Skills for Women: Achieving Impact as a Manager*: 'Speak directly and stand firm when you are interrupted. Statistics show that women allow themselves to be interrupted 50 per cent more often than men. Don't contribute to those statistics' (cited in Cameron 1995a: 37–8).

Well, perhaps we should not blame academic researchers outright for what writers in the self-help genre do with their research findings. However, as Cameron points out (1996: 34), anyone publishing work on a sensitive or contested area needs to be aware of its impact in the world at large.

The trouble with 'dominance'

There are certain problems with the dominance framework. A major drawback is that male dominance is often treated as though it is pan-contextual. But as I've already remarked, all men are not in a position to dominate all women. Such a monolithic perception of patriarchy is useless. In fact, it's less than useless. It is very easily refuted. All a critic needs to do is produce a single counterexample: 'This male dominance business is a load of rubbish, because my mother/grandmother/aunt bosses about my father/grandfather/uncle.' This kind of remark may be all too familiar.

If we are going to make claims about male dominance, we need to be more sophisticated. This involves being more specific. What happens in schools and at home, for instance? How do patterns of male dominance vary across different cultures, and in different contexts within cultures? We need to consider in what institutions, in what situations and in what genres men can and do dominate women, and how those institutions, situations and genres help them to do so. For an example of research into the institution of the family, recall the detailed study I examined in chapter 4 that focused on the dynamics of white American dinner-table narratives. This work revealed not monolithic patriarchal power wielded by fathers over other family members, but something much more interesting. We saw mothers colluding in manoeuvring fathers into positions of panopticon-like control and invulnerability. Parents use the family dinner-table genre of everyday narratives to act out, and enforce, 'father knows best'.

One final observation about the dominance framework needs to be made before I go on to consider problems with 'difference'. Researchers into private language working within a dominance framework face an ethical problem. In researching into private language, you are dependent on people's goodwill. If people allow you to record their private conversations, they are doing you a considerable favour. It may constrain the nature of the results. Quite simply, men are unlikely to be pleased with

the way someone researching into male dominance in conversation interprets their findings. Someone conducting research of this kind among
couples may well have defensive, wounded husbands to contend with. I
have done some research on private conversational talk myself (Talbot
1992a). This was a study of interruptions in which I found that a husband
and wife had different speaker-rights. I found it difficult to work with the
data I had collected and ended up feeling uncomfortable and embarrassed
about what I was doing. My private and professional values and objectives
were in collision, which made me feel uneasy. It is not easy to start getting
personal about people's language habits when they have let you into their
private lives. This is a dilemma for the individual researcher and her willing
'victims' to deal with as they think best.

The trouble with 'difference'

The difference model does not present the ethical, and practical, difficulty
just mentioned (it's possible that this has contributed to its popularity
among language scholars). Tannen's careful neutrality is unlikely to offend
men: 'Nothing hurts more than being told your intentions are bad when
you know they are good, or being told you are doing something wrong
when you know you're just doing it your way' (1991: 297–8). This soothing remark really does sound as though it's addressed to the wounded
husbands I mentioned! Tannen bends over backwards in her concern for
evenhandedness.

Research in feminist linguistics has tended to focus on differences in
the language use of women and men. In the subsections that follow, I
address some of the problems with this overriding preoccupation with
dichotomized gender differences, examining in particular the suppression of power that tends to accompany 'differences' work. In doing this,
I will concentrate largely on Tannen's popularizing books, because they
are well known and influential. Unless otherwise indicated, the problems
addressed are also applicable to other work set exclusively in the differences framework.

The suppression of power

Neglect of power is a major problem with the differences model and with
the cross-cultural miscommunication account that it supports. Most of
Tannen's critics have focused on it (especially Cameron 1992b, 1995a;
Crawford 1995; Freed 1992; Trömel-Plötz 1991; Uchida 1992). Like other

'No no no. He doesn't dominate conversations. He just happens to have a
competitive style'
The demise of dominance

two-cultures proponents, Tannen offers reinterpretations of what has been
identified elsewhere as dominating behaviour (if you can't get a word in,
he's not dominating the conversation; it's just that he happens to have a
competitive style . . .). A major problem with the two-cultures approach –
on its own, as it tends to be used – is that it disregards the *consequences* of
differences, presenting an illusion of men and women being simply equal-
but-different.

This equal-but-different myth tends to go hand in hand with a narrow
focus on individuals and a disregard for broader social considerations. This
is the case with Tannen's work on male and female interactional styles.
The everyday conversational frustrations that Tannen discusses are set
entirely in terms of personal relationships between equals, separate from
social structure and the power asymmetries that it often *imposes* on such
personal relationships. Tannen does not totally reject male dominance as
an explanation for patterns of difference, but her notion of dominance is
severely limited. It is set entirely in terms of individual intention. Recall her
words of soothing reassurance to people who have been told their 'intentions are bad' (quoted above). She focuses on the personal, on individual
men who do things intentionally, and disregards social structure, which
can set men up to act in dominating ways whether they intend to or not.

There is no space in her account for unintentional dominance. The thing is, though, men can dominate whether they intend to or not. Unintentional dominance is a possibility which, try as it may, the miscommunication approach cannot rule out (Uchida 1992: 559). Intentions are not enough to account for gendered patterns of behaviour.

The two-cultures notion itself needs subjecting to scrutiny. It too conceals a neglect of power. The two distinct subcultures in which boys and girls are socialized are presented without any account of *why* there are same-sex play groups in the first place. They are just 'there'. The segregation of the sexes is certainly overstated, anyway. The reality is much more complex, and interesting. In extensive ethnographic studies of two American schools, Barrie Thorne has found complex patterns of mixing and separation (Thorne 1993). She also found evidence that friendship groups outside school tend to be more mixed and cites accounts of friendships between girls and boys going 'underground' in the more public domain of the school (1993: 50).

There is an analogy drawn between sex/gender and ethnicity: cross-sex talk is compared to cross-cultural talk. People from differing cultures misunderstand one another; so do men and women. This analogy is a dubious one. Men's and women's lives are highly integrated, especially in modern societies. Women and men do not exist in totally separate worlds. Mismatches in discourse expectations between, say, British and Indian speakers of English are of quite a different order; they are the outcome of growing up on different continents. Speakers of the male and female conversational styles may have grown up in the same neighbourhood, even in the same house. If, despite this, they really *are* as segregrated as people who have grown up on different continents, then we definitely need to know how, and why. It throws up all kinds of questions – for example, is it voluntary or coerced? What happens to the exceptions?

Underlying the two-cultures view is an assumption that the primary relations between people are single-sex, or *homosocial*. This is unusual, to say the least. Since heterosexuality is the norm, it is far more probable that primary relations are *heterosocial*. So what function do homosocial relations serve? In single-sex groups, children acquire the gender differences needed to support heterosexuality, differences that 'help to construct the heterosexual couple as a unit made up of complementary – but not equal – elements' (Cameron 1992b: 466).

Men's and women's conversational styles, as described, would equip them ideally to take up traditional roles, which ought to make us a little suspicious. There is something familiar about Tannen's innumerable anecdotal examples. Why is this? Could it be, perhaps, that we recognize them because they fit in so well with existing cultural stereotypes? Recall some of the contrasts that Tannen sets up in establishing the two, equally valid, styles:

sympathy	problem-solving
rapport	report
listening	lecturing
private	public
connection	status
supportive	oppositional
intimacy	independence

The left-hand column reminds us that women are nurturers. It could be a celebration of motherly qualities. Moreover, it could be used to support the traditional, conventional idealization of womanhood. The right-hand column could be used in defence of male power and privilege. But why do these differences exist? We are never told. Some of the things that are dressed up as neutral matters of 'style' are actually male privileges.

Now let's consider another item on the list: independence. Here is one of Tannen's anecdotal examples about American couples. 'Linda' is annoyed with 'Josh' because he has invited an old friend of his for the weekend without bothering to consult with her. That same weekend Linda is coming back from a long business trip and would have preferred not to have a house guest. No, Josh is not being an inconsiderate clod, just independent. We are given to understand that, for Josh, 'checking with his wife means seeking permission, which implies that he is not independent' (1991: 26). Several of Tannen's critics have singled this example out for criticism. It's not difficult to see why. As American linguist Alice Freed remarks, a sense of 'entitlement to act entirely on one's own and to make unilateral decisions is part of the social empowerment that men enjoy'. As she says, it has 'precious little to do with communicative style or language' (1992: 145–6). It is at odds with contemporary ideas about companionate marriage or couplehood for one partner to make a decision, about something involving them both, without bothering to check with the other. It strikes me that if 'Josh' values his independence so much, perhaps marriage wasn't such a good idea. I'm sure many men would agree.

Tannen's *You Just Don't Understand* (1991) has proved immensely appealing to the general public. It depicts a world in which power imbalance doesn't seem to exist; women and men coexist as equals. It addresses problems and breakdowns in communication without anyone having to be responsible for them. In her review, Freed identifies the book as part of a backlash against feminism. I think this is an accurate diagnosis. In another review – a very angry one – a German linguist, Senta Trömel-Plötz, complains that 'one searches in vain for concepts like dominance, control, power, politics of gender, sexism, discrimination, and finds two of them mentioned after 200 pages but not explored' (1991: 491). Building on the analogy between cross-sex and cross-cultural communication, the everyday battles of words and wills that beset relationships between men and women are, as presented by Tannen, nothing to do with women's struggles against oppressive behaviour. They just happen because men and women have different interactional styles but don't realize it. There is no unpleasant politics to think about and no one is to blame. The appeal of Tannen's popularized presentation of the difference framework is understandable. It provides a comfortable explanation for domestic disputes without pointing the finger at anybody.

Overemphasis on miscommunication

A difference framework minimizes any blame for 'cross-cultural' tensions by putting the emphasis on miscommunication. Men and women happen to have different interactional styles and misunderstandings occur because they are not aware of them. Tannen's *You Just Don't Understand* was marketed as the solution (emblazoned on the cover of the British edition is the slogan: 'A revolutionary approach to banishing the misunderstandings that haunt our relationships'). Once supplied with the necessary knowledge about these interactional styles, misunderstandings, and the tensions they cause, will be no more.

So the emphasis is on ignorance. Let's go back to the analogy drawn between gender and ethnicity and consider this. When people who have grown up in widely differing ethnic groups communicate with one another, there are going to be problems, because their cultural expectations about communication will be different. For example, in meetings conducted in English between business people from Hong Kong and the United States, the Chinese speakers of English will probably carry over speech patterns from their own language. As a result of this, the native speakers of English are likely to experience difficulties, being unable to tell when important information is being highlighted, for instance. It has been claimed that mismatches of discourse expectations like these – concerning important things like the signalling of new information in a stretch of talk – are behind the

Western stereotype of the 'inscrutable' Chinese (Young 1982). Such failures in understanding come about through one ethnic group's ignorance about another. They can be dispelled by educating people about cultural differences.

As we have already seen, the situation between women and men who have grown up in close cultural proximity is not the same at all. The claim that they are in a comparable state of ignorance is rather surprising, in fact. Within their own language communities, people are acutely sensitive to stylistic variation and used to producing and interpreting different styles as situations demand, as any linguist worth their salt could tell you. We are all used to dealing with differing interactional norms ('remember not to swear in front of your grandmother!'). We can vary our language according to the needs of the social context, in terms of how formal we need to be ('how do you address an archbishop?'), or how technical ('what's the word for those flowers you get on pea plants?'), and suchlike. Contrary to Tannen's account, it is highly improbable that women and men coexist with widely differing interactional styles without even being aware of it. Indeed, that well-known male assumption that when a woman says 'no' she really means 'yes' demonstrates a sophisticated ability on the part of men to anticipate interactional norms different from their own. Far from showing ignorance of the existence of differences between women's and men's styles of talk, it shows an expectation on the part of men that women's speech is patterned differently from their own (Eckert and McConnell-Ginet 1992: 467).

Men and women are not stuck with a single interactional style either. Men, for example, can do both rapport talk and report talk. They are perfectly capable of using what is supposed to be a woman's style, when it suits them to do so. Sometimes men do engage in rapport talk with women; it's known as 'sweet-talking' (Freed 1992: 149).

Fake neutrality

Two-cultures proponents, including Tannen, maintain a carefully neutral position regarding the two distinct interactional styles men and women are supposed to use. Both styles are presented as equally valid. As we have already observed, this stance of careful neutrality fits in with sociolinguistics. In describing language varieties, sociolinguists do not try to establish their relative merits.

Men's and women's styles are supposed to be equal but different. Let's compare this claim with a similar claim about two varieties of English:

Standard British English and Scouse (the local dialect spoken in Liverpool). The accepted sociolinguistic view of these varieties of English is that both are equally valid, linguistically. They are equally valid in the sense that a dialect of a language is every bit as rich in vocabulary and as grammatically complex as its prestige variety, and that a dialect speaker can communicate just as effectively and intelligently with it. In British society at large, however, it is patently not the case that Standard British English and Scouse are viewed as equally valid varieties; there is a social gulf between the local dialect and the prestige variety. Physicians, lawyers and lecturers don't speak Scouse, at least not in their professional capacity, and you won't hear anyone speaking Scouse in parliament. For an American example, try to imagine the chances of a would-be presidential candidate who sounded like a Brooklyn taxi driver, perhaps. The first thing this wanna-be would have to work on would be his or her voice (no slur on Brooklyn taxi drivers intended).

Sociolinguists are not maintaining that the social gulf between local dialect and prestige form does not exist. In defence of stigmatized varieties, sociolinguists have occasionally become embroiled in the wider social world. For example, William Labov has testified in court to the status of Black English Vernacular as a distinct language with its own grammar (not just 'broken English' or 'bad grammar'). He was establishing its validity as a language in order to suppress active discrimination against its speakers in the US education system (the celebrated Ann Arbor case (Labov 1982)).

Tannen, with her claims that male and female interactional styles are equally valid, is actually doing something significantly different. She is not challenging the power differential between the two styles but effectively erasing it. We have already examined the suppression of power in the two-cultures approach to language and gender. Socially, the two styles are *not* equally valid. In Tannen's popularizing books, there is some sleight of hand or, more charitably, slippage between neutral description (which sociolinguistics purports to do) and doling out improving information and advice (which self-help books do). This slippage does women no favours. Accounting for daily conversational frustrations in terms of cross-cultural miscommunication – and selling it to women in self-help books about relationships – takes any pressure off men. Men don't need to change their ways of speaking to accommodate women, women just need to learn to understand them (a one-way pendulum that readers of popular romance fiction will be entirely familiar with, incidentally (Talbot 1995a, 1997a)). To be fair to Tannen, I should say that this is not her intention; she deplores the idea. However, self-help books on 'relationships' are marketed as products for women. It is women who read them and thus, presumably, women who are to be held responsible for resolving the supposed problems of miscommunication between couples that they address, whatever Tannen's intention.

The reification of gender as 'difference'

The past two decades of language and gender research have been overwhelmingly preoccupied with gender differences. Women are cooperative, men are competitive, and so on. By setting the agenda for feminist linguistics as one of establishing that 'men talk like this, women talk like that', it is inevitable that differences are confirmed rather than challenged. This has meant that findings about similarities have, in effect, been suppressed. For example, I presented an account of male–female miscommunication in chapter 5, for which Maltz and Borker (1982) referred to some differences among boys and girls at play established by Goodwin (1980). But in her extensive research on children at play, Goodwin did not only uncover gender differences. She found a great deal of *similarity* in the linguistic behaviour of boys and girls as well.

In some experimental research findings outlined in Freed (1996a), the similarities in men's and women's uses of particular linguistic devices, such as **you know**, far outweighed any differences. Use of **you know** varied according to task, not according to sex of speaker (contrary to one of the early claims considered in chapter 3). Freed reports that she and her fellow researchers inadvertently constructed an experimental space which was gendered as feminine. They found that sex of participants was not a significant variable. Strangely, it appeared to be the *talk* that was gendered; that is, all the participants (male and female) were using a style symbolically associated with women's activities. The spoken genre in which participants were engaged involved them in kinds of interaction stereotypically viewed as female (stereotypes enshrined in the notion of distinct male and female interactional styles).

Gender is represented *as* difference, with gender categories frequently being treated as bipolar, fixed and static. They are sometimes established as though they were complementary pairs, or natural opposites. Books like Tannen's *You Just Don't Understand* do not threaten deep-rooted beliefs in these bipolar categories. They are appealing because they offer solutions to gender problems without making a problem of gender itself. As a consequence of a preoccupation with difference, stereotypes are reinforced, shoring up essentialism in our perception of gender. This is a big problem, as it effectively undermines the emancipatory aim of feminism. Gender-differences work can be, and is, readily picked up by popularizers. It can be used to bolster accounts of men and women available on news-stands that use very traditional sexual dichotomies (for example, John Gray's *Men Are from Mars, Women Are from Venus*).

In the last few chapters, we have encountered a variety of dichotomies, such as informational/interpersonal, public/private and report/rapport. I have commented on the limits to the usefulness of this kind of handy categorization. In gender-differences research there is a tendency to turn masculine and feminine into yet another easy dichotomy. But, as Cameron aptly remarks, '*gender is a problem, not a solution.* "Men do this, women do that" is not only overgeneralised and stereotypical, it fails utterly to address the question of where "men" and "women" come from' (1995a: 42). The challenge for contemporary researchers in language and gender is how to conceptualize gender without polarization.

Beyond difference: the influence of poststructuralism

The 'two-cultures' account presents a static conception of distinct male and female identities, apparently fixed once and for all in childhood. There is an underlying assumption that we internalize society's expectations (that is, incorporate them into our sense of self). But none of the work in the Anglo-American tradition, of which the difference-and-dominance framework is a product, really begins to explain how language, personal identity and social context interact or how this interaction sustains unequal gender relations. There is assumed to be some sort of interplay between language and social structure (except by the earliest practitioners, who tended to assume that the language patterns they studied were simply reflecting social reality). But the links between the individual, language and social structure are assumed, not argued for. The processes by which social conditions affect the insides of people's heads never come into the picture at all.

However, there are other perspectives that specifically address how language is the link between the individual and social structures, rather than assuming the existence of this link. This is where poststructuralism comes in. A key question it asks is: 'How is the individual?' Feminist criticism with a poststructuralist perspective takes language as the site of the cultural production of gender identity (see, for example, Weedon 1997). People's identities are an *effect* of language. Women and men are different because language *positions* us differently. In this view, subjectivity – our sense of ourselves – is something constructed, not pregiven, and our gender identities are not fixed. We take up positions in our enactments of discourse practices; so our identities as individuals are constructed moment by moment. From this view, our sense of self is not fixed and static. It is a process, an 'effect of discourse' which is therefore changeable. This marks an important shift away from commonsensical categorizations and prevents us from being blinded by the obvious (that is: there are men and women, and they are different!). For the American feminist philosopher, Judith Butler, these commonsensical categorizations are 'binary structures that appear as the language of universal rationality' on which our 'hegemonic cultural discourse' on gender is predicated (Butler 1999: 13).

With poststructuralism there has been a surge of interest in language from disciplines other than linguistics and sociology. These days everyone is interested: philosophers, literary critics, historians, psychologists, geographers. As a label, it covers a great deal, including the theoretical positions in the writings of Louis Althusser, Butler quoted above, Jacques Derrida, Michel Foucault, Julia Kristeva and Jacques Lacan. The term covers a range of theoretical positions. Within linguistics, recent engagements with the question of how language is the link between the individual and social structures have been particularly influenced by the work of Foucault (see chapter 7). The appeal of a Foucault-inspired approach is that it presents knowledge and identity as social constructs, and not as essential, immutable truths or entities. Instead language or, better, discourse can be viewed as what our social realities consist of. And since it is what constitutes social reality, it's what constitutes people's sense of themselves as feminine or masculine: that is, our gender identities.

Poststructuralism-influenced work on discourse and gender identity is itself quite diverse. Distinct strands now exist right across the humanities and social sciences. Part III presents some of the work on discourse and gender identity that is informed by linguistic analysis of some kind. Notably absent from this research, in both psychology and linguistics, is the dichotomizing 'men do this, women do that' which characterizes Anglo-American studies in the difference-and-dominance framework. The masculine–feminine dichotomy is not present as the taken-for-granted, the starting point. Moreover, the social identities and relationships of women and men are assumed not to be homogeneous, but to be differently constructed in different discourse practices. We are looking at how women and men are being *made* by these practices.

In this kind of research, a careful avoidance of bipolar categories can be seen very clearly, along with an avoidance of the comparative approach

that goes with such categories. Some analysts are explicit in their grounding in feminist theory and directly or indirectly interrogate categories
such as masculine, feminine, heterosexual, white, middle-class and so
on. 'Exceptional speakers' (this is the title of a contribution by Kira Hall
to *The Handbook of Language and Gender* (Holmes and Meyerhoff 2003))
are increasingly studied on their own terms, rather than as exceptions to
an over-rigid model that is unable to accommodate them. Cases of what
Hall calls 'footnote deviance' (2003: 354) include 'tomboys' and 'sissies',
which a 'two-cultures' account cannot accommodate adequately. Others
are African-American women, whose verbal behaviour does not necessarily fit the pattern for a 'feminine' interactional style based on middle-class
white Americans. This attention to liminal (that is to say, marginal) users
of language has produced new areas of interest within the field of language
and gender. One of these is an emerging field centring on 'the sexual and
gender deviance of previous generations' (Hall 2003: 354) that its practitioners have given the name 'queer linguistics'. A related point is that
there are parallels between developments in the study of gender and that
of ethnicity, where the converse is taking place. With the shift in focus to
gendered subjectivity, there has been increasing attention to masculinities.
Masculinities are being examined as constructed identities, in much the
same way as whiteness is receiving critical attention, rather than occupy-
ing an invisible position as the 'non-ethnic' norm. Language and gender
studies have seen significant expansion to encompass sexual orientation,
ethnicity and multilingualism, and, to some extent, class, involving analyses of spoken, written and signed gendered identities.

I will finish part II with a comment about feminist linguistics. If it is
going to remain feminist, it needs to keep its emancipatory aim in view.
The difference-and-dominance type of work did inspire anti-sexist and
equal opportunities initiatives in the 1980s, but since then its emancipatory
aim seems to have been lost. A poststructuralist view – the view of women
and men as discursively constituted as feminine and masculine subjects in
their actions – is now widely recognized as a valuable alternative. If gendered identities come into being in actions, then they cannot be fixed, they
must be open to change. Drawing attention to this process, and this possibility of change, is potentially emancipatory. Carrying on along the lines
of 'men do this, women do that' no longer is. The challenge now is how to
conceptualize gender without polarization.

In the last part of this book, then, I present research influenced by poststructuralism which examines not gender difference, but the construction
of gender identities. So this approach to language and gender that we are

moving on to is grounded in the assumption that subjectivity is constituted in discourse. In discourse, individuals are positioned as social subjects who are gendered in specific ways.

Further reading

Critics of the 'difference' framework

For recent reflection, see the epilogue chapter in *The Handbook of Language and Gender* (Freed 2003). Two early critical reviews are Cameron (1992b) and Uchida (1992). Freed (1992) and Trömel-Plötz (1991) engage specifically with Deborah Tannen's popularizations of gender differences work. For discussion of how the self-help texts of Tannen and others are actually read, see Cameron (2000). Chapter 6 of Thorne (1993) remains an excellent critique of the 'two-cultures' view of child socialization. Cameron (1998) is a later reflection on the debate over male/female 'misunderstanding' (reprinted in Cameron 2006a). Chapter 3 of Talbot, Atkinson and Atkinson (2003) explores patriarchal power and the role of language in its maintenance. It contains four edited readings and Cameron (1998) is one of them.

Poststructuralism

For poststructuralism and feminism, read Weedon (1997). There is an exploration of tensions between poststructuralist theory and the emancipatory goals of feminism in Baxter (2003). Black and Coward's review of Spender's *Man Made Language* considers poststructuralism specifically in relation to issues of language and gender (1990, originally 1981).

PART III

Discourse and Gender: Construction and Performance

7

Critical perspectives on gender identity

This chapter opens the final part of the book. It is an introduction to study-ing the construction and performance of gender identity in discourse. In this chapter, the focus shifts to the role of language in creating, maintain-ing and changing aspects of people's social identities that are specifically linked to gender. As an example of this approach, I examine the discursive construction of maternity.

Why critical?

Feminism is a form of politics with an emancipatory aim. An important stage in emancipation is identifying mechanisms of oppression. Before change can even be wanted, what appear to be natural aspects of the eve-ryday lives of women and men have to be exposed as culturally produced and as disadvantageous to women (and ultimately, because of this, some men would say to themselves as well). This means beginning with an understanding of how gender is socially constructed.

Critical perspectives on gender identity also have an emancipatory aim. The word 'critical' is meant in a specific way; not just 'being critical' in the ordinary sense, but examining something in order to unearth hidden con-nections, assumptions, etc. One critical perspective can be found in critical discourse analysis (CDA). This is an approach to discourse analysis com-mitted to examining the way language contributes to social reproduction and social change. I provide a basic outline in this chapter. The practi-cal aim of critical discourse analysis is to stimulate *critical* awareness of language, in particular awareness of how existing discourse conventions have come about as a result of relations of power and power struggle. As an approach to discourse analysis, it aims to show 'non-obvious ways in which language is involved in social relations of power and domination' (Fairclough 2001: 229). This involves unearthing the social and histori-cal constitution of naturalized conventions (in other words, of ways of doing things that are so apparently natural they are just 'common sense').

Looking at language critically is a way of denaturalizing it. So critical discourse analysis is useful for feminists. It can be employed in explorations of the social construction of gender. There are numerous branches of critical enquiry into language and discourse issues that are explicitly feminist. The stated aims of feminist stylistics, for example, are 'to ask questions about our commonsense notions of gender and text and to help to create a productive suspicion of all processes of text interpretation' (Mills 1995a). Other distinct strands are discursive psychology (e.g. Edley 2001; Wetherell and Edley 1999), feminist conversation analysis (e.g. Kitzinger 2000; Speer 2005), performative theory (e.g. Butler 1997, 1999), feminist poststructuralist discourse analysis (Baxter 2003), feminist media studies (e.g. Gill 2007; Macdonald 1995; Talbot 2007b), feminist pragmatics (e.g. Christie 2000) and an explicitly feminist CDA (e.g. Lazar 2005a, 2007; Talbot 1995b).

These critical perspectives differ in method and in theoretical emphasis but they share the important insight that gender is not pregiven or static but actively constructed and in flux. Some studies of gender construction place their emphasis on gender as performance. People do not have pre-fixed, stable gender identities; they perform them continuously. Even when we are quite unaware of gender – simply taking it for granted as an obvious and invariable part of our identity, as we do most of the time – even then, we are still engaged in routinely performing gender. Critical perspectives share both an avoidance of gender polarization and a perception of gender identity as *dynamic*. This term has the advantage of giving us another framework beginning with a 'd' to add to the alliterative list: deficit, dominance, difference and dynamic.

Discourse and discourses

I have been using the term 'discourse' quite a lot. Up to now I have not tried to define it, but now we need to stop and consider what it actually refers to. The term is widely and variably used in different subject areas, including linguistics. Linguists who do pragmatics or discourse analysis tend to use it to refer to language use in some way: language as action, or as interaction in specific social situations. For linguists who concentrate on phonology, morphology and suchlike, the term tends to be used differently, to refer to stretches of language longer than a sentence. I have been using it in the first sense: as social interaction in specific contexts. In part II, we looked at the work of a range of discourse analysts, focusing on research into how interaction is gendered in some spoken genres, particularly storytelling and conversation. A large proportion of discourse analysis concentrates on spoken interaction, but discourse can be written as well as spoken.

There is a contrasting, poststructuralist use of discourse which is incorporated into critical discourse analysis. This is to be found in the work of the French philosopher and social theorist Michel Foucault. Discourses for Foucault are structures of possibility and constraint. For example, medicine is a body of knowledge, practices and social identities. Medical discourse defines health and sickness. Take hysteria, for instance: as an object defined by medical discourse, it consists of everything that has been said or written about it. The term is meaningless in itself. What hysteria *is* has shifted from one century to the next. Discourses are historically constituted social constructions in the organization and distribution of knowledge. Medical discourse also determines who has the power to do the defining. Knowledge does not arise out of things and reflect their essential truth: it is not the essence of things in the world. Discourses are constituted in history and society; what is included as truth, access to that truth, who may determine it, all depend on relations of power in institutions. Foucault argues that dominant members of institutions maintain control through discourses by creating order; that is, by being the ones who make boundaries and categories.

Foucault produced historical analyses of discourse and power. He views power not as a property of powerful groups – men, the upper class, capitalists or whatever – but as something deployed in discourse. He investigated the exercise of social power in/through discourses, through the definition of objects and social subjects themselves. As Chris Weedon has pointed out:

> It is in the work of Michel Foucault that the poststructuralist principles of the plurality and constant deferral of meaning and the precarious, discursive structure of subjectivity have been integrated into a theory of language and social power which pays detailed attention to the institutional effects of discourse and its role in the constitution and government of individual subjects. (1997: 104)

In his work, Foucault attends to discourses of the social sciences, which he argues have contributed substantially to making us what we are as people. He writes about how the social sciences have impinged physically on people, constructed them as patients, as legal subjects, sexual subjects and so on. In other words, he argues that practices and relations between people are brought into being as a result of those socially constructed bodies of knowledge that we call 'the social sciences'. He shows that domains of knowledge like medicine and the law – which form social subjects in taking human beings as their subject-matter – are not timeless but historical constructions. In *The History of Sexuality*, for instance, his focus is the discursive constitution of sexual subjects in the juridical system, in medical texts and so on. He describes his purpose in this book in the following way:

> to account for the fact that [sex] is spoken about, to discover who does the speaking, the positions and viewpoints from which they speak, the institutions which prompt people to speak about it and which store and distribute the things that are said. What is at issue, briefly, is the over-all 'discursive fact', the way in which sex is 'put into discourse'. (Foucault 1990: 11)

What Foucault does in his work is to examine the social constitution in language of accumulated conventions that are related to bodies of knowledge. He does this by investigating how power is exercised through these conventions, including how they define social identities. This power is disciplinary. The eighteenth century, Foucault observes, was a time of population growth that brought about problems of poor housing conditions, poor health and suchlike. Indeed, the notion of a country having a 'population', to be managed, cared for and controlled, stems from this period. In contrast with a 'people' – a comparatively indeterminate mass that a monarch could levy tax from – a population was an economic and political problem. It had to be scrutinized:

> At the heart of this economic and political problem of population was sex: it was necessary to analyze the birth-rate, the age of marriage, the legitimate and illegitimate births, the precocity and frequency of sexual relations, the ways of making them fertile or sterile, the effects of unmarried life or of the prohibitions, the impact of contraceptive practices . . . the sexual conduct of the population was taken both as an object of analysis and as a target of intervention. (1990: 25–6)

In this scrutiny, exercised through the authorities of church and state, a new regime of discourses was formed. It was only at this point that notions of 'sexual perversion', 'deviance' and 'unnatural act' became possible. New objects of knowledge began to take shape; in particular, the hysterical woman, the masturbating child and the perverse adult (1990: 105). By the nineteenth century, forms of sexuality and sexual deviance had been characterized and catalogued as medical categories. Among others, the homosexual was born. As Foucault remarks, the 'sodomite had been a temporary aberration; the homosexual was now a species' (1990: 43).

Fortunately, however, the exercise of this power to define is not uncontestable. Counterdiscourses propose alternative versions of social reality. This has important implications for movements committed to bringing about social change, such as feminism. The value of Foucault's conception of discourses lies in its historical and social account of their definition, delimitation and control. His approach can be summarized in the following questions he poses at the end of 'What is an author?': 'What are the modes of existence of this discourse? Where has it been used, how can it circulate, and who can appropriate it for himself? What are the places in it where there is room for possible subjects? Who can assume these various subject functions?' (Foucault 1986: 120).

Discourse as social practice

Critical discourse analysts use the term 'discourse' in both the linguistics sense of social interaction in specific situations and in the Foucault sense. One such practitioner is the linguist Gunther Kress, who refers to the work of Foucault in his characterization of discourse as sociocultural practice. Kress is drawing on Foucault in this description of the defining and delimiting quality of discourse:

> Discourses are systematically-organised sets of statements which give expression to the meaning and values of an institution. Beyond that, they define, describe and delimit what it is possible to say and not possible to say (and by extension – what it is possible to do or not to do) with respect to the area of concern of that institution, whether marginally or centrally. A discourse provides a set of possible statements about a given area, topic, object, process that is to be talked about. In that it provides description, rules, permissions and prohibitions of social and individual actions. (1985: 6–7)

Discourses are historically constituted bodies of knowledge and practice that *shape* people, giving positions of power to some but not to others. But they can only exist in social interaction in specific situations. So discourse is both action and convention. It is never just one or the other.

Figure 7.1 is a representation of this conception of discourse and brings together the two different analytical traditions. It encapsulates the different senses of discourse, presenting language use as a form of social practice. In the centre is the text; it can be spoken as well as written. The text contains formal features, nothing else (grammar, vocabulary and so on). These features are traces of how the text was produced: that is, how it was written or spoken. They are also cues for how it can be interpreted: that is, read

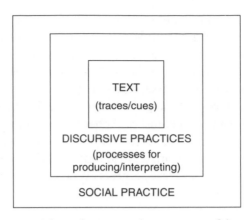

Figure 7.1 Three-dimensional conception of discourse
(Fairclough 1992: 73)

or heard. How a particular listener or reader actually reads or hears a text depends on what resources she has access to for interpreting it. (A very obvious example of resources people need for interpretation is that they must have knowledge of the appropriate language or languages.) The point of emphasizing this need for resources is that it stops us from thinking of texts as though they actually have fixed meanings independently of the social worlds they circulate in. The text's meaning is not already there, except as meaning *potential*. It gets its meaning when people interpret it (and the meaning it gets will not be the same for everybody). This view of text will probably be familiar to students of literature. It does not imply that texts can mean anything, that interpretation is some sort of free-for-all. A text's formal features do impose constraints on what it can mean, how it can be interpreted.

In CDA, textual analysis requires both linguistic and intertextual components. Intertextual analysis involves focus on the genres and discourses that are drawn upon. As it is understood in CDA, intertextual analysis is influenced by Foucault's work on discourse (briefly discussed in the last section) and also by Bakhtin's theory of dialogism (1981). Hybridity is normal; that is to say, there will virtually always be traces/cues of more than one discourse and genre in a given text.

A text is part of the activity of discourse on particular occasions, which is why it is represented in figure 7.1 as *inside* discursive practices. Discursive practices involve both texts and the processes by which people produce and interpret them. Consider a very simple example. When spoken, the words **seller** and **cellar** sound exactly the same; but this is unlikely to confuse, say, stockbrokers at work, because of the knowledge they bring with them as a resource in interpretation. The kind of discursive practice they are engaged in effectively imposes one meaning rather than the other.

The way people respond to texts depends on their social background, hence what they bring *to* the text. Texts construct reading/listening positions which actual readers/listeners have to negotiate with, although whether they accept them depends very much on who they are. This can be particularly clear in the case of mass media publications, which tend to be targeted quite precisely at specific audiences. Think of reading the following in a teenage girls' magazine: 'When you're trying your hardest to impress that hunk in the sixth form . . .' It contains textual cues to presupposed ideas – namely, that there are such things as 'hunks in the sixth form' and that 'you' try very hard to impress them. The reader is set up as someone who already entertains these ideas. A girl of about twelve might accept this reading position; but a woman of forty, probably not!

In figure 7.1, discursive practices are themselves placed within social practice. This is to indicate that discourse is a form of social practice, that language use is not just an individual's activity but a social act. Looking at discourse as social practice makes a commitment to the broader social context essential, since it means discourse analysis has to involve attention to 'the relationship between texts, processes, and their social conditions, both the immediate conditions of the situational context and the more remote conditions of institutional and social structures' (Fairclough 2001: 26). It means paying a lot more attention to the society and history in which discourse takes place than discourse analysts usually do.

This conception of discourse developed in critical discourse analysis provides a valuable framework for studying language and gender. A perennial problem for language and gender researchers is overcoming the sense of ordinariness and obviousness that so much everyday language has, and the accompanying danger of treating everyday experiences as though they somehow occur independently of society. With the model of discourse as social practice that is used in critical discourse analysis, we cannot just forget the social nature of all discourse. It helps to counteract the tendency for the discourse in which we perform our gender identities to be naturalized.

Gender identity and subject positioning

A single individual is placed in a wide range of positions as a social subject. These are known as *subject positions*. They are set up in discourse. A person does not exist independently of them; she is constituted *as a person* in the act of working within various discourses. From the beginning of her entry into social life she is positioned within varied institutional and societal structures, which bestow upon her specific social roles. In consequence, we can consider any individual as a constellation of subject positions bestowed by different discourses. Social subjects take up positions in activities within institutions and social formations. In this sense they are effects of discourse, rather than its producers. For example, it is only by entering into medical discourse that a person becomes a doctor. Her subject position of doctor is an effect of medical discourse. She is not its author. She didn't invent it.

People enter into different subject positions in discourses. These can shift in an individual's lifetime, or indeed within the course of an hour. Consider the tensions experienced by a woman who is responsible for the daily care of an elderly relation while at the same time being a full-time wage earner. What she is expected to be, and to do, as a gendered person is clearly not constant. An individual's subjectivity is not fixed, invariant and 'unitary'; it is diversified and potentially contradictory. Recall your own changing experiences: perhaps in transition from school to college, or school to work, or returning to education as a mature student after years of full-time employment, or maybe in transition from bringing up a family and part-time employment to becoming a full-time student at university. We all experience shifts during our lifetime, taking on different gender identities in different communities or cultures. These produce tensions, as conflicting values, assumptions and objectives impinge upon us and shape us.

These contradictions are part of our gendered identities. We all harbour contradictory desires and aims. Consider the contradictions surrounding bodily demands on women as workers. What people can see and what they believe to be true or right don't always match up. Many women have contradictory ideas about what they can and should do as domestic workers (such as cleaning up after incontinent elderly relations or carrying heavy children about) and what they are capable of as paid workers. As domestic social subjects – as wives, mothers, daughters – women are expected to do whatever work is necessary in the maintenance of their families, regardless of how arduous and unpleasant it may be. But when it comes to the job market, arduousness and unpleasantness are used as reasons for excluding women from doing what is traditionally men's work, on the basis of beliefs about femininity. The contradiction does not exist only in the minds of these women. It is present as a consequence of real relations within the family and the economic world. They may be unaware of the contradiction between the two subject positions imposed on them, or be aware of it but feel powerless to change the social conditions which bring it about.

People are brought into existence as social subjects whose identities appear self-evident to them. This self-evidentness gives us the illusion of self-determination, of being able to pull ourselves up by our own boot-straps, an illusion a French discourse analyst, Michel Pêcheux, calls the 'Munchausen effect' (from Baron Munchausen's amazing feat of jumping across a crevasse while holding himself aloft by his own pigtail). It goes against the grain, perhaps, to think of ourselves as processes, as being con-structed by elements we are mostly not even aware of. But we are, since we are defined and delimited in discourse (as patients, students, fathers . . .) both by being talked about and written about, and as talkers and lis-teners, writers and readers. We are 'subjugated knowers' and constrained actors. Our sense of self, of autonomy as thinking individuals who have a command of language, is constituted in discourse.

However, though self-determination is an illusion, this does not mean that people are passively shaped. People are not just acted upon; they are active in their own construction. They are busily involved in the construc-tion of gender identities, especially their own. They *perform* their gender identities. If we think of gender as performance, it can help us to steer clear of a false impression that people are just passively put together by discourse, like robots on a production line. A gendered identity is, if you like, 'a performative accomplishment' (Butler 1999: 179). Reflecting on her work on performativity, Butler explains:

> The view that gender is performative sought to show that what we take to
> be an internal essence of gender is manufactured through a sustained set
> of acts, posited through the gendered stylization of the body. In this way,
> it showed that what we take to be an 'internal' feature of ourselves is one
> that we anticipate and produce through certain bodily acts. (1999: xv)

Butler's ideas are particularly valuable in discussion of sexualities and I return to them in chapter 11.

The concept of subject positions is central to all approaches to dis-course analysis influenced by poststructuralism. Discursive psychology, for instance, examines shifts in subject positioning within and across conversations:

> Subject positions can be defined quite simply as 'locations' within a
> conversation. They are the identities made relevant by specific ways

of talking and because those ways of talking can change both within and between conversations (i.e. as different discourses or interpretative repertoires are employed) then, in some sense at least, so too do the identities of the speakers. However, . . . we must remember that people are also the masters of language, the creators of texts (Edley 2001: 210)

The construction of identities may be far from passive, as the following study of an American TV panel discussion amply demonstrates (Bucholtz 1996). This study looks at the language patterns of two African-American women who were panellists. The panel discussion was broadcast shortly after, and in direct response to, the nationwide civil disturbances in the United States in 1992 (this civil unrest followed a jury's acquittal of four Los Angeles police officers who had been charged with brutally beating Rodney King, an African-American man). Mary Bucholtz argues that the panel discussion, as a genre, is itself a combination of the genres of interview and conversation. There is tension between the conventions of each. The two women challenge the interview-like conventions being imposed by the moderator (LF). They subvert his institutional authority, imposing more egalitarian, conversation-like conventions (see chapter 5). They do this in various ways, including by breaking down the one-way question–answer format.

The short extract below shows one of the women (EH) initiating this disruption. Notice that she begins by conforming to the interview norms which have been operating so far. By initially asking permission, she is acknowledging (and perhaps pointing out) that she does not have the right to ask questions within the existing format:

EH: Can I ask ⌈a question?⌉
LF: ⌊Yeah⌋ Mhm?
EH: Do we have to be so *dry* in ⌈here?⌉
LF: ⌊Nuh⌋ (.) please
EH: Can we talk across the-=
LF: =Jump in=
EH: =I mean can we be *real* ?=
LF: =Yes heh=
EH: =It's getting on my nerves okay th(h)ank y(h)ou

(Adapted from Bucholtz 1996: 276–7)

Bucholtz argues that in breaking down the one-way question–answer format and producing a lot of minimal responses and suchlike, characteristic of informal conversations, these women are reframing the discussion into a format more congenial for them as African-American women. She points to black feminist theorists who have argued that there is a distinctive black feminist epistemology, or theory of knowledge (Collins 1990; hooks 1984). In this epistemology, knowledge is arrived at by means of open discussion – something that the panel moderator's approach is making impossible.

The two women also use some elements of African-American vernacular in place of Standard American English, the latter being the variety conventionally used in formal settings such as TV panel discussions. They sometimes use phonological features distinctive of the African-American variety of English, such as simplification of consonant clusters (so that **just** becomes **jus'**, for instance). They also use some vocabulary recognizable as African-American vernacular forms, such as **brother** and **cool out**, in the sense of 'black man' and 'withdraw' respectively (Bucholtz 1996: 279).

By means of these and other strategies, the women impose their own kind of cultural space. 'These strategies', Bucholtz observes, 'allow the speakers to subvert their own imposed position in the interaction by constructing social identities and patterns of alignment for themselves that do not conform to the roles assigned to them by the institutional norms of the discourse' (1996: 278). The two women are acting politically (of course, the changes they succeed in bringing about are only effective in a local and temporary way). In doing so, they are asserting their social identities as African-American women. They publicly perform these social identities.

A study of discourse in education, conducted by Victoria Bergvall (1996), rests explicitly on a performative view of gender. She looks at verbal interaction among engineering students, examining how gender identities are constructed and enacted and focusing particularly on the discourse in classes and small group discussions. Engineering is traditionally a masculine domain and although women now study to become engineers too, it is still a highly androcentric area, both in education and elsewhere. Traditional notions about gender identities prevail. Bergvall observes that this creates big problems for women engineering students. They are caught up in conflicting demands to which they must respond. On the one hand, there is a social need to behave in stereotypically 'feminine' ways, if they wish to take part in heterosexual social and sexual relationships (in other words, the men will only date 'proper' women). On the other hand, if they are going to succeed in their studies, they must assert themselves and their views, which is liable to put them in competition with fellow students. This involves assertive, competitive behaviour, perceived as 'masculine'. So the female engineering students both perform 'being feminine' for their male fellow students – by conforming to expectations that they should use speech patterns displaying supportiveness, cooperativeness, tentativeness and suchlike – and also present themselves as assertive and competitive. That is, they contrive to do both.

Bergvall observes that fixed categories of masculine and feminine are really no help at all in accounting for the speech patterns of the female engineering students, patterns which suggest they are responding to the competing stereotypical gender roles of asserting and facilitating. Within the 'difference' framework we examined in part II, these women could only be accounted for as aberrations. Such a range of 'masculine' and 'feminine' behaviour from women is only explicable in terms of gender as performative. The performance model does not focus on 'dichotomous differences expected under polarized, categorical roles of feminine and masculine, but on the fluid enactment of gender roles in specific social situations' (Bergvall 1996: 175). The female engineering students appear to be responding to conflicting pressures by creating new gender identities for themselves, apparently without being aware of doing so.

The discursive construction of maternity

As an example of a study taking a critical perspective, this section examines the discursive construction of maternity. When a woman becomes pregnant, she is drawn into a discourse of antenatal care, a part of the larger medical discourse. The avowed aim of antenatal care is to provide care for a pregnant woman and her unborn baby throughout pregnancy so that both of them are healthy at delivery. Antenatal care involves regular tests on both woman and foetus, screening for defects, diseases and other possible hazards. It also routinely includes provision of advice on diet, exercise and suchlike, and instruction on what to expect when the big day finally arrives. Antenatal care discourse occurs in a wide variety of genres. Genres that women in industrialized societies become involved in when they are pregnant include antenatal classes, interview-like consultations with physicians, obstetric examinations, hospital check-ups, midwife visits and so on. Language plays a more central role in some of these genres than it does in others.

Why look at the discourse of antenatal care? Well, discourse is a social practice that contributes to the construction of knowledge, and the construction of people's identities and relationships. Like it or not, women's social identities are tied up in their childbearing capacity. Medical discourse is an important site of struggle over the domain of childbirth and the formation of women's identities as mothers. The medical discourse on pregnancy and childbirth is not the only one, but it is more powerful than any other, and more widespread. Antenatal care discourse is upheld by the power behind the medical institution, power exercised by the medical profession. It is contemporary society's most influential discourse on the social phenomenon of maternity.

A fascinating study of the discursive construction of maternity was conducted by Sarah Kiær, a Danish scholar, when she was both a graduate student at Lancaster University and an expectant mother (Kiær 1990). The contrast between her identities as scholar and as 'mum-to-be' was quite startling. Her research was triggered off by her experience of being addressed differently once she became 'officially' pregnant; in other words, once she had seen her physician and started attending a clinic. She had an uneasy sense of being *turned into someone else* by the social interaction side of pregnancy. In her study, she examines the articulation of antenatal care discourse across a range of genres, both spoken and written. Her main sources are the antenatal classes that she attended and meetings with her physician in his surgery (both of which she audio-taped, as well as being a participant-observer). She refers to various printed materials as well, such as a Pregnancy Book handed out to expectant mothers at the antenatal clinic. Her work also includes a history of the medicalization of childbirth, an essential component in her critical study of antenatal care discourse.

What Kiær focuses on is the space that pregnant women take up in the discourse of antenatal care. She attends to the way pregnancy is constructed as an illness, with women as patients and labour as a series of medical procedures. She investigates the power relations being acted out in the different genres, the attributes assigned to mothers in antenatal care discourse, and how these contribute to the perpetuation of unequal power relations.

The routine consultations she had with her physician had an interview format, with the doctor in control of the talk throughout. He typically produced a string of statements and questions intended to elicit brief yes–no responses from her, checking on whether the baby was moving, whether her fingers were swelling up, and suchlike. This format gave her the limited role of respondent, and made it difficult for her to ask any questions herself. Topics discussed in these consultations were her physical functions (such as blood pressure) and the baby. This kind of depersonalized talk constructs the mother as a patient 'suffering from the pathology of pregnancy' (Oakley 1984: 213) and as an object carrying a baby and a set of symptoms.

In antenatal classes, mothers are instructees. The instructors describe labour as a series of actions performed by medical practitioners, not by the mothers themselves. The focus is on hospital procedure, which pregnant women need to be prepared for if things are to run smoothly. To put it another way, antenatal classes are 'ideological programming' of women for hospital care. In fact, in the antenatal classes Kiær recorded, they neglected to inform women adequately about choices and rights in labour.

Both these spoken genres articulate antenatal discourse. Kiær points to an interesting difference between them. In the doctor–patient interviews, the pregnant woman is constructed as a patient. The talk is likely to remain recognizably medical, of a kind you might encounter in any visit to a general practitioner. In the antenatal class, the pregnant woman is constructed as a patient-to-be. The class seems to be an initiation into patienthood using a combination of medical discourse (which is impersonal) and a discourse of motherhood and the family (which is more personal, about community and shared experience).

Both types of discourse are part of antenatal care; they are naturalized within the medical institution. The medical profession uses them to exercise power through consent (rather than by force, as they would if women were legally obliged to submit to antenatal care). Pregnant women participate: it's the natural thing to do. For antenatal care to succeed, women have to be convinced of the need for medical supervision. The routinized medical procedures – including the doctor–patient interviews – emphasize the assumption that something might go wrong. Pregnancy is a medical condition, constructed as an illness (as in the parody in Monty Python's *The Meaning of Life*: 'don't worry, we'll soon have you cured!'). Women in labour are constructed as patients (who must not do anything themselves, because they are 'not qualified!'). In fact, Marjorie Tew, a medical historian, relates that the twentieth-century trend towards hospitalizing mothers may have had as much to do with professional rivalry between doctors and midwives as with the needs of the mother and child: 'The policy of the increasing hospitalization of birth advocated by doctors, allegedly to improve the welfare of mothers and babies, was in fact a very effective means of gaining competitive advantage by reducing the power and status of midwives and confirming the doctors' ascendancy over their professional rivals' (1990: 7).

Since the eighteenth century, a basic assumption of the medical profession has been that women are no good at giving birth. They need an expert to take charge. A delivery is conducted by a trained medical practitioner, not the pregnant woman herself. For example, Sharoe Green Maternity

Unit's publication states, in a section on home confinements, that: 'You will . . . need a midwife to deliver you at home.' The woman producing the baby is never represented as the person doing the delivering; she is never the grammatical subject of the verb **deliver**. It is either represented as something the midwife does *for* her, as we've seen, or as something that happens *to* her, as an agentless process. 'During the third stage [of labour], the placenta is delivered', says a pamphlet produced by obstetric physiotherapists. Pregnant mothers are patients, ignorant about their condition and a potential danger to themselves and their babies. In the course of the twentieth century, pregnancy and childbirth became completely medicalized: 'With the definition of all pregnancies as potentially pathological, antenatal care obtained its final mandate, a mandate written by the medical profession in alliance with the population-controlling interests of the state, and one giving an unprecedented degree of licence over the bodies and approved life-styles of women' (Oakley 1984: 2). The medical profession has the right to define what it is to be a good mother and to determine what women need to know about childbirth.

In the British healthcare system, leaflets and booklets proliferate. Expectant mothers receive handfuls of them. These are informational and instructive texts, issuing commands to readers. For example, a leaflet entitled 'Reduce the risk of cot death', produced by the Department of Health in 2004, addresses the reader with imperatives such as: 'Do not let anyone smoke in the same room as your baby', 'If your baby is unwell, seek prompt advice' and 'Cut smoking in pregnancy – fathers too!' (Somerset 2006). The various publications distributed by the maternity clinic tend to be highly normative. Kiær found that, as well as telling a pregnant woman how she is going to feel, these printed materials tended to assume a particular, traditional kind of household and husband–wife relationship. For example, a handout she received at Royal Lancaster Infirmary had a heading 'Can my husband watch the scan?', which assumes of course that mothers are married. In the Baby Book from the same health authority, a section on 'How you will look' details changes to hair, skin and nails, and recommends 'using a good hand lotion and rubber gloves to protect your hands and nails when you are doing the household chores'. This presupposes that you do the household chores, and will continue to do so throughout pregnancy (even though you can scarcely bend over to tie your own shoelaces . . .). On similar lines are suggestions about asking your husband to 'help' with the housework. These publications are also normative in assuming you feel positive about pregnancy and at the prospect of baby itself. They invariably open with 'Congratulations!', for example. Many, perhaps most, women's feelings about being pregnant are actually quite mixed and, even if they have decided to go ahead with it, they may not be altogether sure whether congratulations are in order.

The Sharoe Green Maternity Unit's handbook of 1996 (produced in a different health authority) is less overtly normative in its assumptions about the kind of family structure pregnant women are part of. It avoids assuming that couples are married, frequently using the neutral **partner** or alternative terms of reference: **husband/partner**, **father/partner**. In contrast with 'Can my husband watch the scan?', partners in unmarried couples are not explicitly excluded by 'only fathers/partners are able to see the scan'. Indeed, if the couples in the illustrations weren't so resolutely heterosexual, even a gay couple might not feel entirely excluded.

However, it still marginalizes women without partners. Single parents-to-be feature, briefly, in a leaflet detailing state benefit entitlements, and nowhere else. But there are signs of some effort to use language that does not alienate large numbers of women (in other words, the pamphlet producers are responding to pressures for language reform). A (very) small proportion of the printed materials handed out to expectant mothers are written in Hindi, Gujurati, Punjabi and Urdu, as well as in English, taking into account the ethnic diversity of the Preston area, which the Sharoe Green Maternity Unit serves.

The care about terms of reference in printed materials that I noted above suggests a change is taking place in the way the medical profession defines motherhood. Mothers are not stereotyped as housewives, for instance, and may be acknowledged as workers if it is pertinent, medically speaking. For example, a leaflet produced by the Toxoplasmosis Trust states that 'it is important for pregnant farmers to be aware that toxoplasmosis can be caught from sheep at lambing time'. Being married and a housewife no longer seems to be central to the definition of a good mother in medical discourse.

As well as having the right to define what it is to be a good mother, the medical profession has the right to determine what women need to know about childbirth. As Kiær has observed, what women need to know is largely a matter of training as patients-to-be. In the medical world, the handling of large numbers of people consists of routines. Expectant mothers, like other patients, are passive recipients of care who must comply in these routines. They need to be familiarized with childbirth as a series of medical procedures. A person who refuses to be a good patient – by trying to take control or by refusing to comply – would be disruptive.

However, the passivity required of mothers is variable, which may make it all the more difficult to perceive. The goals of obstetric physiotherapists mean that they do not want women to be entirely passive patients. In a pamphlet describing the three stages of labour, produced by physiotherapists, they are recommending coping strategies for the woman in labour at each stage. In strong contrast with antenatal care discourse elsewhere, this pamphlet represents the midwife and the birthing woman as collaborators. Moreover, the woman's body knows what it's doing: 'Be aware of what your body is telling you to do.' This sensible advice is likely to encourage self-confidence. It is not echoed by other medical practitioners who, as we have seen, set themselves up as the ones telling the mother what to do. Tew is deeply critical of the severe limits set on women's active participation and responsibility in the birthing of their own babies:

> In most spheres of human activity, confidence is of great importance in leading to successful results. In no sphere is this more true than in childbirth where the physiological processes are so intimately dependent on psychological states. In the sphere of maternity care the obstetricians' objective was to make their profession the sole repository of confidence.... It inspired the confidence of the lay public, but most critically, it destroyed the confidence of mothers in their own reproductive efficiency. (1990: 10)

Another relatively active role for the expectant mother in antenatal care discourse is as formulator of a birth plan, as clinics sometimes recommend. It brings her in as decision-maker (making her feel involved, as well it might!). Her main decision, though, is probably what pain relief to have and one of the multiple choices – transcutaneous electrical nerve stimulation, or TENS – is only a choice for the economically advantaged, since it has to be paid for by the individual (unlike most healthcare in Britain, which is paid for through taxation). All in all, choice may be more illusory than real. It is more a matter of medical procedure being presented *as if* there are choices.

We have been looking at a particular area of medical discourse, focusing on the construction of pregnancy and birth as medical conditions. Mothers are shaped as patients, whose docility, obedience and overall passivity are required for care to succeed. But medical discourse does not just exert its shaping power over patients. It structures practitioners too. Members of the medical profession are themselves constructed and constrained by medical discourse. After all, not just anyone is permitted to 'deliver' babies, or conduct obstetric procedures. You have to sit examinations, acquire qualifications (Oakley reports occasions when court action has been taken against fathers for practising illegal midwifery, that being the midwifery profession's view of unregistered home births attended by the partner alone (1984: 214)). The entry requirements for the medical profession are rigorous. For practitioners, entry into medical discourse involves even more 'ideological programming' than for patients.

Finally, antenatal care discourse is not a static body of knowledge, practices and subject positions. It undergoes change. Changes happen, not just in the rather familiar way of advances in medicine (a view of change solely in terms of scientific progress, which is itself ideologically charged), but also as a result of struggle within and across social institutions. I have already noted a shift towards the representation of care in the National Health Service in terms of patient choice – a change brought about under Thatcherism (the 'Patients' Charter'). Changes in medical procedure happen as a result of pressure groups, both within the National Health Service (in the case of Britain) and from other bodies, such as the National Childbirth Trust. This sort of change comes about because of struggle over the defining and determining powers that medical discourse bestows on practitioners. In the case of antenatal care, this may include what goes into women's training as patients when they become pregnant, determining what women need to know about childbirth. Curiously, for pregnant trainee-patients, some medical procedures may only become visible as they are becoming outmoded. For example, the shave/enema dual procedure may be mentioned in the outline for a birth plan as something to be 'discussed' with the midwife, after an assertion that it is not routinized. These procedures, which used to be a matter of routine, were not even mentioned in earlier publications purportedly preparing women for their experience/ordeal.

Examining constructions of gender identity

How might antenatal care be otherwise? Perhaps it's hard to imagine alternatives, but on inspection I think it is clear that antenatal care constructs the people involved in specific ways. So there must be alternatives. Tew refers to 'birthing attendants', rather than midwives, a rewording that alters our perception of the relationship between women in childbirth and their assistants. I remarked on the normativeness of offering congratulations, which puts pressure on women to feel a particular way about the prospect of having a baby. But is that the only way to feel? With the increasing numbers of teenage pregnancies, are congratulations always in order? In fact, there are other kinds of talk about pregnancy, in which it is taken for granted that you *don't* want to be pregnant.

In addressing these kinds of issues we are examining the social construction of common sense surrounding maternity in an industrialized society. Critical discourse analysis can help us to get past the obviousness of everyday experience, the naturalness of patterns of talking, of ways of representing people. It can be used to scrutinize commonsensical notions about gender identity, in the cultivation of 'productive suspicion' about texts (Mills 1995a: 21). Here is a useful set of questions posed by Kress (1985: 7) for overcoming the commonsensical quality of single texts:

1   Why is this topic being written about?
2   How is this topic being written about?
3   What other ways of writing about the topic are there?

In attempting to break through the barrier of commonsense perception, it is often worth looking for tensions, contradiction and conflict. It may be fruitful to look for shifts across discourses and genres, as I did to some extent in examining how maternity is discursively constituted. Consider also the generic tensions in the panel discussion study looked at in this chapter.

Critical discourse analysis often has its starting point in another discipline. A historical perspective – a view of how present-day practices came about – is particularly important. The remaining chapters present detailed studies, providing suggestions for issues, textual features and so on worthy of scrutiny. In them, I am not examining what women do and what men do, but the production of people as men and as women. In this chapter and in part III as a whole I give a lot of attention to critical discourse analysis, but I am not advocating or trying to impose a single approach to examining constructions of gender identity. CDA itself is not a single approach in any case. People who identify what they do as CDA want to align themselves with an existing, somewhat diverse body of work. Within this body of work some aims are held in common: namely, the objective of exposing power relations, attention to broader social context and, with specific regard to gender studies, absence of polarization into 'men do this, women do that'.

Further reading

Discourse and identity

Benwell and Stokoe (2006) provides an overview of theoretical and analytical methods for studying identity. It is strongly focused on how to put them into practice and is very useful.

Critical discourse analysis

Bloor and Bloor (2007) is a clear introduction to the principles and practices of CDA. A very usable textbook combining CDA and systemic functional linguistics is Young and Fitzgerald (2006).

Some key readings are Fairclough (1992, 2001), Fairclough and Wodak (1997) and Wodak and Meyer (2001). For the application of CDA to the media, see Fairclough (1995, 1998) and Talbot (2007b) and, to fiction, see Talbot (1995a). Examples of intertextual analysis can be found in Fairclough (1992, 1995) and Talbot (2005, 2008). Two constructive critiques are Hammersley (1997) and Stubbs (1997).

Subject positioning

This is covered in the general CDA readings. A useful read for clarifying the sense of continuous process is Davies and Harré (1990), a social psychology journal article. See also Mouffe (1992). Mills (1995a) has a good chapter on gender and reader positioning. See also Talbot (1995a), especially ch. 2.

Pregnancy and parenthood

On the language of pregnancy, see Freed (1996b, 1999). Two detailed critical histories of the medicalization of pregnancy and childbirth are Tew (1990) and Oakley (1984). Some readings on the politics of pregnancy and parenthood representations are Lazar (2000, 2005b), Marshall and Woollett (2000), Page (2003), Rúdolfsdóttir (2000) and Sunderland (2002, 2004). For a study of the vilification of lone mothers in the British press and politics, see Atkinson, Oerton and Burns (1998), and, for mothers as 'unworthy' recipients in the American Welfare System, see Pelissier Kingfisher (1996a, 1996b) (there are extracts from and discussion of the latter in chapter 2 of Talbot, Atkinson and Atkinson 2003). Carabine (2001) examines nineteenth-century unmarried motherhood in an interesting demonstration of Foucauldian genealogical analysis.

8

Consumerism

In this chapter, I ask: how do genres like advertising and magazines help to establish and consolidate particular kinds of identity for women and men? How can we shed light on these processes by analysing the language of these kinds of genre?

Femininity

Some theorists of femininity maintain that it is entirely a matter of sexualization, a matter of learning to view yourself from the man's point of view and of perceiving your sexuality *as* your identity as feminine (MacKinnon 1982). In this view, the need for a gendered identity forces women to see themselves through men's eyes, and to cultivate feminine characteristics that they expect men to want from them. As a consequence, women's self-esteem is caught up in their appearance and desirability to others, particularly to men. As Ros Coward, a British critic and scholar, explains:

> Most women know to their cost that appearance is perhaps the crucial way by which men form opinions of women. For that reason, feelings about self-image get mixed up with feelings about security and comfort. Self-image in this society is enmeshed with judgments about desirability. And because desirability has been elevated to being the crucial reason for sexual relations, it sometimes appears to women that the whole possibility of being loved and comforted hangs on how their appearance will be received. (1984: 78)

The way women look is vitally important: the success of social relationships hangs on being desirable, and being desirable is all about visual impact.

Conventional kinds of feminine appearance are shaped by the mass media, fashion and related industries. Being feminine involves, among other things, a particular mode of consumption. A conventionally gendered appearance requires a good deal of grooming and, especially for women, beauty work. A feminine identity has to be worked at. This is work that most women are happy to do. It is an everyday aspect of women's lives and through doing it they can hope to establish for themselves acceptable social identities as women. This presents us with a rather different perspective on femininity. Looking at femininity this way does not discount the overwhelming importance of the visual, and its probable consequences, but it does present femininity as more than a matter of sexualization. In this view, women are not just turning themselves into 'sex objects'. They are actively involved in self-creation. We could turn **feminine** into a verb, to **feminize**. When women go shopping for clothes and cosmetics, they make decisions about how to feminize themselves.

Femininity spans institutions, discursively organizing women's lives. We can consider it as a particular structuring of social space. As such it is a conglomeration of concepts, themes and images, and of kinds of social relation and social practice. Femininity is articulated in and through commercial and mass media discourses, especially in the magazine industry and in the fashion industries of clothing and cosmetics. But most of all, it is articulated on women's bodies, by women themselves.

Women and consumerism

In modern industrial societies, gender identities are determined by capitalist social conditions and constructed in capitalist social relations. Women have a lifelong relationship with consumerism. As wives and mothers, women are very often responsible for most of the shopping for their families, if not all of it (notwithstanding the drastic changes in shopping habits brought about by the spread of supermarkets in the second half of the twentieth century). Women are also caught up in something we can call 'consumer femininity'. This enters into women's daily lives in the material and visual resources that they draw upon to feminize themselves; that is, both the products they buy and the concepts, practical skills and suchlike that they need to cultivate in order to use them. The know-how for using products is acquired through talk with other women, or from magazines. So consumer femininity also enters women's daily lives in the social relationships they engage in. It is a major influence on patterns of friendship, especially among teenagers.

Consumer femininity is, to a large extent, a construction of the mass media but, as I said, it is articulated on women's bodies. Women actively participate, spending on it their creative energies and time, as well as their money. Fashion and beauty standards are shaped by the manufacturing, advertising, fashion and magazine industries, which offer a range of material and symbolic resources for creating femininity. In participating in consumer femininity, a woman constructs herself as an object requiring work, establishing a practical relation with herself as a thing. This work is always required: no one can approximate the kinds of appearance offered without effort and expense. So, as Canadian sociologist Dorothy Smith remarks, 'women's bodies are always imperfect. They always need fixing' (1988: 47).

Women's magazines have had close historical connections with consumerism practically from the start. The very earliest magazine-like journals were publications for an aristocratic readership, but by the middle of the nineteenth century there were also publications catering for the rapidly expanding middle classes in Europe and the United States. These magazines for an aspiring middle-class readership 'offered their readers – the socially climbing wives and daughters of the professional and business classes – guidance about what to buy, wear and do to further their aspirations' (Ferguson 1983: 16). Like their aristocratic predecessors, they contained features on fashion, readers' letters and responses, fiction and so on. Unlike them, these magazines also dealt with topics and activities relating to women's unpaid work in the domestic sphere of the home. Their readers were not leisured aristocratic ladies, but household managers. Magazines started to run practical features on aspects of household management. These included recipes, knitting patterns and articles on the management of household servants.

The beginnings of what I'm calling consumer femininity can be seen in these mid nineteenth-century publications. Magazines played an important part in the growth of the fashion industry in the nineteenth century. *The Englishwoman's Domestic Magazine*, like its rivals, covered the latest Paris fashions. But as well as offering images for consumption, it also began to offer the means for matching them, in the form of paper patterns (Beetham 1996: 78). These were not cheap, but they did bring Paris fashions into households that could not afford the real thing. Magazines have had a central role in 'democratizing' fashion, paradoxically making widely available the 'exclusive' clothing designed for an elite group. The availability of paper patterns bridged the gap between the fashion plates and the domestic managers of middle-class households, enabling them to create themselves as approximations of the image. In this, they were producers – perhaps employing the services of a dressmaker – as much as consumers, but the practical effort to recreate themselves in accordance with the media image is clearly there. Margaret Beetham, a British magazine historian, remarks that traditional notions of femininity were being undermined:

> A feminine ideal which centred on appearance and dress threatened to rewrite not only class distinction but a definition of femininity in terms of the domestic and the moral. . . . the fashion-plate represented a woman not only primarily beautiful, rather than useful or good, but one constructed as an object to be looked at rather than an actor or a self. (1996: 78)

Women's lifelong relationship with the marketplace places them in the subject position of consumer in diverse discourses. This subject position is part of the femininity offered in women's magazines, since 'feminizing practices' involve the use of commodities. As a matter of necessity, magazines have become saturated with the genre of advertising (advertising has been the main economic support of the magazine industry since the end of the nineteenth century; the cover price of a present-day 'glossy' would not cover the cost of the paper it is printed on). Because of pressure from manufacturers and their advertisers since the consumer boom of the 1950s, it has become increasingly difficult for magazine editors to include anything that is not directly related to promoting products. As a consequence, the definition of femininity as a mode of consumption has intensified in magazines.

The sex sell

Very little that finds its way into magazines escapes being packaged as a commodity. Not surprisingly, sex is commodified and offered to readers for their consumption. It is used to sell another commodity: the magazine itself. Consider a few 'sell lines', headlines from the covers of magazines:

> Why sex is good for you (*Marie Claire*, Nov. 1996)
>
> Easy ways to a BETTER BODY, BETTER JOB, BETTER SEX LIFE (*New Woman*, Feb. 1996)
>
> 1,000 men confess. What makes a woman UNFORGETTABLE in bed (*Cosmopolitan*, July 2008)
>
> Sex & work. What he's really thinking about in the office (and it ain't just spreadsheets) (*Cosmopolitan*, July 2008)

Each of these headlines advertises an instructional feature inside the magazine. It is not only in instructional texts like these that the topic of sex crops up. It often appears in another genre as well – the personal narrative – where it is presented as a commodity in its own right. Interestingly, the two most recent examples above are both a hybrid of the genres of instructional text and confessional narrative. Three more cover headlines illustrate my point about commodification:

MEN WHO PAY FOR SEX LESSONS (*Marie Claire*, May 1996)

A woman confesses: 'My night with a male hooker' (*Cosmopolitan*, Nov. 1995)

'I pay men for sex' – Ten women explain why (*Marie Claire*, Feb. 1994)

So sexuality, too, has become a mode of consumption. In representing sex as a commodity to be consumed, the magazines clearly transgress traditional codes of behaviour governing sexuality, particularly women's sexuality. This is at odds with the traditional view of male–female relationships taking place within the institution of the family. There is certainly nothing romantic about it. The reader is constructed as a modern, liberated woman. What makes these short first-person narratives worth telling is their transgressiveness. While the sexual element makes them interesting, they are only newsworthy because of the element of transgression (Caldas-Coulthard 1996: 256).

The study of 'sex narratives' was conducted by a Brazilian linguist, Carmen Rosa Caldas-Coulthard. In her analysis, she uses the Labovian model of story structure that I used on an oral narrative in chapter 4. In magazine stories, as in newspapers, what appears in the headline is the condensed summary, or abstract; for example, '"I pay men for sex" – Ten women explain why'.

Story abstracts in magazines actually appear three times: on the cover, on the contents page and heading the features themselves. When reappearing on the contents page and heading the actual feature, the abstract ('What, in a nutshell, is the story about?') is often reworded and is likely to include some of the orientation ('Who, why, what, where, how?') as well. The headline above, for example, is rewritten in the contents as: 'Why Women Go to Male Prostitutes – Ten women talk to Clare Campbell about hiring men for sex'. Here the supposedly quoted text is gone, replaced with an authorial voice. There are also the barest of orientation details. The headlines above the feature itself are different again, elaborating with further orientation details:

Why Women Go to Male Prostitutes
Men who charge for sex can be found in hotel bars, or through escort agencies, personal columns and ads in newsagents' windows. Clare Campbell talks to ten women who have hired male prostitutes.

The main text that follows consists of ten first-person narratives. In magazine and newspaper stories, the orientation stage tends to be spread out more than in oral storytelling, with additional details being introduced as the story proceeds. In the collection of ten separate narratives, each has a heading identifying the narrator by first name, age and occupation, for instance, 'Irene, 37, housewife and mother', 'Yasmin, 44, charity fundraiser'. This is followed by further orientation detail in a formulaic pattern. Family links are used to identify the protagonists – they exist in relation to husband and children – and a situation indicating a problem is established:

> Richard, my husband, hasn't made love to me for ten years. We have a lovely twelve-year-old son called Liam.
>
> I'm twice divorced . . . I have a beautiful and successful daughter of 24.

Caldas-Coulthard observes that the evaluative elements accompanying the complicating action and resolution that follow are overwhelmingly negative. She notes consistent use of the same vocabulary – guilt, loss, shame, misery:

> I felt guilty about the expense at first.
>
> I am deeply ashamed of doing it.
>
> I felt miserable about it afterwards . . . I have always been left with that same feeling of loss.

Women who pay for sex evidently suffer.

This sex narrative study shows up some of the contradictions characteristic of women's magazines, and indeed of print media more generally. The stories take up the transgressive topic of sexual involvements independent of love, marriage or even friendship. The article is apparently non-judgemental; it positions its readers as sexually independent and 'liberated'. But it is ultimately condemnatory. Caldas-Coulthard remarks that 'the sex narratives provide readers with forms of sexual deviance and prohibited love affairs but maintain a moral attitude of condemnation towards the facts portrayed' (1996: 268). The narrators are represented as ordinary people, presenting authentic first-person narratives of their personal experiences: confessional types of narrative. But the shifts in voice between versions of the abstract and the rest of the stories introduce ambivalence, so that it is not clear whether they are fact or fiction. The apparent quotation on the cover is presented as a real person's 'own words', but it is not to be found in any of the stories. The separate sex narratives are supposed to be authentic, but they are heavily mediated by the writer of the article. Texts in journalism are always multi-authored; the stories from 'real people' have been transformed into copy and processed by a series of editors and subeditors before reaching the page. As Caldas-Coulthard says, 'The apparent "factuality" is a fiction' (1996: 258). The transgression offered by the feature entitled 'I pay men for sex' is placed safely in a fantasy world. Similarly, a study of the *Cosmopolitan* global 'brand' concludes that the 'fun, fearless female' is fearlessly having fun in 'a neutral fantasy setting, well removed from reality' (Machin and Thornborrow 2003: 463).

Multiple voices in magazines

In the early years of publishing, the term **magazine** itself was not firmly established. Other names used in the titles of such journals were **repository**, **museum** and **miscellany**: for instance, *Christian Mother's Miscellany*, *Lady's Monthly Museum*, *Ladies' Fashionable Repository*. Before the word **magazine** took on its predominant modern meaning – as a particular kind of publication containing diverse elements – it used to refer to a place where miscellaneous things are kept, a storehouse. In this earlier meaning, incidentally, it is close to the French word **magasin** that is still used for a large shop or department store.

Magazines have always been multivoiced, both in the sense of containing diverse discourses and genres and in the sense of having multiple authorship. Early magazines relied heavily on their readers as authors; the modern distinction between amateur and professional authorship did not really exist. Readers' contributions to eighteenth-century publications were not confined to the letters page as they are for the most part today. Readers also provided copy in the form of stories, articles, verse and even, on occasion, translations of recently published scholarship. Margaret Beetham cites the 'Notes to contributors' section of *Lady's Magazine*, in which a harassed editor berates a translator of Rousseau's *Émile* for not submitting instalments on time (1996: 20). These contributions were not paid for and appeared in print anonymously. However, they did place magazine readers as members of a community of writers and readers, rather than just as reader-consumers. In this respect, early magazines were similar to some modern 'fanzines' (amateur magazines produced by fans). As journalism became increasingly professionalized, it is likely that contributions from women decreased, although the practice of anonymity makes it difficult to tell for sure (Ballaster et al. 1991: 71).

Magazines are not homogeneous, and they never have been. Diversity is a key characteristic. They draw on a wide range of genres and discourses, addressing their readers in many different voices. Genres – conventional frameworks for interaction – include the letters page, advertisements, various kinds of advisory, instructional and information-giving features, fictional narratives, 'true' stories. Discourses – kinds of knowledge and practice – include journalism, discourses of economics, the family, fashion, science (selectively drawn upon in the 'health and beauty' sections) and, very selectively, feminism. A discourse on the family is perhaps less visible in the glossies than in the service magazines. It is none the less present, as we saw in the sex narratives in the last section.

There is a consistent core of discourses and genres throughout magazines, which set up for readers consistent constellations of subject positions. The service magazines centre on domestic consumption; the glossies address the reader-consumer as an independent individual. There is room for some variation, of course. *Marie Claire* is notable for its regular articles on human rights, which bring in a political discourse. A piece of reportage dealing with Burma's military dictatorship, for example, is explicit in its criticism of the Burmese tourist industry (*Marie Claire*, Nov. 1996). It is introduced in the features section on the contents page as follows:

> REPORTAGE
> EXPLOITED How Burma's people
> are being brutally treated in order
> to create a holiday paradise

Such reportage is less frequent in other glossies and is rarely, if ever, found in the service magazines. As well as positioning the reader in some form of political discourse, *Marie Claire*'s human rights features still implicitly offer the reader a subject position as consumer. It is, however, a rather different reader-consumer from elsewhere in the same publication. It offers consumer selectivity and discernment on political grounds, a form of consumer power sometimes called ethical consumerism.

As we have already observed, magazines are diverse and often contain contradictory elements. You can pick up any magazine and find examples, but the contradictions in *Marie Claire* are particularly striking. Their presence in the magazine is openly acknowledged by its editor and not viewed as a problem (cited in Caldas-Coulthard 1996: 251). In the midst of all the glamour and gloss, it is not unusual for the impossible ideals of female appearance to be engaged with critically, as in a Janet Street Porter interview with Annie Lennox:

[JSP]:   when you look through magazines, you're bombarded by images
          of physical perfection, which make you feel like a failure.

[AL]:   It really gets to you at a certain point. You cannot live in a society that bombards you with perfection without being affected by it. (*Marie Claire*, April 2008)

Adjacent articles appear to undermine one another. For instance, an opinion piece by Body Shop founder, the late Anita Roddick, headed 'Why I love my wrinkles' follows a feature called 'Skincare special: how to stop your skin ageing' and another on 'Anti-ageing eye treatments' (*Marie Claire*, Nov. 1996). However, the article in praise of wrinkles also functions as a promotional feature for Body Shop products. All three are advertising skincare products.

So when is an ad not an ad? When it's an advertorial. The genre of advertisement has encroached on the space taken up by other genres in magazines; the boundary between advertising and editorial material has become blurred. I mentioned earlier the difficulty editors have in including anything in a magazine that is not directly related to product promotion. Magazines started to carry advertorials in the late 1930s.

These consumer features are advertising passed off as editorial content; they now make up a large proportion of any publication. There are sometimes attempts to demarcate boundaries between kinds of genre. Large display ads are visually distinct from the written text of a feature, for instance, or written text may be given a small heading announcing that it is a 'promotional feature' or an 'advertisement'. But product-promoting material is far more widespread than these labels and visual signals indicate. The voice of advertising is virtually always present.

Power relations

Media discourse is one-sided, with one group of people doing most of the talking/writing. Their addressees are a mass audience; formed of individual people, of course, but not known to them as such. Producers of mass media discourse have to guess whom they are addressing. They have to construct an implied reader/viewer – an imaginary person in the target audience – and address that one. Their guesswork is very well informed, however. With sophisticated market research at their disposal, they are not shooting in the dark, by any means.

There is no doubt that the mass media are influential. People working in the media are in a position to shape other people's ideas. The producers of mass media texts are in a powerful position. However, things are not as straightforward as they may seem. Who are these empowered producers of magazines? The groups of people who actually put together each issue are hardly free agents. Their actions, as subeditors and so on, are under the immediate control of the editor, who is in turn constrained by company policy, which is determined by profit-making. As Cynthia White, a magazine historian, has observed, modern magazines are 'run according to strict business methods and are answerable to cost-accountants' (1970: 181). The magazine industry's profit is made through advertising revenue. In effect, manufacturers and their promotion departments occupy most of each publication because, as well as buying advertising space, they also supply magazines with a lot of advertising copy, in the form of information about products. This information provides the basis for many of the editorial elements of magazines. Indeed, advertorials are demanded by manufacturers as a condition for placing their ads in the first place. So an actual issue of a publication like *Marie Claire* comes into existence in a relationship between the publishers (for *Marie Claire*, European Magazines Ltd) and a wide range of manufacturers and their promotion departments.

What are the consequences? The powerful influence of business interests limits the range of voices permitted into magazines. This amounts to censorship. In publications that are dependent on advertising revenue from companies producing cosmetics and other beauty products, critical perspectives on 'health and beauty' are unlikely to be heard. Even the *Marie Claire* feature in praise of wrinkles simultaneously supports what Naomi Wolf calls the 'beauty myth'. The feature is illustrated with photographs of various well-known 'older women' who are still conventionally beautiful and, as we saw in the last section, it is in any case a promotional feature for Body Shop products. Advertisers have withdrawn accounts from publishers who have stepped over the line (Wolf 1990: 81). In the absence of critical voices, the reader has only a cosmetics company's own view on their products, a view voiced in the advertorials and the ads themselves. As Wolf caustically remarks, any 'woman who buys a product on the recommendation of beauty copy is paying for the privilege of being lied to by two sources' (1990: 82).

Censoring effectively goes on in the processing of visual images too. The standard practices of airbrushing and, more recently, computer enhancement eliminate blemishes from the smoother-than-life faces of models. A computer can transform an already waif-like model into an anatomical impossibility. Real women's faces and figures are seldom to be seen, especially in the glossies. Photographs of 'real people' are limited to certain genres. When they do appear they are in 'relationships' features (as in 'Reunited with the daughter conceived through rape', *Marie Claire*, Nov. 1996) and in 'reportage', like the feature on Burma mentioned above.

Text population

Magazines are multivoiced, as we have seen. They are 'populated' with an indeterminate number of voices (Talbot 1992b). All texts are multivoiced in the sense that they always have earlier texts embedded in them. Texts, and the discourse in which texts occur, always have histories. Consider, for example, an interview appearing in a magazine. The text of the interview in print is clearly linked to an earlier discourse when the interview itself took place. Many other texts precede the printed text, from discussions with the editor to memos to the printers. The discourses in which they occurred were part of the production process of the printed magazine interview. The editor's voice has shaped the words on the printed page, even if she wrote none of the copy and there are no detectable traces of her influence; she can be said to be part of the text's population.

Often, however, there *are* traces of people's voices, real or imaginary. A particular text may be multivoiced because it contains various characters, or a variety of attitudes or perspectives. These voices may be interacting, engaging in dialogue. Perhaps surprisingly, one voice may be the reader herself, or rather, the implied reader. The implied reader's voice is present in the following extract. It is taken from an 1890s issue of *The Queen*, and the implied readers are London socialites, pitied by the writer for not living in the peace of the countryside:

> You poor creatures, still confined to the bricks and mortar of Babylon, must take your amusements and pleasures where you can get them. But wherever you take them you have to accept fatigue as the inalienable condition. Now, we in the heart of the country have no such fatigue, and our enjoyment is all the more complete in consequence. You love music, do you? and you go to the opera, to concerts, to the Albert Hall, to hear this singer and that – these pieces or those. That is, you go into a crowded assembly, where the air is absolutely poisonous, and you come away with a headache born of the noise and bad air, the rush to and fro, the clatter of the streets, the shaking of your vehicle, the mistimed hours of dinner and bed. We, on the contrary, sit on the lawn and listen to the linnets and the thrushes – or we saunter up and down the long walk in the tender evening stillness, while the nightingales challenge one another from bush and branch, and make such music in the moonlight as Theocritus knew and Horace enjoyed. (*The Queen*, 12 Sept. 1891)

The writer presents the London socialite's arguments in favour of life in the big city, then contests them at some length and contrasts the inferior 'amusements and pleasures' of London with those offered by the countryside. The fourth sentence seems to be a repetition of what the reader has said. We could reconstruct the passage as a dialogue, like this, filling in the reader's voice:

Writer: We in the heart of the country have no such fatigue, and our
           enjoyment is all the more complete in consequence.
[Reader: But I love music. In London, we have the opera, concerts, the
           Albert Hall.]
Writer: You love music, do you?
[Reader: Why yes I do! Why, only last week I heard several celebrated
           singers, performing some superb pieces.]
Writer: You go to the opera, to concerts, to the Albert Hall, to hear this
           singer and that – these pieces or those. That is, you go into a
           crowded assembly . . .

and so on. (Those interested in magazines might like to know that *Queen* – as it was known in the 1960s - was merged with *Harper's Bazaar* in 1970, but eventually dropped from the masthead of *Harper's and Queen*.)

In the above example, I have supplied the reader's voice. The following is an extract from the letters page from a more recent, but also defunct, publication called *Jackie*, a British magazine for pre-teenage readers. I have taken the extract from a study examining shifts in the writer–reader relationship in *Jackie* between 1970 and 1990 (Wilmot 1991). The writer is consenting to a reader's request to print a photograph of a particular film star: 'Oh come on, . . . still I suppose that's no reason, is it? (No!! – the readers.) So here's the young whippersnapper himself' (*Jackie*, 11 Aug. 1990, quoted in Wilmot 1991: 34). As Wilmot observes, *Jackie*'s copywriters were very fond of this strategy of explicitly simulating a reader's voice (1991: 40). It had declined by 1990, but could still be found in the 'Chatback' section of the magazine. These days, this is routinely done by copywriters in a highly formulaic way, as we could see in the examples presented in the 'sex sell' section earlier in this chapter. So-called first-person pieces in magazines routinely have the voice of the protagonist in the headline, including entirely imaginary ones (as in 'I'm afraid of the big bad birth' in an advisory piece in *Pregnancy and Birth*).

Multiple voices can be spotlighted by focusing on certain textual features. Sometimes the presence of voices may be obvious, as in the case of speech representation (often called reported speech), where a voice is explicitly foregrounded for the reader with quotation marks. It may in fact have been conjured up from nowhere, like the *Marie Claire* headline

'I pay men for sex'. The voice is made even more explicit with a report-ing clause as well (as with 'A woman confesses: "My night with a male hooker"', where the verb contains the verbal process of **confessing**). Here there is a voice and someone purported to produce it too. Voices may be detectable simply by focusing on verbal and mental processes. When verbs like **think, say, know, like, prefer** or nouns like **belief, opinion, wish** and suchlike crop up, there are traces of someone's utterances or ideas embed-ded in the text. In the following – taken from a *Cosmopolitan* article on the 'philosophy' of *feng shui* – the writer is voicing an implied reader's thoughts and observations: 'If you're single and would prefer not to be, look around your home. You'll probably notice a lot of solitary objects' (*Cosmopolitan*, Nov. 1995, p. 62).

Less obviously, a writer may implicitly speak for someone else. Writers do this when they give someone else's reasons or justifications for some-thing. In doing so, they assume access to that person's thought processes. The next example is from the reply to a letter on a problem page for young readers. The letter-writer is apprehensive about going out with a boy because of a scar remaining from a road accident when she was younger. The response attends to this apprehension: 'Maybe it's just because you're getting a little older and a bit more self-conscious about your appearance?' (*Jackie*, 18 Mar. 1989). Here the writer is not only assuming access to the girl's thought processes but the authority to establish what her motiva-tions were. This writer is being tentative in her assumption (as indicated by **maybe, a bit**). In other cases, a writer may simply 'report' other people's motivations.

Magazine texts are also multivoiced in the sense that their copywriters (already composite beings) shift subject positions as they take up different discourses, some of which we noted above: the family, fashion, home eco-nomics, politics and so on. They also shift position as they move from one genre to another: from an advisory role to interviewer, from the writer of a fashion history article to advertiser, from agony aunt to clairvoyant. Genres establish expectations about how interaction will proceed. These can be like *scripts*, which, as the theatrical metaphor suggests, are represen-tations of people's expectations about the parts taken up by participants. A script for interviewing sets up expectations about the kinds of question–answer pairs likely to occur and about who will be doing the questioning and answering. Some genres are more obviously script-like than others. Instructional texts, such as recipes or exercise routines, follow a relatively rigid format and the copywriter's role as instructor is clear.

One method for identifying the subject positioning of copywriters is to look at *classification schemes*. Focusing on classification schemes provides a way of examining vocabulary and topics that goes beneath the surface, so to speak, to the frames of knowledge (mental representations) that they establish. An advertising voice, for example, sets up schemes of classification for us, marking out the world we live in. In women's magazines, classification schemes that proliferate relate to the kinds of appearance or 'looks' offered as standards by the fashion industry and to the itemization of the body as a visible object requiring work. Readers are encouraged to discriminate facial shapes, skin tone and 'problems', hair colour, etc. These classificatory areas may be new to readers; encountering them forms part of a reader's initiation into feminizing practices. Each area itemized requires a different product and different treatment. Other important classificatory areas which are essential for a feminine education are the range of commodities needed to approximate the different 'looks', for which practitioners need to acquire the ability to make fine discriminations of colour, shape and texture.

Simple observations about *grammatical choices* can help to pinpoint a particular voice, or shifts from one voice to another. Kinds of grammatical choice frequent in advertising copy reflect the focus on a commodity and its availability, rather than the processes of its production. Very often a product may simply be represented with a photograph, captioned with name, stockist and price, without any grammatical relationship formally established between them at all. Or a product may have an attribute (some desirable quality) attached to it with the verb **be** or **have**, in a simple sentence such as 'They have no added perfume or colour' or 'They're ideal for even the most sensitive skins.' In contrast, when a copywriter takes on the voice of a fashion historian, she or he will tend to use a lot of phrases specifying time, particularly prepositional phrases like 'in the sixties' and 'during the eighties'.

The voice of a friend

As we have seen, the subject position of advertiser can be found throughout magazines. There is another persona taken up by magazine copywriters very frequently, namely that of a friend. This subject position – an important member of the text population of a magazine – merits a section to itself. However, in focusing on this component of the copywriter's composite identity we will need to give further attention to another inhabitant of the text: the reader.

A defining characteristic of modern magazines is their distinctive addresser–addressee relationship. In the early years of magazines, there seems to have been a great deal of interplay between magazine producers and their genteel readership. Readers, as potential contributors of copy, were members of a community of writers and readers, rather than simply reader-consumers as they are for the most part today. Traces of friendly interaction with individual reader-contributors can be seen in the earliest publications. However, by the end of the nineteenth century, journalism had become fully professionalized and readers' contributions were restricted to the letters columns. The market also broadened to include a lower-middle-class readership. The friendly, informal voice that eventually became explicit editorial policy required *simulations* of two-way interaction and of closeness. It started in Britain in *My Weekly*, a new down-market publication in 1910. In this magazine's first editorial, the editor claimed to know her readers (which of course she did not) and offered them friendship. Various critics have characterized the friendly voice of women's magazines as the voice of a sister, or female confidante (Leman 1980; McRobbie 1978; Winship 1987).

In the absence of readers actually known to them, magazine writers have to imagine them. This postulation of an implied reader involves the synthesis of friendly interaction. A practice called *synthetic personalization* (Fairclough 2001: 62) is now widespread in the mass media. It has three facets: an impression of two-way interaction, an informal style that is closely linked to positive politeness and the establishment of common ground. The way synthetic personalization is achieved varies between publications. There are, however, some common elements, such as direct address to the reader.

Direct address to you is extremely common on magazine covers: 'Bikini body GUARANTEED. YOU CAN STICK TO THAT DIET', 'HOW TO MAKE YOUR MONEY LAST A MONTH!' (*Cosmopolitan*, July 2008). The use of the pronoun **you** in questions and statements is very frequent in other copy, like this question at the beginning of a health and beauty section: 'Is stress showing on your face?' (*Marie Claire*, Nov. 1996, again). Direct address is also very frequent in the wording of display ads, when there is any wording at all (many modern display ads, especially in the glossies, contain few words other than the product name). The pronoun **we** is also frequent. Sometimes it refers to the magazine editorial only (the exclusive **we**), as in this feature headline: 'Trust us . . . it's good to feel vulnerable'. Sometimes it refers to the editorial and the reader together (the inclusive **we**), as in the subheading to the same feature:

> We all have our wobbly moments, when life seems like a tightrope from
> which we're about to fall. But there is a positive side to vulnerability – it
> brings us great insight and the opportunity to think, understand and
> make changes to our lives that leave us feeling stronger than ever before.
> (*Cosmopolitan*, Nov. 1995, p. 148)

The inclusive **we** here contributes to an impression that magazine writers
and readers are a group of people with a lot in common.

Such pronominal usage contributes to the synthesis of interaction. We
have already seen the simulation of interaction in the last section, in an
extract from *The Queen* from 1891. The impression of community and
gossip has long been a feature of magazines for women. Direct address to
the reader as **you** is not exclusive to twentieth-century publications. In the
extract from *The Queen* we saw the reader being addressed as **you**. It did
seem to be using the pronoun **we** rather differently, however, making a
contrast between 'us countrydwellers' and 'you cityfolk', rather than using
it to establish the magazine's writers and readers as a community. In fact
it would hardly have been necessary to work at establishing the readership
as a community. *The Queen* was a society magazine, read by the upper
class. The group identity is clear enough from the society column with the
heading 'Upper Ten Thousand', as the aristocracy called themselves.

One aspect of the friendly voice in magazines which appears to have
changed a great deal is the level of formality. In modern magazines, the
voice of a friend is informal. An informal style is closely linked to positive
politeness (see chapter 5). Features associated with positive politeness are
very common indeed in modern magazines. In some publications, especially those for the young, the copywriters have a noticeable tendency to
mimic the supposed language of their target audience: a way of claiming to
be 'one of the gang'. Most magazines for young people contain relentless
attempts to use the current slang; they crack jokes (usually bad puns) and
pepper the text with exclamation marks. A simple way to highlight this
strategy is to contrast the informal vocabulary in an ad's main text with the
formality of its small print (which will be in some form of legalese).

In fact, this mimicry of the target audience is part of a more general tendency. Magazines, like other mass media texts, implicitly claim that their
writers and readers think the same way and do the same things. In other
words, they assume shared values and norms, shared common sense. The
pursuit of 'beauty', for example, is simply taken for granted in women's
magazines. The expenditure of time and effort is assumed to be worth-
while and not questioned. The body is fragmented and itemized, since
each part requires separate attention if it is to be beautiful. An ad for hair

remover asks: 'Are you doing enough for your underarms?' This question presupposes that *you should be doing something*; the need to do beauty work on your armpits is presented as shared wisdom. Concepts, preoccupations and anxieties are presented as though they already exist in the readers' daily lives.

Many presuppositions establish a vague common sense, as in this example: 'Compliment [*sic*] all the great ethnic fashions around just now with a soft romantic style like this one from Schwarzkopf' (*Jackie*, 18 Mar. 1989). Here the copywriter is setting herself up as the kind of person who takes for granted a presupposed idea: *there are great ethnic fashions around*. She is also setting up the reader as a like-minded 'fashion-conscious' person. A significant contribution to the writer's establishment of an identity for herself and a friendly, 'close' relationship with the reader is achieved through claims to common ground like this one, and to her assumption of shared knowledge and experiences. The writer's establishment of a friendly, 'sisterly' identity is wrapped up in her construction of an implied reader. We can say little about the constructed writer without also considering this reader.

In examining the common knowledge established in a text, then, things to look out for are presuppositions attributed to the reader, to **us** or simply to some vague 'common sense' (*Are you doing enough for your underarms?*, *Lipstick as we know it, Complement all the great ethnic fashions around* . . .). We have also seen that the inclusive **we** contributes to the impression that magazine writers and readers are a group of people who have a lot in common. (I have just used the inclusive **we** in the previous sentence; since you are reading this section, I am assuming you share my knowledge of what I have written in it!) A study of an article in *New Woman* called 'Learning to talk . . . to your lover' presents a list of assumptions drawn in as shared knowledge. A single sentence from the article contains three examples of the inclusive **we**:

> From the day we decide who's going to sleep on which side of the bed, we are negotiating with the man we love about everything from fidelity to finances.

Siobhan MacErlane comments as follows:

> This sentence makes a lot of assumptions and claims for 'us'. Apparently 'we' are all heterosexuals; 'we' sleep with the man we love (forget it if you're a strict Catholic – unless of course you're married); 'we' love a man if we sleep with him (a dose of morals here for us); and 'we' constantly negotiate within our relationships (they could well be right about

the bed, i.e. that we sleep in one, though some homeless . . . women could be excluded from this as well!). (1989: 15)

The writer of the *New Woman* feature takes a lot for granted. Attention to frames of knowledge and classification schemes can also reveal concepts presented as shared knowledge. For example, in a feature on a hairstyle, the hairstyle is the topic for which we have a frame, a mental representation. However, we also need to draw on other, implicit frames to understand it. In the following, it is assumed that growing your hair is something you actively try to do: 'Trying to grow your hair but getting to that horribly straggly stage?' (*Jackie*, 18 Mar. 1989). It also sets up a classification scheme. It is presupposed that there is a stage which is 'horribly straggly', presumably one of several other hair-growing stages. For its young readers (between ten and twelve) this feature is probably creating these concepts, but they are presented as something we all know about.

In looking at how the copywriter establishes a friendly persona, then, we need to consider writer–reader interaction, especially its simulation, mimicry of the audience's language and, above all, the establishment of a shared common sense.

I opened this chapter with a discussion of women's active performance of femininity. I then went on to examine how women's magazines construct 'consumer femininity' for their readers. Alongside the fashion and cosmetics industries, the magazine industry offers women resources for carrying out feminizing practices on themselves. Consumer femininity, then, is ultimately a feminine identity that women achieve for themselves when they buy and use commodities. Of course, it is not only magazines that position women as consumers. Women are also central as consumers on television, both in the advertising breaks between programmes and on teleshopping channels. I looked at the discourse of antenatal care in the last chapter. The packages that women are presented with at antenatal clinics are full of advertising material; the subject position of consumer is part of being an expectant mother.

Consumer femininity is not the only kind of feminine identity, however. Femininity takes different forms, so we should really use it in the plural and speak of femininities. Women's identities are not only formed by consumerist discourses. Employment, personal relationships, the family – these all contribute to constructing women's identities. Class and ethnicity structure women differently, so that being feminine is not the same for every woman.

Men as consumers

Over the past few decades, men too have been increasingly hailed as consumers and persuaded to part with their disposable income (or, indeed, extend their credit card debt). In Britain, it is likely that the men's magazine has made a significant contribution in bringing about this shift. As I've already noted, magazines are predicated on consumption and shot through with consumerist discourses. In Britain, modern men's lifestyle magazines started in the 1980s. They were very much associated with the notion of the 'New Man'; previously magazines for men in Britain were either pornographic or hobby-based (home improvements, cars, gardening, music and so on). The new lifestyle magazines were a huge commercial success (possibly because of deregulation that opened up marketing and advertising revenue). They developed out of the style and music press and legitimized consumption for men, positioning them as knowing consumers. It was difficult terrain, however, with the need to negotiate around both the feminine space of the glossy style magazine and the men's market of soft porn. In respect of the former, it is interesting to note that the term used in men's magazines for health & beauty and fashion (as women's magazines know them) is 'grooming'. In contrast with women's glossies, cover models for *Arena* and *GQ* were well-known men in the leisure industries (such as the film director David Lynch). In an interesting potential contradiction, overwork was normalized, according to a study of over-lexicalization in a single issue (Tetlow 1991). In the issue Tetlow examined, she also noted that the 'breadwinner'/worker aspect of hegemonic masculinity (see chapter 9) was being overdetermined.

Loaded was launched in 1994 and had a different approach. It was followed almost immediately by the relaunch of *FHM*. The editors claimed to be creating a new genre that was resolutely immature and 'laddish'. For example, an editorial heralds the reassertion of a youthful form of traditional heterosexual masculinity. The editorial is chatty, ironic and resistant to the preoccupation with 'grooming' (that is, health, beauty and fashion):

> *Loaded* should be rammed full of the things that people go on about in the pub and that stuff like health and perfume should be left to the adult mags. Remember, grooming is for horses. (James Brown, editorial 1995; quoted in Jackson, Stevenson and Brooks 2001: 77)

Initially, cover models were still men, but behaving badly ('celebrities' with 'lad' credentials). As with the women's magazines discussed earlier, synthetic personalization is abundant. It tends to be realized somewhat differently, however, with banter and abuse in abundance (Benwell 2001, 2004; Talbot 2007b).

The grooming products mocked in the early *Loaded* editorial are now far less problematic for magazines and advertisers than they were previously. Advertising agencies have focused their creative energies on how to package commodities that are perceived as feminine to a male consumer. Marketing personal care products for men involves appeals to masculine values and preoccupations. The branding of some grooming products available in the United States provides an illustration. The punning use of military metaphors can be seen in the product names of a Billy Jealousy skin care range, produced by a Texas-based company. Their facial moisturizer, for example, is Combat Lines. Their anti-aging serum About Face is another example, endorsed by *Men's Health Magazine* as 'worth adding to your grooming arsenal' (billyjealousy.com). The promotional text for their cologne jokingly presents it as dangerous:

> ILLICIT, the perfect prescription for today's sophisticated bad boy.
> WARNING: Keep away from heat, flame, minors and probation officers.
> ILLICIT can only be shipped via ground due to hazmat regulations.
> (www.billyjealousy.com. Retrieved 29 March 2008)

Men are clearly being caught up in itemization of the body as a visible object requiring work, with education in discriminatory practices essential for that work. They are increasingly achieving the subject position of consumer masculinity when buying and using commodities. So are men turning into 'metrosexuals'? The rapid growth of the grooming market suggests that this may indeed be the case. The term 'metrosexual' first appeared in print in 1994, in an article by the British columnist Mark Simpson, entitled 'Here come the mirror men':

> Metrosexual man, the single young man with a high disposable income, living or working in the city (because that's where all the best shops are), is perhaps the most promising consumer market of the decade. In the Eighties he was only to be found inside fashion magazines such as *GQ*, in television advertisements for Levis jeans or in gay bars. In the Nineties, he's everywhere and he's going shopping. (Simpson 2006)

An American author of self-help books, Michael Flocker, uses the term in a somewhat broader sense that includes men of all ages, particularly celebrities. In an interview promoting his book *The Metrosexual Guide to Style* on CNN, he discusses the case of Arnold Schwarzenegger:

O'Brien: Let's go through a few of the people who would be considered metrosexual. Among the people you have on the list, Arnold Schwarzenegger. Why does he qualify?

Flocker: He's a card carrying member. You know. . .

O'Brien: He is?

Flocker: Yes, he's admitted to having hundreds of pairs of shoes, all his clothes are tailor-made. He's always impeccably groomed and is seen coming and going from the spa regularly. He has a manicurist, a pedicurist. He leaves nothing to chance.

O'Brien: And no one is going to call him a girly-man to his face.

(www.edition.cnn.com/TRANSCRIPTS. Retrieved 29 March 2008)

Here Flocker is describing the grooming practices of an affluent former Hollywood actor and professional body builder. Schwarzenegger's masculinity has to be worked at and involves a particular mode of consumption: the professional grooming work that is part of the life of a screen actor.

Few men are comfortable with such high-maintenance consumer masculinity, however. In some focus group work with 'ordinary' men in Scotland, Bethan Benwell found that the young men in her study had ambivalent responses to men's magazine content, particularly the advertisements for grooming products. In her data, a 'troubled subject position' is revealed by laughter as one of the interviewees admits to 'doing a Nivea thing' in response to an advertorial (Benwell and Stokoe 2006: 198). This ambivalence is, of course, well recognized by advertisers, who are not slow in conducting focus groups themselves. I have already mentioned the compensatory appeal to interest in all things military in some Texan grooming products. There is a study of magazine advertising and features on skin care which presents an interesting contrast in marketing strategies of 'anti-ageing' products for women and men (Coupland 2007). Among its interesting findings is the suggestion that the scrutinizing gaze of women is being presented as a significant issue for men.

So, these days men's bodies are imperfect too. Boys and young men are starting to display anxieties previously associated with women and girls. Masculinizing strategies of more traditional kinds are the subject of the next chapter.

Further reading

Consumerism

For consumer femininity, see Smith (1988); also Talbot (1992b, 1995b) and ch. 5 of Benwell and Stokoe (2006). Andrews and Talbot (2000) deals with women in consumer culture. There is some interesting work on shop-by-television and gender identity (Bucholtz 1999, 2000). See also Richardson (1997) and ch. 8 in Talbot (2007b). On the subject of consumer masculinity and the metrosexual, readings include Edwards (1997) and Harrison (2008). I have already mentioned an interesting article on 'consumerized solutions' to ageing (Coupland 2007).

Advertising

Goffman's classic *Gender Advertisements* (1978) continues to be interesting for its interpretations of posture and gesture. For four volumes providing comprehensive coverage of advertising language, go to Cook (2008). For feminism and 'postfeminism' in ads, see Gill (2007), Lazar (2007) and Talbot (2008).

Magazines

For a detailed history of British magazines for women, read Beetham (1996). See also Winship (1987) and White (1970). For detailed analysis of magazine readers and how they actually use their magazines, read Hermes (1995). Turning to the language of magazines, McLoughlin (2000) is an excellent place to start. See also chapter 4 in Delin (2000) and chapter 3 in Matheson (2005). Talbot (1992b) presents a framework for examining a 'text population', focusing on an advertorial in a British magazine for pre-teenage girls; working within the same framework, Talbot (1995b) examines the offer of friendship in the advertorial. Osterman and Keller-Cohen (1998) considers quizzes in American and Brazilian teen magazines. Caldas-Coulthard (1996) and Machin and Thornborrow (2003, 2006) examine women's magazine features on sex, while McLoughlin (2008) focuses on 'sex specials' in two teen magazines. Nakamura (2005) covers Japanese fashion magazines.

There is less available on magazines for men and most attention to language is from Bethan Benwell (2001, 2002, 2003, 2004, 2005). See also Talbot (2007b).

9

New men and old boys

This chapter is about men and masculinities, change and resistance to change. Like the previous chapter, it considers how we can shed light on these things by analysing language. It presents studies of constructions of masculine identities in the everyday life of young men in a variety of cultural contexts. It also examines contemporary representations of hegemonic masculinity and resistance to its subversion in magazines and newspapers.

Masculinities

I argued in the last chapter that femininity has to be worked at. It is not just a natural consequence of being female. The same can be said for masculinity. Indeed, it has a kind of fragility or brittleness to it. Boys put enormous effort into being masculine. They need to distance themselves from their mothers, to repress the early intimate bond with the parent who nurtures them. This, at least, is the case presented in Nancy Chodorow's work in object-relations theory within sociology (Chodorow 1978). In this view, male children must distinguish their own identity as masculine from the identity of their female parent, leading to anxiety and compulsive performances of maleness. Boys have to prove their masculinity, constantly. Put this way, it sounds like a neurosis. We also need to bear in mind that boys and men have a lot to gain from masculinity. Boys soon learn that it is highly valued, something worth achieving. By performing masculinity, men can expect to reap respect, prestige and the right to command: the 'patriarchal dividend' (Connell 2005: 81).

Masculine and feminine identities are effects of discursive practices. Masculinity is performed by individuals, of course, but it is not an individual property or attribute; it is formed within institutions and is historically constituted. Like femininity, it is discursively produced and its articulation spans institutions. Like femininity, it can be viewed as a conglomeration of concepts, themes and images, and of kinds of social relation and social practice. But what is it? What does it look like? The answers to these questions are not simple. There are different versions: masculinities. *Hegemonic* masculinity is the dominant form, the one that counts as normal, that traditionally has the blessing of the church, the support of the state and, ultimately, has all the force and obviousness of common sense. Hegemony is not achieved by force – although that helps – but by consent. Robert Connell, an Australian sociologist, explains: 'Hegemonic masculinity can be defined as the configuration of gender practice which embodies the currently accepted answer to the problem of the legitimacy of patriarchy . . . It is the successful claim to authority, more than direct violence, that is the mark of hegemony (though violence often underpins or supports authority)' (2005: 77). He stresses that it is not 'a fixed character type, always and everywhere the same' (2005: 76) but constantly shifting. We need to examine how hegemonic masculinity exists in relation to subordinate masculinities, and in relation to women.

Men's ascendancy is institutionalized in the patriarchal institution of the family, in which women and children are subordinate to men. There is notable similarity between traditional households in different cultures and across classes, with wives being responsible for the domestic servicing of men (in other words, they look after their bodies: see they have food and clothes to wear). Note that I am not just saying that men dominate women. In the workplace, too, there is an unequal sexual division of labour across classes and ethnic groups. The global domination of men over women is a structural fact, demonstrable with statistics on the labour market, incomes and wealth, government and other sites of power (for some facts and figures, see Connell 2005: 82).

Some of the key concepts, practices and relations surrounding hegemonic masculinity in industrialized societies are rationality, heterosexuality, hierarchy, dominance, violence and being 'the breadwinner'. Men have given themselves a privileged position with regard to rationality. Women were long excluded from the rational, controlling discourses of science and bureaucracy and these discourses are still strongly associated with a specifically middle-class masculinity. Bringing in the 'family wage' is deeply entrenched as masculine in a wide range of discourses. Work is part of being a 'real man'. A study of the men's magazine *Arena* suggests that men are defined in terms of their employment. In the frequent features on celebrities, they are profiled as highly work-oriented and overwork is normalized. In an article on work-related stress, the writer addresses the reader as a workaholic 'and although the article is purportedly problematising overwork, the abundance of lexicalisations (the overachievers, hard work fetishism, the work dodger, work related deaths, cattle wagon commuting) seem instead to reinforce and naturalise the situation' (Tetlow 1991: 33). In terms of the men's magazine market, *Arena* in the early nineties was trying to do things that are no longer necessary - namely, legitimizing consumption for men and negotiating a position in the 'feminine' space of the British lifestyle magazine – and this article was doing some of this cultural work. But man-the-wage-earner is a fairly recent aspect of hegemonic masculinity anyway, which shows how gender identities are enmeshed in history and in economic structures. It has its origins in industrialization, in the creation of 'workplace' and 'home' as separate domains and the exclusion of women from paid employment that this enforced. Consider a rather different defining characteristic articulated in the Cohen Brothers' film, *Oh Brother Where art Thou?*: 'You ain't no kinda man if you don't have land.'

Another key practice in enactments of masculinity is violence. Male violence is legitimized to various degrees across institutions: from school sports to the state institutions of military and civil force. The army and the police are licensed to use violence. They provide 'protection' that is perceived as masculine (interestingly, however, women's increasing presence in the police may be altering this perception, according to a study of police-work in Pittsburgh (McElhinny 1995) – I return to this study in the next section). Of course, many of the people on the receiving end of police and military aggression are men. Connell identifies two patterns of violence. One of these sustains dominance over women: intimidation, from street harassment to murder. Another sustains the boundaries among men: from 'queer bashing' and gang fights to full-scale international warfare (Connell 2005: 83).

Hegemonic masculinity depends upon subordinate masculinities. Since the late nineteenth century, homosexuality has been a key subordinate masculinity. Other subordinate forms are imposed on men at the bottom end of social hierarchies. There are also oppositional forms. Connell identifies an oppositional 'protest masculinity'. The following, from a description of one of his case studies, characterizes this form of masculine identity: 'violence, school resistance, minor crime, heavy drug/alcohol use, manual labour, motorbikes or cars, short heterosexual liaisons. There is something frenzied and showy about it' (2005: 110). Later in this chapter, I present displays of a kind of masculine identity cultivated by young working-class men, typically in gangs (the study, by Pujolar (1997a, 2001), refers to it as 'simplified masculinity'). Both Pujolar and Connell describe a form of masculinity adopted by young men with little hope of rewarding employment, marginalized by these poor job prospects and poor housing. It is a marginalized masculinity, reworking elements of hegemonic masculinity in the context of poverty. It is an identity shaped by deprivation.

Hegemonic masculinity embodies cultural ideals. Cultural expressions of male ascendancy are endemic in the media. Consider the larger-than-life model of hegemonic masculinity embodied in James Bond, for instance, over the years. However, real social power does not reside in big muscles, displays of bravery or doing your own stunts, or, indeed, posing with firearms. Power resides elsewhere: in being at the head of a multinational corporation, a general leading an army, a senator or an MP. However, media manifestations support masculine power. It seems likely that such fantasy images help men to draw on and rework aspects of hegemonic masculinity. They give all men some investment in, some access to, the patriarchal dividend. As Connell observes, 'a large number of men have some connection with the hegemonic project but do not embody hegemonic masculinity' outright (2005: 79):

> It is tempting to treat them simply as slacker versions of hegemonic masculinity – the difference between the men who cheer football matches on TV and those who run out into the mud and the tackles themselves. But there is often something more definite and carefully crafted than that. Marriage, fatherhood and community life often involve extensive compromises with women rather than naked domination or an uncontested display of authority. A great many men who draw the patriarchal dividend also respect their wives and mothers, are never violent towards women, do their accustomed share of the housework, bring home the family wage, and can easily convince themselves that feminists must be bra-burning extremists. (2005: 81)

They can be said to be complicit in the 'hegemonic project'.

A lot has been published on masculinity in recent years. There has been a proliferation of popular psychology books on the subject, some of them bestsellers. Perhaps the best-known is Robert Bly's *Iron John*: a book that seeks to find relevance for modern men in Jungian archetypes found in myths and folklore, lifted out of their context and with complete disregard for their cultural origins (first published in 1990). There has also been a good deal of research on masculinity in the social sciences and in cultural studies. Standing out from all of it is Judith Halberstam's uncoupling of masculinity from men (1998).

Little of this work focuses on language, however. To date, only one edited collection focuses exclusively on language and masculinity (Johnson and Meinhof 1997; but see also Coates 2002). Not all the contributions in the volume work within a critical discourse analysis framework, but they are not incompatible with it. Some of the research I refer to in this chapter is drawn from this collection: namely, a college fraternity election meeting studied by Scott Kiesling, Deborah Cameron's discussion of American students gossiping about 'fags', Joan Pujolar's examination of everyday street-talk among Catalan men and my own study of a British newspaper's coverage of a sexual harassment conviction.

Dominance and control

Social ascendancy does not make life all plain sailing for men. There is a requirement imposed on individuals, an expectation that they will *embody* male dominance and control. They have to perform it. This is not to say that this constraint imposed on men by masculinity is like the constraints femininity imposes on women. The expectation for men to be embodiments of dominance may be tough, but it is hardly as restrictive as the expectation that women will *not* be dominant. Moreover, as Kiesling concedes: 'when a man constructs a powerful identity, it is usually connected in some way to "real" power. . . . a man's powerful identity is *rewarded* (with power), whereas a woman's non-powerless identity may be *punished*' (Kiesling 1997: 65–6). Nevertheless, men are expected to perform dominance and control. Kiesling looks for discourse strategies used by members of a college fraternity in Virginia to create and demonstrate power. In this section, I present some of his findings and then turn to two other perspectives on male dominance and control: fictional representations and women doing 'men's work'.

Men's positions of dominance are bestowed on them within institutions; they do not attain them by their own efforts alone. We have already observed this in Elinor Ochs and Carolyn Taylor's study of the 'Father knows best' dynamic in chapter 4. They found that fathers are set up, generally by mothers, as primary audience, judge and critic of other family members. In saying to their offspring, 'You wanna tell Daddy what happened to you today?', women contribute to the construction of hegemonic masculinity.

A fraternity hierarchy

Participation in a 'frat' community forms part of male students' preparation for the world of work. The young men are acquiring social practices in anticipation of careers in which they have positions of dominance. As such they have big investments in hegemonic masculinity. The frat communities of

US colleges have a closed, self-contained, hierarchical social structure. They can only be entered from the bottom. Full members, known as 'brothers', initiate prospective new ones. These 'pledges', as the probationary members are called, are second-class citizens. A 'pledge' is treated like a servant, totally dependent on his 'pledge educator'. He is put through an initiation not unlike in a military boot camp before he can become a full member (Kiesling 1997: 69). Even after initiation, the newly qualified member is subordinate to the older ones. This hierarchical structure has a good deal in common with the master–apprentice hierarchy found in London print shops by Cynthia Cockburn, a British sociologist (Cockburn 1983).

Below are some speakers' contributions at an election meeting. Fraternity election meetings are public, official occasions. At them, members must demonstrate their authority in stating their views and preferences. At this particular meeting, four candidates are being considered for the office of 'chapter correspondent', a position traditionally held by a young, recently initiated member. The candidates have made speeches and then left while the rest of the meeting discusses them. I will just contrast the strategies used by two speakers for constructing powerful identities for themselves. The first of them, 'Darter', is a new initiate and he does not usually speak in meetings. Here he speaks out in support of one of the candidates (his delivery is very rapid):

1	Darter:	Um *Ri:tchie* may come off like he's really
2		like a dumb ass and everything but uh
3		he's like one of the smartest people I know
4		y'know I went to high school with him
5		and he was like ranked *fifth* in our class
6		(.) and he can he can write like rea:lly well
7	Kim:	He's *A:s*ian man, what do you expect?
8	Speed:	((sarcastic)) Is he really?
9	Darter:	I mean he he *types* like unbelievably
10		(..) quick (.) um I just think this would be
11		a good position for him to hold because
12		he's a really good writer (.) I mean I've
13		read a lot of papers of his

(Adapted from Kiesling 1997: 73)

Darter uses mitigation and hesitation in stating his views. In lines 9–10, the conditional 'would' frames his statement as a suggestion and he mitigates it with 'I just think'. He bases his right to speak on the specialized knowledge he brings: he knows the candidate from high school. In lines 11–12, he justifies his stated opinion, explicitly highlighting the reasoning behind it ('because he's a really good writer'). He presents himself as knowledgeable, but tentative about the value of the knowledge he has to offer.

In contrast, a fourth-year member, 'Mack', presents himself very differently. He has been 'pledge educator' of the younger members present at the meeting, and also of one of the candidates under consideration. Mack uses very little mitigation and bases his right to speak on his position, not on the knowledge he brings. He is nominated to speak by the president, 'Mick', who is chairing the meeting (Kiesling does not say whether Darter is nominated or not). The other participant, 'Pencil', is the graduate adviser:

1	Mick:	Mack
2	Mack:	*Okay* (..) This is *it* (..)
...		
3		we need to look at what we have left here
4		(.) and there are certain positions that
5		everybody fits into perfectly (.) Ernie
6		does *not* fit into this (.) I'm not sure
7		where Ernie fits in just yet
8	?:	historian
9	Mack:	*but* I: a:m afraid that we are going to
10		waste uh one of the few brains *left* (.) in
11		someplace that that uh historian has
12		potentially been a non-existent position
13		(.) uh I think for a couple semesters
14		yahoo took some pictures
15	Pencil:	We're talking about chapter correspondent now
16	Mack:	what's that? I know
17	Pencil:	and he can hold *both* positions
18	Mack:	I understand that (.) But he won't (..)
19		I see- I see *Kurt-* I see Kurt- I see *Kurt-*
20	Pencil:	Then talk about chapter correspondent
21		(.) point of order
22	?:	we have we have four left
23	Pencil:	point of order

24	Mack:	I see Kurt as chapter correspondent (.)
25		not Ritchie damn it

(Adapted from Kiesling 1997: 75–6)

Mack sets himself up as an authority figure in various ways in this extract. Unlike Darter, he does not justify his statements or modify them with modality markers. His contribution begins with a categorical statement: 'This is it'; or, as Kiesling puts it, he begins 'by serving notice that his word is gospel' (1997: 76). His delivery is slow and authority-laden, in contrast with the rapidity and hesitancy of Darter's speech. He uses the inclusive **we** to speak for the group as a whole in his blunt categorical statements in lines 3 and 9. With devices such as the existential statement in line 4 ('there are certain positions . . .'), he presents his opinions as simple facts. In lines 9–14, he seems to be trying to highlight his authority as 'elder statesman' by displaying knowledge of the history of the fraternity. When called to order by Pencil, he makes his choice of candidate in a statement worthy of a visionary (lines 19 and 24): 'I see- I see *Kurt*- I see Kurt- I see *Kurt*- . . . I see Kurt as chapter correspondent.' He gives no reason at all for his preference.

There are non-verbal cues to the hierarchical positioning of participants at the meeting. The pecking order among these young men determines where they sit in the classroom where the election meeting is taking place. The older ones sit on the right, the younger on the left. Mack has seated himself as far to the right as possible. No one has taken a seat on the extreme left, which is hardly surprising (1997: 77).

Representations

Male dominance and the 'natural' controlling hand of men in the public domain can be found in representations of masculinity across cultures. Gender hierarchies can often be seen in visual representations. As part of a study of non-commercial advertising in Spain, JoAnne Neff van Aertselaer examines a government-produced comic book informing the public of changes implemented by the Socialist administration (Neff van Aertselaer 1997). Gender equity has been among the policies and social programmes of the Socialist-run government in Spain. Yet the comic was a pre-election device for winning votes, not in itself an agent of social change. In its presentation of an 'ideal Socialist family', it visually reinforces existing gender identities rather than trying to represent new ones. On the comic's cover, the mother is presented as, quite literally, at the centre of the family (1997:

164). Inside the comic, there is little action outside the home on the part of women, but women frequently gaze admiringly at men doing things. This provides another reminder that women contribute to constructing hegemonic masculinity. Men do not take up positions of dominance by their own efforts alone.

The dominant male also inhabits fiction, and he is never more in control than in 'action' adventure stories. In a study I made of a horror novel by James Herbert, the male protagonist's control of the situation is awesome (Talbot 1995a: 123–37). The novel I looked at was *Lair*, the second in Herbert's trilogy about giant mutant killer rats. In a passage that I look at closely, one of these sinister mutants is scurrying around in a dark corridor, menacing the protagonists, and a whole horde of them is gnawing its way through the door. There are two female characters in the scene; one of them is badly injured and unconscious, the other simply frightened. Both of them – conscious and unconscious – are little more than pieces of baggage being dragged up and down the corridor by the hero, making the controlling male hand rather too literal to take seriously. In my study, I demonstrate the extent of his active involvement and control of the situation by examining the distribution of transitive and intransitive verbs. That is, I show the extent to which the grammar of the passage establishes him as the one who is making things happen. Most of the verbs for which he is the grammatical subject are transitive (verbs like **reach**, **grab**, **take**, which take a direct object). In contrast, the actions of the other protagonists, including the rat, are represented with intransitive verbs (verbs like **lean** and **watch**, which do not have to take a direct object). Here is a short extract, containing the verbs mentioned:

> Jenny leaned back against the far wall and watched in fascinated horror. Pender reached her and shielded her body . . . 'Luke. Come here quickly.' It was Will calling from the gloomy end of the corridor. Pender grabbed Jenny's arm and took her with him. (Herbert 1979: 146)

To me the whole scene is like a comedy routine, but it certainly wasn't meant to be.

Male control is also central to other genres of fiction. In romance fiction for women, masculine dominance and aggression are eroticized. In the romance novels published by Harlequin Mills & Boon, the objects of desire are always powerful figures, charismatic and influential; and they always intimidate the heroine (Talbot 1995a, 1997a). In fact, most of them are bullies. The larger-than-life heroes in a lot of popular fiction, and the extent of their control over heroines, make it possible to read them as parodies of patriarchal power. Exaggerated masculine aggression, physical strength and muscularity are contrasted with equally exaggerated feminine passivity, weakness and flaccidity. This is never more true than in popular romance fiction. The following passage is taken from a recent romance novel. The setting is an auction; the hero has just jokingly reassured the heroine that if she starts bidding rashly he will clap a hand over her mouth. His strength to overpower her is presented as erotic:

> Her glance fell to his hands. Lean-fingered, tanned, they were more than capable of physically silencing her. She had a momentary vision of them, dark and strong against the transparent pallor of her skin, and swallowed, appalled at the flicker of forbidden excitement it aroused in her. (Donald 1990: 22)

In this passage, the eroticized power is located in the character's hands. The passage also illustrates another frequently used device. There is a visual contrast of the woman's 'transparent pallor' and the darker, tanned skin of the man's hands. Eroticization in Harlequin Mills & Boon depends on the maximization of gender difference.

Men's work

But let's return to the real world. Police work, as a job requiring strength and sometimes violence, is perceived as masculine. But what do women have to do when they take up 'masculine' jobs, and what happens to the jobs' perceived masculinity when they do? These are two issues addressed by Bonnie McElhinny in her study of the police in Pittsburgh (1995, 2002). As a consequence of a long-term affirmative action programme in Pittsburgh, women now make up 25 per cent of the police force (there is a similar figure for the presence of African-American women and men). Advisers to women trying to enter the domain of masculine 'blue-collar' jobs (that is, jobs seen to involve physical strength and ability) recommend various strategies involving the manipulation of gender markers. This includes advice on clothing and suchlike: 'Women are frequently coached, for instance, to wear long-sleeved shirts and bulky sweaters to suggest upper-body strength, and well-worn boots to suggest familiarity with doing "hard" work' (McElhinny 1995: 220). Paradoxically, women in 'masculine' jobs need to perform gender in order to make gender invisible.

In the case of police work, the uniform provides the visual masculine 'camouflage'. The women officers McElhinny interviewed also spoke of having cultivated emotional distance as part of a professional persona.

One interviewee, a white woman, describes it like this: 'When I'm at work I always feel like I have to be so gruff, you know. And normally I'm not like that. Sometimes I try to be like such a hard ass. I don't smile as much' (1995: 225). However, she is not simply performing as a male impersonator. The same interviewee goes on to report that, having noticed that her African-American women colleagues 'kinda command respect', she has started to cultivate their 'slang' and 'tone' (p. 226). When questioned about their ability to perform in a job requiring strength or violence, the women redefine these qualities as institutional. As they point out, police power resides in being police officers, not in wielding brute force. The job is increasingly bureaucratized, requiring detailed report writing. The competence of police officers lies in cool, emotionless efficiency rather than in physical ability or exertion. This aligns women in the police force with the younger, college-educated men. The presence of women in the police, while perhaps not changing the perception of it as masculine, is contributing to its shift from a 'blue-collar' masculine job to a more middle-class form of masculinity.

The importance of being hetero

Heterosexuality is central to hegemonic masculinity. It is, however, dependent on subordinate masculinities, especially homosexual forms, since it must negate them. These subordinate masculinities need not be clearly defined; in fact, hegemonic masculinity prefers it that way (Connell 1987: 186). This section focuses on the marginalization of gay masculinity, examining spoken interaction among men in Spain and in the United States and homophobia in the British press.

Several of the contributions in Johnson and Meinhof's book on masculinity (1997) have been influenced by poststructuralist views of language and of identity construction. Joan Pujolar, for instance, explores how young men in working-class neighbourhoods in Barcelona actively construct their masculinity in interaction. Taking a dialogical approach, he examines how their identities are constructed in dialogue. The multivoicedness is particularly clear because the 'voices' he examines include distinct languages and accents. Deborah Cameron's chapter in the same volume examines the enactment of heterosexual masculine identity by a group of American students, achieved in part by their highly cooperative gossiping, about 'fags'. Cameron calls this 'performative gender work', and she uses it to demonstrate just how misleading the familiar characterizations of male and female conversational styles are. What both these studies reveal are performances of forms of masculinity that depend upon homosexuality for their definition.

The 'antithesis of man' among US college students

Five American friends at leisure chat over a drink while watching sport on TV. Deborah Cameron examines the highly cooperative talk of these young men, in which they jointly produce a picture of several despised classmates. One of the victims of this all-male gossiping is labelled 'the antithesis of man' (1997: 53).

In chapter 5, I considered the distinct conversational styles attributed to women and men. These familiar characterizations – based on distinctions between competition and cooperation, report and rapport, and so on – are not very helpful here. These young men collaborate with one another, building on each other's contributions and frequently using supportive devices. Here is a short extract of such cooperative talk:

```
Ed:      he's I mean he's like a real artsy fartsy fag
         he's like (xxx) he's so gay he's got this like
         really high voice and wire rim glasses and
         he sits next to the ugliest-ass bitch in the
         history of the world ⌈and
Bryan:                        ⌊and they're all hitting on
         her too, like four guys ⌈hitting on her
Ed:                              ⌊I know it's like
         four homos hitting on her
```

(Cameron 1997: 56)

One thing that is particularly noticeable about this extract is the high frequency of **like** (**you know** is also used frequently elsewhere in this conversation). The functions of **like** in American English are complex and multiple. It sometimes functions as a hedge. The occurrences in this passage do not seem to be functioning that way, but do relate to the building up of group involvement and consensus. They contribute to the establishment or presupposing of common ground, by marking given information. They are also probably markers of high involvement in the talk, occurring most frequently when other features are present indicating excited involvement: high pitch, loudness, swearing and so on.

These young men are united in their shared perception of gays as alien. Curiously, the victims of their gossip are probably not gay at all. They are criticized for perceived deviance in their gender identity, for their failure to match up to standards of masculinity. Having a high-pitched voice, not dressing well, 'hitting on' (showing sexual interest in) an ugly woman – these flaws mean they don't make the grade as men, therefore they are homosexual. In engaging in this gossip about supposedly gay classmates, the young men are performing heterosexual masculinity. Such displays are apparently a common occurrence. Gay-bashing keeps at bay the 'dread spectre of homosexuality' (Cameron 1997: 51) that haunts all-male groups. It is not necessary when women are present, when heterosexual masculinity can be demonstrated in other ways.

Real men in working-class Catalonia

Pujolar studied the everyday life and talk of two groups of young men and women from working-class neighbourhoods in Barcelona. Barcelona is the capital of Catalonia, a region of northern Spain with its own language, Catalan, which is the administrative language of the region and used in schools. Speakers of Spanish in the region are descended from immigrant workers and tend to be working-class. The groups Pujolar studied contained a mixture of Catalan and Spanish speakers. He invented a name for each of the groups, calling them the 'Rambleros' and the 'Trepas'. The Rambleros are named after the 'Ramblas', the typically Catalan pedestrian avenues of their neighbourhood. He named the 'Trepas' after a term they used themselves, which he thinks was formerly used by Spanish-speaking parents to address their rebellious or noisy children (Pujolar, personal communication).

For the Rambleros men, the streets were for public performance. They frequently engaged in verbal duelling and fighting, public displays of masculinity. The taunting and teasing they engaged in sometimes took the form of playful threatening demands for fellatio. Pujolar gives an example of a series of exchanges initiated by one of the men, Andrés, suggesting that they go for a sandwich. By way of response to this suggestion, Luis offers his genitalia instead:

Andrés:	aquel? eh vamos al bocata	Hey, let's go to that sandwich place?
Luis:	mira (.) si quiere	Look (.) if you wanna eat
	comer (.) te puedes	(.) you stick your snout between
	amorrar entre mis	my legs, you know?
	patas sabes?	

(Pujolar 1997a: 89)

This response both rejects the suggestion and, apparently, hints at the possibility that Andrés is homosexual (and not that *Luis* is homosexual, as one might be forgiven for thinking). Andrés makes a retort that responds to both potential meanings:

Andrés: pues chico con esto no   Well kid, with this I wouldn't
          me llega pa nada   really have enough

(1997a: 89)

This retort is followed by mock offers of genitalia by the other members of the group, which Andrés rejects in similar fashion. In doing so, he both defends his initial proposal – to go and eat – and makes disparaging implications about their penis size. By doing this, he retaliates for the slur on his own heterosexual masculinity. The episode is concluded with a boast about penis size from one of the men, an utterance which is both threatening and friendly at the same time:

Ricardo: mira (.) te pongo yo la   Look (.) I stick my cock into
          polla en la boca es que   your mouth and there won't be
          no te cabe colega   enough room for it, mate

(1997a: 90)

The episode is an example of a distinct genre of verbal duelling. The Rambleros men use this speech genre in their performance of a particular form of masculinity associated with heterosexuality, verbal aggression, physical size and strength. This episode also shows the curious way in which the men's assertions of (heterosexual) masculinity are tied up with a preoccupation with homosexual sexual behaviour.

The Rambleros men voice their masculinity in other ways as well. They speak in accents containing southern Spanish Andalusian elements, particularly the musical intonation patterns characteristic of an Andalusian accent, despite not being from that region (Pujolar 1997a: 96). In Catalonia, the Andalusian accent carries working-class, or peasant, associations and therefore also connotations of 'simplicity' and 'authenticity'. Also connected with this construction of 'authenticity' is the men's distancing from formal kinds of talk. In the group discussions that Pujolar organized with this group, the men would not engage in formal talk, as the women did, and used ridicule and humorous 'dirty talk' as challenges to it.

So their 'simplified masculinity', as Pujolar names it, is performed by various means, including creative swearing, confrontations and insults – the last two being keyed as playful activities in his data, rather than serious ones. The women in the same group tended to perform what he calls 'intimations', that is, displays of intimacy in pairs. Interestingly, he notes that the women's organization of intimacy displays and mutual self-disclosure greatly facilitated his entry into the group. Though he reports initial awkwardness with these displays, through them the women were able to function as mediators: both to explain to him the background to the men's jokes and banter and also to explain his research to the men. He makes another interesting observation when he acknowledges that, despite the amount of attention he received from the women, he evidently found them less visible. He initially presents them as peripheral, as Paul Willis (1977) did in his work among groups of young working-class people in the UK. Fortunately, unlike Willis, Pujolar did not stop there. Having presented the agendas and the loud, highly visible group activities of the Rambleros men, he acknowledges the need to reverse his focus and 'try to conceptualize what women were seeking and what they brought into the social spaces' that he investigated too (2001: 68). Pujolar counters the inevitable tendency to dichotomize gendered behaviour in the groups by stressing that they are mixed and, in the case of the Rambleros, highly cohesive, aware that he would otherwise be fostering the fallacy of male and female subcultures existing independently.

The other group of men and women Pujolar spent time with were the Trepas. This was a rather different group, more politically aware, and he found more subversion of traditional gendered behaviours than among the Rambleros. The Trepas men and women were critical of the sexist attitudes and behaviour of working-class men, especially those who harass female colleagues at work, whom they mockingly represented speaking with Andalusian accents. In other words, they mimicked the accent as part of their rejection of the form of masculinity cultivated by the Rambleros men. They themselves used relatively standard forms of Catalan and Spanish, peppered with the specialized language of the inner city. This is a drug culture argot carrying connotations of working-class masculinity and associated with *la penya*: the poor youth of Spain.

Among the Trepas, subversiveness, transgressiveness and resistance to authority were perceived as manly, rather than the fighting and similar risk-taking that the Rambleros went in for. The Trepas men did a good deal of heavy drinking and drug-taking, or at least talked about doing so, and in their conversations they frequently created humorous pretend dialogues involving imaginary non-transgressive individuals. These men heaped ridicule on outsiders – that is, anyone not sharing their transgressive agenda of drug-taking and drinking – speaking Catalan in silly voices to do so. In the following example, Pepe is beginning an account of an occasion when he got drunk on a certain kind of beer (Catalan in italics):

Pepe:	cogí una cogorza con esa	Got drunk like hell with this shit
	mierda el otro día tío	the other day, lad
Mauro:	ah es cerveza no?	Ah. It's beer, isn't it?
Ayats:		((in a silly voice))
	Ah (.) sí sí (.)	Ah! Yes yes.
	et fots un	Drink a couple
	parell i a (xx)	and (xx)
Pepe:		((in a silly voice))
	sí nen (.)	Yes boy.
	posa molt	It really gets you

(Pujolar 1997a: 100)

The Trepas men here are using Catalan voices to animate some imaginary silly people as middle-class, inauthentic and, above all, unmasculine. This exploration of masculinity in a multilingual context by Pujolar illustrates very clearly the extent to which gender identities are embedded in local practices and the importance of examining gender in conjunction with class and ethnicity.

'Guilt over games boys play'

This final exploration of the construction of heterosexual masculinity is rather different. It arose from two distinct interests: homophobia in the press, on the one hand, and critical discourse analysis on the other – specifically, the use of CDA for focusing on the reader's complicity in the production of meaning and its implications for constructions of identity in the act of reading (Gough and Talbot 1996).

Val Gough and I looked at a single letter and reply from a problem page in a British tabloid newspaper, which had been given the heading: 'Guilt over games boys play'. The letter itself is from an adult man who is anxious about some homoerotic experiences that he shared with his best friend when they were both still schoolchildren. As adults, he and his friend are both actively heterosexual (he is married, his friend has a girlfriend) but, he says, he still experiences a confusing combination of guilt and curiosity. The letter, in other words, is a sighting of the 'dread spectre of homosexuality' (Cameron 1997: 51) that hovers around male friendships. The reply to it, which Gough and I concentrated on, banishes that spectre. This exorcism is performed by Marje Proops (at the time the doyenne of British 'agony columns'). Proops's reply reassures him that he is 'normal'. Her overall message is that homosexual experiences like his are legitimate, as long as they occur in the context of a development towards confirmed heterosexual, 'normal' relations: 'Many heterosexual men have a passing curiosity about homosexuality, and that isn't a bad thing. It compels you to make choices' (*Sunday Mirror*, 17 Jan. 1993).

As Gough and I observe in our analysis, in order to make coherent sense of these two sentences, a reader has to entertain all sorts of background assumptions. There are two explicit cohesive links which help to join them together. The first is straightforward enough: 'It' links back to 'passing curiosity'. The second cohesive connection is between 'you' and 'Many heterosexual men'; 'you' therefore functions as a generic pronoun refer- ring to a heterosexual male subject. Since the pronoun 'you' also refers specifically to the letter-writer, it has a dual function: as both a generic and a specific pronoun. But there is also an implicit **because**, a causal link, between the two sentences, which is *not* cued textually. A reader has to bridge the gap by inferring two things. The first inference that must be made is that heterosexuality and homosexuality are separate sexualities: an easy inference to make since, as I've said, the 'you' addressed is constructed as heterosexual. The second inference is that interest in homosexuality is valid in so far as it reinforces this separate heterosexual identity (Gough and Talbot 1996: 220–1). These inferences, contentious as they are, are needed to make coherent sense of the two sentences. If they were stated they would be much more noticeable, hence much more likely to be challenged. As they stand, they are unlikely to be contested by a reader, especially an unreflective heterosexual one, even though – or precisely because – she or he is complicit in their creation.

Inferences and presupposed ideas are part of the 'common sense' that a reader needs to draw upon in order to read a text as coherent. They are assumptions about the social world that are set up in such a way that they are not asserted, but readers still need to supply them to make sense of texts. Whether they are noticeable or not depends on the reader. They may be very visible for some readers, as the assumption about the preda- tory nature of male heterosexuality is for me in this extract from Proops's reassuring reply: 'You made [your choice] many years ago when you began to pursue women . . .' (*Sunday Mirror*, 17 Jan. 1993). Here it is presupposed that the letter-writer 'began to pursue women' (cued by the 'when' beginning the second clause). This presupposed bit of 'common sense' rests on an assumption that the male sexual drive is naturally predatory, which is, to say the least, debatable.

Proops was outspoken in defence of homosexuals for decades before the legal reforms of the 1960s. There is nothing reformist about her reply to this letter, however. In this instance she is reassuring the letter-writer that his masculinity is unambiguously heterosexual. In the process, she is reinforcing some very conventional notions about sexuality. Though she deplored the oppression of gay men, she was evidently aware of the importance of being hetero.

Change and resistance

Masculinity has undergone many changes in recent decades. One remarkable development has been the growth of 'gay liberation' and the oppositional form of masculinity it fosters. Straight men too, given the changes that have taken place in women's lives, have been forced to make adjustments: accommodating to life with women in paid employment, rejecting oppressive male behaviour, participating more in childcare. For a while in the 1980s, the media even started talking about the birth of the New Man. There are clearly economic constraints on changes in masculinity, however. The institution of the family is central to hegemonic masculinity and the family unit is still inevitably structured by work possibilities, by economic inequality in the workplace. Such a situation is self-perpetuating. High levels of male unemployment and the so-called 'feminization' of the workplace have changed the terrain in recent years, but overall a man's wages are still likely to be higher and he is more likely to have job security. But masculinities are not fixed. I have already remarked on the comparative recency of a key element of hegemonic masculinity: the breadwinner role. It may be that homophobia is a recent 'invention' too, since the classification of sexualities ('heterosexual', 'homosexual') only dates back to the late nineteenth century.

Not acting in conventionally gendered ways can be a risky business and 'gender crossing', as Pujolar points out, is a delicate matter (1997: 92). Nevertheless, gender identities are not fixed and changes do take place, sometimes for the better. Among the groups of young people Pujolar studied, there were some people, both men and women, who did not conform to norms of gendered behaviour. Among the Trepas, the more politically conscious of the two groups, he came across feminist-informed criticisms of men's sexist behaviour. Whether we go so far as to believe that the New Man lives, breathes and walks among us (and I think a healthy scepticism is in order), it has to be said that feminism, in its impact on women's lives and in its critique of masculinity, has had considerable influence. If it is to carry on doing so the criticism must continue.

This is where critical discourse analysis can be useful. With its focus on social reproduction and social change, CDA can be used to expose the social construction of gender identities and to challenge passive acceptance of the status quo. In this chapter so far, I have examined some men's performances of masculinity, focusing on dominance and control and the importance to them of heterosexuality. I finish it with some attention to responses to change, looking at college classrooms and the media.

'It's good for her': derision and silencing in a college discussion group

Two American sociolinguists, Victoria Bergvall and Kathryn Remlinger, have turned to CDA in examining educational discourse, specifically college discussion groups as a public domain that continues to be male dominated. They attend to 'the reproductive and resistant academic discourse of teachers and students' in classroom discussion (Bergvall and Remlinger 1996: 454). In addition to an interest in continued male dominance of language in the public domain, underlying their study is a commitment to student-centred education, essential both for students' full engagement in their own education and for valuable practice in coping with public kinds of talk (in this, Bergvall and Remlinger are taking issue with a restrictive, reproductive view of education that sees students as passive sponges, soaking up information supplied by teachers). In their investigation, they examine certain discourse practices in the classroom, then use their findings reflexively, by taking them back to the participants themselves. Their application of CDA is intended to 'transform harmful practices by informing us and our students about such problematic, repressive forms of discourse and showing us how to practise more liberatory strategies' (1996: 454–5).

The study focuses on the dynamics of discussion, on students' collective involvement in educational tasks. In it, Bergvall and Remlinger distinguish between *task-continuation* and *task-divergence*. Task-continuation refers to contributions that add to collaborative engagement in a verbal task. In an educational context, this is generally within an agenda set by the teacher; for instance, in a literature class, the discussion is probably pre-arranged by the teacher's selection of a text. Some divergent behaviour may also be collaborative, in that it diverges from the teacher's agenda but builds on the educational task; for example, bringing in new issues not addressed by the teacher. Such divergence from the teacher's set agenda may be viewed positively as empowering for students, since it gives space for dissent. It may be liberatory for students and is important in a challenge to the reproductive view of education.

By task-divergence, Bergvall and Remlinger mean less constructive forms of divergence: turns that function to sidetrack or derail the discussion task. In their analysis they identified task-divergence on the basis of absence of focus on the academic task and predominantly phatic and expressive function (1996: 467). Here is a small example, divergence through an aside in a linguistics class:

(F Prof = female professor)
F Prof: What's the past tense of drink? I drink I-
Sarah: drank
F Prof: drank (.) I have-
Sarah: drunk
Jim: [((audible whispering to Steve)) I have been drunk
F Prof: [I have drunk (.) Okay

(1996: 467)

Jim's digressive turn in this extract sets him up as autonomous, rather than a member of the larger collaborating group. He uses it to assert personal power, by focusing attention on himself at a local level. It is intriguing to see, in this little boast about boozing, an echo of the transgressiveness of the Trepas group of men discussed in an earlier section. Is it a little humourless to take issue with his lightening of what may have been a rather dry lesson about irregular verbs? Well perhaps, but he is not offering his joke for the group as a whole and he is setting himself apart from the group discussion (along with his colleague, Steve, whether Steve wants to be or not). The aside is task-divergent: 'Such humorous asides may seem to be natural extensions of the task, but they are actually task-divergent because they establish individual power and open a limited second floor rather than foster group norms of cooperation and accommodation to the main floor's task-continuation' (1996: 467–8).

At the same time as asserting his own autonomy, Jim is challenging the female teacher's authority. In an interview, he identified himself as the 'class clown', a role adopted exclusively by men in Bergvall and Remlinger's data. Interestingly, it seems that a specific kind of disruptive behaviour – the class-clown role – is linked with the performance of a transgressive form of masculinity.

My focus now is change and resistance to change. While men traditionally dominate public forms of talk, the active participation of women in college classes is now widespread. Bergvall and Remlinger have found that, to reassert the status quo, task-divergence is sometimes used in a repressive way to belittle fellow students and discourage their active participation. What follows is an example of a student being the subject of open derision, in the form of harsh laughter and derisive asides. It took place in a literature class, during a discussion of Toni Cade Bambara's 'Blues ain't no mockin' bird'. At one point in this short story, which centres on a poor rural family who keep chickens, the grandfather deals with a predatory hawk by nailing it alive to the barn door, in order to attract its mate. One student is struggling to make a comparison between the barbarous killing of the hawk, as she sees it, in the story and the slaughter of dolphins in the tuna-fishing industry:

(M Prof = male professor; MS = male student, unidentified)

1	Veronica:	Well wait a second (.) all right (.)
2		this is an example (.) I'm not trying to
3		make a judgement or anything but look at
4		the whole debate about you know right
5		now (.) about tuna and they're talking
6		about the drift nets that kill dolphins and
7		whatever (.) you know when they (.)
8		I mean it's like well (.) do people need
9		those tunas to (.) you know produce food
10		n and all that kind of stuff for people?
11		but you (.) but we don't think that it's right
12		for them to (.) to kill the dolphins along
13		with em so how is it right to you know
14		[to kill the hawks
15	Marie:	[(who's killing?)
16	Class:	((extended laughter, 5+ seconds, increasingly loud and harsh, with several bouts of laughter by different people, including Marie. More asides underneath))
17	Marie:	(inaudible aside)
18	Louis:	all ri::ght

19	Marie:	[(xxx)((laugh))]
20	M Prof:	⌊are these people environmentalists?⌋
21	Greg:	not really (.) I ⌈don't think they ⌉really care
22	MS:	⌊it's good for her ⌋(xx)
23	Marie:	⌊((laugh))

(Bergvall and Remlinger 1996: 468)

Marie's remark in line 15 indicates confusion at Veronica's rather lengthy attempt at an analogy. Marie may be querying the relevance of Veronica's point to the discussion task, as the teacher does more explicitly in line 20. Her comment certainly puts an end to it, triggering extended, loud laughter and various asides within the group. In line 22, a clearly audible, derisive aside is directed against Veronica by MS (a male student, unidentified). The net result is to silence her.

It is true that Veronica's attempted analogy is a bit of a muddle, but other students make contributions that are equally confusing. However, it is the more outspoken female students – who have successfully broken out of the mould of silence or reticence in public talk – whose domination of the floor is challenged in this way. Again, notice that it is not just a matter of men dominating women. In this example – the silencing of Veronica – Marie is a key player. She does not do the same to male students. Bergvall and Remlinger remark that this silencing is 'a troublesome indicator of opposition to assertive, "substantially engaged" female students that we have seen elsewhere in our data' (1996: 470). However, there is transformative potential in bringing into the college classroom attention to the dynamics of discussion groups like these, as they propose.

Media containment

There have been changes in masculinities over the past couple of decades, but I think we must be cautious. It seems to me that piecemeal changes simply serve to sustain hegemonic masculinity. They do not put it under threat. This somewhat pessimistic view is shared by Robert Hanke, writing about US television and hegemonic masculinity (Hanke 1992). Hanke, coming from an American cultural studies perspective, is primarily writing about fiction, throwing cold water on enthusiasm about representations of 'new men' in TV situation comedy. However, his argument holds for non-fictional performances of masculinities too.

The dominating, authoritative male abounds on prime-time TV in the action-adventure, sports and news programming, but is not to be seen in domestic comedies like *Thirtysomething*. But, says Hanke, we must not mistake 'the synchronic variety of images of men for diachronic change' (1992: 192). In other words, just because there are lots of different kinds of representation of men about at the same time, it does not mean that change is taking place. After all, there has always been variety in the available representations of men. Hanke poses a key question: how is masculinity redefining itself in order to remain hegemonic? It can comfortably incorporate such things as domesticity and interest in relationships, as long as it glosses over real inequities. Hanke is primarily discussing changes in the way characters in fiction are depicted, but the argument holds for non-fictional performances of masculinities.

Consider an item in the British press containing a favourable report of a sexual harassment conviction. It appeared in the *Sun*, a politically conservative daily newspaper targeted at a working-class audience. This news coverage surprised me. Legislation against sexual harassment in the workplace has come about because of a feminist counterdiscourse on gender. The *Sun* is not where I would have expected to read a favourable account of feminism in practice. Yet there it was. The article was rather overshadowed, however. It appeared on 'page three', the home of its customary topless pin-up, known as the 'page three girl', whose image occupies over half the page. So the page it appeared on was dominated by the image of a woman wearing a hat, and little else. And, I must say, the article was not exactly serious in tone. The guilty party was the owner of a seafood business, so that puns, on the theme of fish, were abundant, starting with the headline: '£6,000 bill puts randy fish boss in his plaice!' Nevertheless, side by side with a familiar sexist discourse on gender, here, via an industrial tribunal, was an articulation of feminism (the article never uses the f-word – which is, of course, feminism!).

I was very interested to see how the article exploited ambivalence. It was absorbing, so to speak, the threat posed by feminism and deflecting the blame for practices like harassment away from 'your average *Sun* reader' and on to a sexually ineffectual, middle-class scapegoat. The report – half joking, half serious – provided the male *Sun* reader with a cosy distance from the villain of the piece, despite the obvious parallels that can be drawn between sexual harassment and 'normal' male behaviour, such as ogling the pin-ups on 'page three' (Talbot 1997b).

I think this piece of news coverage demonstrates how resilient masculinity is. The problem for hegemonic masculinity is that its legitimacy has been put under threat. Its stability lies in its very flexibility. It can take on board apparently incompatible elements. For me, the single newspaper article illustrates the capacity of masculinity to adapt to, even assimilate, opposition. This flexibility enables it to withstand larger, more disruptive structural changes.

I will end this chapter on masculinities by considering another response in the press to the pressure exerted by feminism. In the early 1990s, the men's magazine *Arena* ran a semi-serious opinion piece on a new kind of masculine identity: the New Lad. It suggests one way in which masculinity is redefining itself in order to remain hegemonic. This hybrid creature is claimed to be a combination of the New Man and the unreconstructed Old Lad. Helen Tetlow's analysis of this article (1991) involves, in part, pinpointing how the writer's highly subjective views on these supposed categories of masculine identity are presented as universally held common sense.

Consider the following, a single sentence from the *Arena* article: 'the death of the New Man has coincided with the birth of an identifiable though slippery subspecies which has emerged as a muted response to the embarrassing vacuum left by the New Man's ignominious non-appearance' (see Tetlow 1991: 47). This sounds very authoritative, as though he knows what he's talking about. He writes with categorical certainty, using no hedging, no tentative **I thinks** or **maybes**. Indeed, elsewhere in the article he uses intensifiers; for example in maintaining that something is 'blindingly obvious' (1991: 48). The sentence sounds quite technical too, as though he is drawing on scientific discourse. There are a lot of processes hidden inside noun phrases: this is a grammatical feature known as nominalization, a characteristic of scientific kinds of discourse. Nominalizations actually leave out a lot of information about how, why, when and suchlike.

In fact, as Tetlow shows, there are a lot of questions that can be asked about the sentence, addressing precisely these hidden processes:

Text	*Hidden processes*
the death of	when did he die?
the New Man	how? why?
has coincided with	
the birth of an	when was he born?
identifiable	identifiable by whom?
though slippery subspecies	
which has emerged as	
a muted response	who responded? why was it muted?

| to the embarrassing vacuum left by | embarrassing to whom? |
| the New Man's ignominious non-appearance | when and why did he not appear? who felt ridiculous as a result? |

The *Arena* article provides no answers to these questions. The commonsensical appearance of the writer's opinion is achieved by means of a convenient vagueness. This supports the position of wise cynicism he moves on to later in the article: 'Basically, the New Lad aspires to New Man status when he's with women, but reverts to Old Lad type when he's out with the boys. Clever, eh?' (Tetlow 1991: 54).

Further reading

Theorizing masculinity

Connell (2005) and Segal (2006) are both key texts. See also Benyon (2002), Gardiner (2002), Kimmel, Hearn and Connell (2004) and Whitehead (2001).

Control and violence

Adams, Towns and Gavey (1995) presents a rhetorical analysis of New Zealand men's talk about their own violence against their partners. See also extract and discussion in chapter 3 of Talbot, Atkinson and Atkinson (2003). Two other studies of men's accounts of their own violence are Ehrlich (2001) on Canadian courtroom testimonies and Hearn (1998) on interviews with British prison inmates. A multimodal analysis of children's war toys can be found in Machin and Van Leeuwen (2009).

Homophobia

I have already mentioned the study of 'gay-bashing' talk in Cameron (1997). See also Coates (2003), especially chapter 3. A fuller account of the problem page study referred to is in Gough and Talbot (1996).

   A full account of the research on youth culture in Catalonia is available in both English and Catalan (Pujolar 1997b, 2001). See also extracts and discussion in chapter 5 of Talbot, Atkinson and Atkinson (2003).

10

Public talk

This chapter outlines recent work on discourse and gender construction in professional public contexts. It focuses on the marginalization of women's voices in specific workplaces which are masculinist Communities of Practice (these terms are defined below), including broadcasting and politics. It concludes with some attention to hostile media representations of women in work.

Women and the public sphere

Historically speaking, the public sphere has been an exclusively male domain. It still is in some traditional societies. In chapter 1, I mentioned a contemporary tribal people in Brazil known as the Karajá. Social roles for men and women among the Karajá are very clearly defined. According to tradition, only the men may hold official positions requiring public address.

Public language tends to be formal and to convey status; public speakers are generally in positions of authority. Even the exceptions – such as speakers on Hyde Park Corner, preachers and ranters in general – tend to be men. In societies where high status and authority are for men only, women must be kept silent in the public sphere. The apostle Paul, writing in the first century AD, was quite clear about it. 'Let your women keep silence in the churches', he said, 'for it is not permitted unto them to speak . . . And if they will learn any thing, let them ask their husbands at home: for it is a shame for women to speak in the church' (St Paul's First Epistle to the Corinthians, 14: 34–5). Whatever he actually intended by this pronouncement, 2,000 years ago, there is one thing we do know, and that is that it was widely used in the Christian world to justify the continued exclusion of women from positions of authority in the church.

This was in line with the pronouncements of the Greek philosophers, another major influence on Western beliefs. Aristotle, for example, wrote that women should be prevented from taxing their brains with things like political activity, because it would dry up their wombs. Until well into the nineteenth century, Aristotle's claim fuelled attempts to frighten women away from public speaking with dire warnings about it inducing sterility (Jamieson 1988: 69). Daring to address the public – whether orally or in writing – was damaging to a woman's reputation for many centuries. The 'virtue' of an eighteenth-century woman who had novels published was highly suspect. Women as preachers were widely ridiculed. The English language has a remarkable variety of words for vocal women, all of them condemnatory: **scold**, **shrew**, **gossip**, **nag**, **termagant**, **virago**, **fishwife**, **harpie**, **magpie**, **jay**, **parrot**, **poll**, **harridan**, **(castrating) bitch**, **battle-axe**. I'm glad to say that some of them have gone out of fashion.

Being forced to remain silent, to have no public voice, is like being invisible. As Robin Lakoff remarks, women are still not free of the restrictions traditionally forced on them:

> Silence is analogous to invisibility. . . . in ancient Athens women of the upper classes were not supposed to appear in public at all (literal public invisibility), in fundamentalist Muslim societies, women must be veiled in public (symbolic public invisibility). We pride ourselves on our liberation from those humiliating constraints. We tend not to realize how recent and partial our liberation really is. (1995: 29)

In traditional rituals such as weddings, it is often still men who do all the speech-making. In the Anglo-American Christian tradition, speeches are made by the bride's father and the best man. The bride is literally visible, to be sure – her role is to look lovely – but she is publicly silent (and often, in fact, veiled).

Historically women have been excluded from prestigious and potentially influential kinds of discourse. While women in most industrialized societies are no longer barred from such discourses, they are still marginalized in many public contexts. As Cameron points out, the problem is not so much access to public talk at all as continued marginality in

> those settings, genres and ways of using language that carry the greatest weight of cultural authority for the community as a whole. Female voices are most obviously unwelcome in contexts where the community's most cherished values are ritually and solemnly affirmed, using a formal or elevated register of language to discuss 'the great subjects' in a quasi-'sacred' institutional space – the Parliamentary chamber, the courtroom, the church. (2006c: 8)

In Britain, for example, the debate over the ordination of women continues to rumble on. Women have been eligible for the Anglican clergy since the 1990s, but those women who have entered the ministry have tended to be marginalized and subordinated, as Clare Walsh's research on the Church of England has demonstrated (Walsh 2001).

In chapter 6, I referred to an experimental study by Alice Freed, in which she concluded that the experimental space she had set up, and the talk that was taking place within it, were gendered. Walsh draws upon Freed's insight that settings may be gendered to argue that forms of talk in the public sphere are primarily masculine (and masculinist – a term I will return to in a moment). As she observes, what we perceive as professional norms of conduct are better viewed as masculinist:

> historically the minority status of women within public sphere institu-
> tions, such as Parliament and the established Church, means that the
> dominant discursive practices which circulate in these domains are those
> associated with white middle-class male speakers. Through habitual use,
> these masculinist discursive norms have assumed the status of gender-
> neutral *professional* norms, as have male-oriented patterns of behaviour.
> (Walsh 2001: 1)

By referring to these discursive practices as 'masculinist', Walsh is indicat-ing that over the centuries they have been historically constituted along with hegemonic forms of masculinity. She offers the term as an alternative to 'patriarchal' in order to avoid the impression that women are intention-ally denied full access or participation (2001: 25n).

In entering institutions like Parliament and the church, then, women are entering Communities of Practice (Eckert and McConnell-Ginet 1992; Lave and Wenger 1991) that have previously been the preserve of men. Eckert and McConnell-Ginet define a Community of Practice as 'an aggre-gate of people who, united by a common enterprise, come to develop and share ways of doing things, ways of talking, beliefs, and values – in short, practices' (Eckert 2006: 183). Since women are participating in masculinist Communities of Practice, they are highly likely to experience a sense of marginality; as Eckert puts it, they feel like 'interlopers' (1998: 67). In such contexts, women have more than their own anxieties to contend with. They are also likely to encounter men's defence of their own privilege, as we will see in the next section, which attends to women's experiences in the debating chamber of the British House of Commons.

Politics

The Palace of Westminster in London is of fairly recent history (the current building was only completed in 1870), but there has been a House of Commons debating chamber since the fourteenth century. Women have been eligible to enter it since 1918, but rarely did so until 1997. Over hundreds of years a masculinist Community of Practice has evolved, with an organizational structure that harks back to another age and is resistant to change. The long and irregular hours cater for the landed gentry of an earlier era and certainly not for present-day politicians with childcare needs. The Commons is rather like a gentleman's club 'fashioned by 500 years of men-only shortlists' (King 2005). To this day, it is equipped with a rifle range but has no crèche! The debating chamber itself is designed for adversarial encounters. The floor between the two ranks of benching is marked with red lines, traditionally two sword-lengths apart; an MP may only speak from behind one of these lines (House of Commons Information Office 2009: 4). While actual swordplay is presumably no longer a problem in the House, metaphorically speaking it is still very common:

> The style of debate in the House has traditionally been one of cut-and-thrust . . . This style of debate can make the Commons Chamber a rather noisy place with robustly expressed opinion, many interventions, expressions of approval or disapproval and, sometimes, of repartee and banter. (2009)

A highly combative style prevails in debate, as it does in relations between Party members more generally. Walsh observes that this is further aggravated by the Party Whip system 'which effectively means that a culture of bullying is not only tolerated, but is integral to the Parliamentary system' (2001: 69).

After a Labour landslide victory in 1997, there was an influx of women into the British House of Commons. How these women fared in the debating chamber is the subject of a recent study (Shaw 2006). Sylvia Shaw based her study on sixty hours of video-recorded material filmed between 1997 and 2001, and semi-structured interviews with women MPs. Most of her interviewees spoke of their 'terror' of speaking in the House. Shaw concedes that the prospect probably has the same effect on many male MPs but points out that men don't have to contend with 'the sexist barracking and negative media representation commonly directed at women MPs' (2006: 82). A former Liberal Democrat MP, Jackie Ballard, has commented that behaviour at Westminster 'falls way below the standards you would allow in any workplace, particularly in terms of sexist language and so on' (Somes, Moran and Lovenduski 2005). Shaw argues that the debating chamber – for centuries the exclusive preserve of a male, white, upper- and middle-class elite – is not a level playing field: it disadvantages many men and all women. As a genre, commons debate is highly rule-governed.

In particular, there are rigid chairing conventions and formal address requirements. An ability to operate within this genre with ease displays membership of the Community of Practice. Conversely, failure to use this so-called 'parliamentary language' constructs a speaker as a peripheral figure in it – a newcomer or 'interloper'.

The rules of engagement in Commons debate are enforced by a moderator, known as the Speaker. Mr/Madam Speaker is responsible for maintaining 'order' in the debating chamber. Chairing conventions and terms of address are highly formal and stylized. Here is an example of a woman MP tangled up by these rules. She begins to make a powerful and articulate speech, initially free of hesitation, fluent and apparently confident. In line 9, another MP asks for permission to comment, which she grants:

FMP   = female Labour MP (name not supplied)
JH   = John Hayes (male Conservative MP)

1	FMP:	the problem the police faced (.) was the fact that
2		they were institutionally racist (.) institutionally
3		incompetent and institutionally corrupt and
4		I would say that corruption is the twin brother
5		of racism (.) and it affects us all and this why
6		the debate is so important (.) and the Lawrence
7		inquiry is so important for white people as
8		well as black people
9	JH:	would the right Honourable Lady give way
10	FMP:	yes
11	JH:	I'm very grateful to the Honourable Lady (.)
12		the Honourable Lady is telling this House
13		is she the police suffers from institutionalised
14		corruption (.) leaving aside that outrageous
15		claim (.) doesn't she realise that by blaming
16		an institution collectively (.) by assuming
17		there is some unconscious collective guilt (.)
18		she is letting off the hook (.) those officers
19		who are certainly guilty of these charges (.)
20		because they are hiding behind the very sort
21		of collective allegations that she makes

When the speechmaker responds to this intervention, she starts running into difficulties. She addresses her challenger directly, realizing her error and apologizing in line 26:

```
22   FMP:      thank you (.) well if we can look at the issue
23             you raise by perhaps taking another -ism
24             and another institution (.) just to see whether
25             (.) the point you make is correct or not
26             oh I'm sorry
27   Speaker:  o- o- order the Honourable Lady must use
28             the correct parliamentary language
```

She acknowledges her difficulty with the constraints of the conventions, in an implicit apology to the Speaker. She then resumes her speech in line 31, addressing her addressee in the appropriately indirect way, in the third person, as 'the Honourable Gentleman':

```
29   FMP:      Mr Deputy Speaker I suffer from an inability
30             to get that into my mind even after two years
31             in this house (.) yes um the Honourable
32             Gentleman er opposite um will perhaps look
33             at another example we can use another -ism
34             I was saying and a- another institution
35             lets take sexism (.) and lets take (.) parliament
36             lets take the House of Commons (.) lets look
37             across the benches here (.) and in fact when
38             one woman opposite and twenty-six men (.)
39             on the opposition benches (.) now surely
40             you would not deny that that means we have
41             an institution which is biased against women (.)
42             would the Honourable Gentleman deny that
43             I presume he would not (.) now equally equally
```

After initial disfluency on resuming her speech, she regains her grasp of her subject, but reverts to direct address in line 44, which prompts a second intervention by the Speaker:

```
44             (.) so you would say (.) well I- sorry the
45             Honourable Gentleman
46   Speaker:  order the Honourable Lady must think carefully
47             before she chooses her words (1.0)
48   FMP:      absolutely right er (.) Mr Deputy Speaker er
49             the Honourable Gentleman just said yes
50             he would deny that there is a discrimination
```

51	against women when effectively there are no
52	women well two women at this moment in time
53	sitting on the benches opposite

(speech continues)

(Shaw 2006: 86–7)

Here we have an example of a woman struggling to comply with the discursive norms of the House. It is perhaps a little surprising that Shaw found no examples of men doing the same. In her corpus of data, male newcomers kept a low profile in the House; they were either silent or simply absent.

In an earlier study, Shaw (2000) found that legal interventions – asking the speechmaker to 'give way' – were equally distributed across male and female MPs' contributions to debate. It was men, however, who performed almost all illegal interventions. There were various rule-breaking ruses that only men engaged in: barracking and cheering were very frequent, as was hijacking the floor with illegal interventions that went unchallenged (such as 'oh *rub*bish Winterton (.) you really are a *si*lly man' (Shaw 2006: 93)). Women did not indulge in such disruptive rule breaking. As newcomers to the Community of Practice, they needed to be 'beyond reproach' and on their best behaviour (2006: 96).

Of course, before the influx in 1997 there had been a small number of women in the House who managed to operate successfully in its masculinist environment, the most prominent among them being Margaret Thatcher, the only female prime minister to date. The way she styled herself as a leader is well documented (e.g. Fairclough 2001). The late Gwyneth Dunwoody, a senior Labour MP, earned grudging respect for her aggressive behaviour – and the affectionate nickname of Mrs Badger. An obituary recalls this comment: 'I don't mind being called a battleaxe. They are well made, very sharp, and largely very efficient in what they do' (White 2008). Yet women in the political arena continue to be seen as the exception to the norm. Interviews with women in the European Parliament indicate that they are acutely aware of their identities as exotic exceptions, or 'special birds' (Wodak 2003: 692). The media are also male dominated; in their masculinist institutional discourses, women politicians are always at risk of being marginalized and trivialized. Infamously, the record of 101 female Labour MPs voted into Westminster in May 1997 was reported in the British press as the arrival of 'Blair's babes' (*Daily Mail*, 8 May 1997). This patronizing collocation was the caption to an annotated photograph. Here is some of the accompanying commentary:

> The women frothed out of Church House, Westminster, in a multi-coloured tide. It was like the Chelsea Flower Show meets the Girl Guides, as the fuschia [*sic*] suits loved by the likes of Margaret Beckett (No. 83), and Barbara Follett's glittering emerald green (No. 74), mingled with more sombre browns and beiges. (*Daily Mail*, 8 May 1997; cited in Walsh 2001: 45)

The verb **frothed** and the preoccupation with visual impact trivializes the arrival of all these women on the political scene (Walsh 2001: 45).

The media reproduce and circulate entrenched ideas about the place of women in the political sphere. In her autobiography, Hillary Rodham Clinton remarks on expectations of her role as first lady. The White House press corps expected her to project herself as either a feminist professional figure or a traditional homemaker (Clinton 2003: 140). Another no-win situation arose for her during the Democrat presidential nomination race that she ran in herself, according to Melanne Verveer (her chief of staff when she was first lady):

> She has made it to a point that no previous woman has made it to in our country, in terms of being a really viable candidate for president. But I think in the process of demonstrating that one is competent and tough enough to be commander-in chief, in the process of presenting that image, the reaction is 'well, perhaps in doing that she's not likeable', yet if one presents herself as soft and likeable, which she also is, the perception is she's not tough enough. So it's this double bind. (Brockes 2008: 22)

Here we have that all too familiar double-bind, that 'damned if you do, damned if you don't' predicament noted in chapter 3, that Robin Lakoff identified in the 1970s. Commentators on the nomination contest between Clinton and Barack Obama have suggested that being masculine in itself gives a candidate greater capacity to embody the desired qualities of a leader: 'the advantages of masculinity are . . . not least in the scope it gives a candidate to embody those politically vital virtues of a capacity for change and a capacity for protection, the capacities for both a degree of aggression and a degree of care' (Evans 2008). I return to media representations of women in employment in the final section of this chapter.

Broadcast interviews

In current affairs broadcasting, the political 'hard news' interview is an elite genre. The interviewer role is a prestigious one. It has been character-ized as 'tribune of the people' (Clayman 2002), since it involves expressing concerns on behalf of an audience. A recent study of media celebrity argues that the people's tribune identity has evolved into a form of celebrity, a 'public inquisitor' (Higgins 2010). This role involves engaging in particular forms of aggressive, inquisitorial dialogue. The study considers Jeremy Paxman and John Humphrys, two prominent figures in British broadcasting who have extended the remit of this elite discursive role to media genres other than the 'hard news' interview (Paxman, for instance, enacts it on the BBC quiz show, *University Challenge*). In this section I consider the interviewing styles of these anchor-interviewers on the high-profile programmes with which they are principally associated: *Newsnight* (BBC2) and *Today* (BBC Radio 4). I also consider the experiences of Sue MacGregor, a feminist broadcaster, in joining the *Today* team.

A well-known characteristic of Paxman's interviewing style is his dogged persistence, with a tendency to repetition and interruption in grilling his interviewees. An extreme case was an interview in 1997 with a Conservative politician, Michael Howard. In it, Paxman recycled the same question twelve times or more. Here is a short passage containing two of them (in lines 3 and 8):

```
     MH:    Michael Howard
     JP:    Jeremy Paxman
1    MH:    I was entitled to express my views?
2           I was entitled to be consulted=
3    JP:    =Did you threaten to overrule him
            [
4    MH:    I- I was not entitled to
5           instruct Derek Lewis and I did not
6           instruct him and the truth of-
7           the truth of the matter is that ((fades))=
            [
8    JP:    Did you threaten to overrule him
```

Here is another short passage from a little later in the same interview. Howard is speaking very slowly, while Paxman's speech at times is very rapid:

```
1    JP:    I note you're not answering the question
2           whether you threatened to overrule him
3    MH:    ((extremely slow delivery)) well the- the
4.          important aspect of this (.) which it's
5           very clear to bear in mind
```

```
6          (i:s this)-
           [
7   JP:    >>>I'm sorry I'm gonna be frightfully rude
8          but-<<<
9   MH:    yes (you can)-
           [
10  JP:    >I'm so(h)rry<
```
((several seconds of indecipherable simultaneous talk))

In line 7, Paxman's formulaic apology functions as a negative politeness strategy, presumably softening the impending face threat of yet another repetition. Then, in line 10, another appears to be oriented to the severe breakdown in turn taking. Here Paxman is the dogged interviewer subjecting his interviewee to a gentlemanly grilling. It illustrates the confrontational interviewing style of the public inquisitor, with the high degree of simultaneous talk, dislocated turn taking and the interviewer's overt challenges in imposition of his agenda. (In fact, the producer's voice in his ear was telling him to stall for time – he was just doing as he was told. And, strangely, the interviewee's answer was no anyway!)

Like other interviewers, Paxman frequently employs an ambiguous 'double-voicing' tactic in his questioning strategies. There is a three-way distinction between speaker roles or 'voices' that is sometimes useful, especially in dealing with complex media discourse. The person whose views an utterance presents is the *Principal*; the one who composes the utterance is the *Author*; the one who merely utters it is the *Animator* ('the talking machine' (Goffman 1981: 167)). Broadcast journalists, being supposedly committed to neutrality, standardly present the views of others: that is, they 'animate' them. A simple example of such animation of the words of others is when a news interviewer makes reference to a soundbite that has just been played. Distinctively, however, Paxman sometimes uses the pose of merely animating the views 'authored' by others to insult his interviewees, while maintaining an allegedly neutral stance. Such questions can be highly aggravated and face-threatening, as in his question in lines 5–11:

```
    JP:    Jeremy Paxman
    DD:    David Davis
1   JP:    David Davis could the Conservatives win
2          the next election with David Cameron as
3          leader
4   DD:    (.) I reckon they could (.) yeah
```

5	JP:	In that case why should they (.) choose a
6		man (.) described by your colleagues to us
7		as (.) and these are direct quotes as a
8		thug a bully an adventurer (.) disloyal
9		(.) congenitally treacherous (.) and
10		winner of the whips' office shit of the
11		year championship
12	DD:	(.) how flattering

In lines 5–11, Paxman is animating the alleged words of Davis's Conservative colleagues. The ambiguity lies, of course, in his own alignment with them. From Davis's ironic response (line 12), it is apparent that he considers the pose of neutrality to be a transparently empty one. It forms part of an opening gambit of a type commonly employed by Paxman.

Paxman's on-air persona as an inquisitor figure was celebrated in a fifteen-minute Sunday supplement on *The Westminster Hour* (BBC Radio 4, 18 June 2006), which I have examined elsewhere (Talbot 2007b). It is entitled 'How to beat Jeremy Paxman' and its presenter identifies him as 'Britain's number one interrogator'. This is an interesting feature in that it offers a representation of a highly valued discursive style, how the BBC chooses to represent one of its own current affairs 'celebrities': as a heroic persona. The implied listener of the feature is invited to take the position of a hypothetical MP preparing to appear on *Newsnight*: 'you've thought through the arguments (.) but are you ready for the whole body experience?' The contact sport metaphor underlying this question sets Paxman up as some kind of discursive pugilist or wrestler. The feature frames the dogged grilling in the first two extracts above as 'a legend' and the face-threatening opening gambit in the third extract as a wily cricket strategy: 'bowling a bouncer'. The sport metaphors contribute to building a representation of Paxman interviews as gentlemanly sportsmanship. Not only does the broadcast text valorize the discursive fisticuffs of gentlemanly, sportsmanlike interviewers like Paxman, it presents them as an essential part of the democratic process, since, for as long as the 'political process dictates (.) that the truth . . . cannot or should not be told (.) if Paxman didn't exist (.) you'd probably have to invent him'.

The masculinist culture of the newsroom has been widely noted (e.g. Born 2002, 2004; van Zoonen 1998). One consequence of this is that the female voice is marginalized. In an autobiography, Sue MacGregor recounts her experiences as a broadcaster in a masculinist Community of Practice in BBC Radio (MacGregor 2002). When she joined the team of

BBC Radio 4's flagship news programme *Today* in 1984, the prestigious slots went to her male colleagues, John Humphrys and the late Brian Redhead, while she was given 'soft news' stories to cover. When a female editor took over two years later (Jenny Abramsky in 1986), a change might have been expected. However, she continued to be consigned to a subordinate position, with the lion's share of the big set-piece interviews going to the men in the newsroom. This junior position was apparently reflected in her salary, which was substantially less than the men's, despite a declaration of a 'basic policy that there is an equivalence between them all' (Donovan 1997; cited in Walsh 2006: 123). Cast as the female side-kick in the broadcasting team, she recollects that while her colleagues were initially kind and helpful, as she gained in confidence they appeared set on undermining it, with 'some devastating put-downs. Any stumble on my part would be noticed and marked with a grin. Once [Redhead] thrust a piece of paper with the word "FOOL!" written on it in front of me as I finished a live interview' (MacGregor 2002: 229).

Like Paxman, Humphrys's interviewing style is frequently aggressive and inquisitorial with a 'tendency to engineer on-air verbal punch-ups' (Walsh 2006: 129). Walsh points to continuity with the aggressive, hectoring style of debate in the House of Commons (2006: 124) but questions the effectiveness of his 'yah-boo style of interviewing' in helping the public to make informed distinctions between political parties and their policies. In contrast, MacGregor, as a feminist broadcaster, took up what Walsh has called a 'critical difference' stance in the *Today* newsroom (2006: 130). She rejected masculinist assumptions about how political interviews should be conducted. Walsh notes that MacGregor's interviewing style is more readily defined by what it refrains from than what it includes – no persistent interruptions, no entrapment questions, no belligerent hectoring (2006: 131). She frequently engaged in small talk with guests before the interview to put them at ease, which presents an interesting contrast with Paxman on *Newsnight*. According to Michael Howard (one of the interviewees featured above), Paxman deliberately makes *Newsnight* guests feel uneasy, by ignoring them or looking bored before they go on-air (Talbot 2007b: 122).

In diverging from the interviewing practices of her male colleagues, MacGregor performed effective political interviewing that engaged the audience, rather than being, in extreme cases, a literal turn-off. She achieved this by probing rather than sparring, by focusing on issues rather than engaging in personal disputes. Walsh demonstrates that MacGregor is quite capable of holding politicians to account without resorting to such aggressive confrontation. An Australian feminist linguist has come to a similar conclusion about a woman interviewing a politician on television (Winter 1993). Walsh, indeed, concludes that Humphrys's interviewing style is not so much necessary for democracy as self-indulgent. However, it is MacGregor who is 'criticised for being too-too aggressive and interrupting too much' (MacGregor in interview with Walsh (2006: 134)).

Women in charge: dealing with the double-bind

Practices of masculinist communities have become naturalized as simply professional practices, as already noted. In common with women in broadcasting, women in leadership positions also find themselves in a double-bind. On the one hand there is an expectation that they will behave in ways that are considered to be acceptably feminine, while on the other hand they need to behave professionally, which requires behaviour that is perceived as masculine. A team of New Zealand sociolinguists have conducted a large empirical study of workplace discourse, a key outcome of which was insight into varied responses to the challenge that this double-bind poses for women in positions of leadership. The Wellington Language in the Workplace Project produced a nuanced, contextualized exploration of gendered styles across a wide range of workplaces. It sought to 'erode traditional associations between femininity and ineffectiveness on the one hand, and masculinity and seniority on the other' (Holmes 2006: 26–7).

The project includes a case study of a senior manager in a multinational commercial organization. This case study focuses on a woman in charge of fifty staff who has adopted a 'queenly' persona (2006: 55) which enabled her staff to defer to her authority *despite* her femaleness. Holmes describes this as a 'slightly ironic and distant, but very functional' persona that 'resolved the problems of authority, but also allowed her to express her femininity when appropriate' (2006). From the data offered, this identity seems to have been assigned to her by her staff, rather than one she has cultivated herself. She was openly nicknamed 'Queen Clara' by her staff and happy to share in jokes around this persona, as in the extract below, taken from a small team meeting. The meeting involves six men and seven women and Smithy is about to chair it. He opens by asking her about the British queen mother, who had recently been in the news because of a hip operation:

1 Smithy: how's your mum?
2 Clara: sorry?
3 Smithy: she broke her hip didn't she?
4 Clara: my mother?

5	All:	((laughter))
6	Clara:	what are you talking about?
7	XF:	((laughs)) the queen mother
8	Dai:	((laughs)) the queen mother
9	Clara:	oh
10	All:	((laugh))
11	Clara:	my husband and I ((using a hyperlectal accent and superior tone))
12	All:	((laugh))
13	Clara:	are confident that she'll pull through
14	All:	((laugh))

(Holmes 2006: 56)

It is clear from lines 2, 4 and 6 that Clara is puzzled to start with. Once she understands that Smithy is initiating a joke, however, she is happy to play along and parodies the queen's upper-class voice in lines 11 and 13. Small-talk like this is typical at the boundaries of meetings and she is quite capable of participating. However, she is also highly authoritative. In the next extract, taken from another meeting, she issues blunt directives, which are not only unmitigated but aggravated by repetition:

1	Harry:	looks like there's been actually a request for screendumps
2		I know it was outside of the scope
3		but people (will be) pretty worried about it
4		maybe if you-=
5	Rob:	=we can quickly show you that
6	Clara:	no screendumps
7	Matt:	we-
8	Clara:	no screendumps
9	Rob:	(x)
10	Peg:	((sarcastically)) thank you Clara
11	Clara:	no screendumps
		[ ]
12	Matt:	we know we know
13		you didn't want them and um er we've
		[ ]
14	Clara:	((using a 'robotic' voice)) that does not meet the criteria

((several reasons provided why screendumps should be allowed))

15	Clara:	thanks for looking at that though
16	Sandy:	so that's a clear well maybe no
17	Clara:	it's a no
18	Sandy:	it's a no a royal no
19	Clara:	did people feel disempowered by that decision
20	Peg:	((sarcastically)) no
21	Clara:	((laughs))

(Adapted from Holmes 2005: 50–1)

In line 6 Clara vetoes 'screendumps' – that is, printing off material from the screen. She then interrupts Matt to repeat the veto in line 8 and repeats yet again in line 11, following Peg's sarcastic thanks. In line 14 she follows up with explicit reference to some criteria that have already been agreed. 'Disregarding conventionally polite (and stereotypically "feminine") ways of disagreeing with one's colleagues', Holmes observes, 'Clara is here "doing power" very explicitly, using a stereotypically "masculine" strategy of simply stating what is to happen' (2005: 51).

Holmes notes Clara's apparent awareness of the abrasive effect of her uncompromising manner. This is suggested by her positively polite follow-up in line 15 ('thanks for looking at that though') but most explicit in her tongue-in-cheek remark in line 19: 'did people feel disempowered by that decision' (2005: 52). There is something else that supports this view that I'd also like to pick out. This is to do with her 'robotic' delivery of 'that does not meet the criteria' in line 14. In presenting her justification in such a distinctive and quirky fashion at this point, Clara appears to be self-ironizing. She has just delivered a terse veto, three times in identical form. She is justifying her veto by rigid adherence to operational criteria, mechanistically abiding by the rules. This odd 'robotic' delivery seems to be reducing the face threat, through self-mocking humour, of her uncompromising position as their boss.

Other team members use humour too, frequently milking the ongoing 'Queen Clara' joke. In the extract, Sandy, her deputy manager, appears to be deploying it to sound out Clara's position. She responds to Clara's positively polite thanks with a suggestion that she may be wavering in her resolve, with the internally contradictory 'so that's a clear well maybe no' (line 16). She then echoes Clara's further unequivocal negative ('it's a no') with reference to her 'queenly' status: 'it's a no a royal no' (line 18).

In organizations in New Zealand being hard-nosed and adversarial is normal behaviour (Holmes 2006: 10). Yet women's compensatory use of humour and self-deprecation was very frequent in the Wellington workplace discourse that was examined in the project (for other examples, see Holmes and Schnurr 2005; Holmes and Stubbe 2003b; Marra, Schnurr and Holmes 2006). It seems that being hard-nosed, while necessary, poses problems for women:

> while it is officially acceptable for women to 'do power' explicitly in the workplace, there is an underlying pressure to counter or neutralize the effects of the authoritative and 'masculine' strategies entailed in doing so with more 'feminine', supportive and collegial or self-deprecating behaviours. (Holmes 2005: 52)

Elsewhere in the Wellington project data, a 'maternal' persona is discussed (Holmes and Stubbe 2003a, 2003b). A 'motherly' way of exercising authority has been suggested in studies elsewhere, including the United States (e.g. Kendall 2003), Spain (Martín Rojo and Esteban 2005) and the United Kingdom (Mullany 2007). It has been characterized by the use of face-saving strategies, particularly indirect forms for directives and a high degree of mitigation. Shari Kendall conducted a contrastive study of one manager's directive use at home and at work. Her ironic result was that, by these measures, the manager was more 'maternal' with her subordinates than she was with her daughter at home! But these 'queenly' and 'maternal' personas are not, in any case, actual subject positions occupied by the women leaders to whom they are attributed (the subject position of queen is bestowed on very few indeed). Rather they are familiar female stereotypes being deployed in the workplace, to cope with the anomaly of the woman boss. Stereotyping involves simplification, reduction and naturalization. It is generally negative, it works to maintain the status quo and it plays an important part in hegemonic struggle (Hall 1997; Talbot 2003). Returning for a moment to Clara, the 'queenly' persona attributed to her is highly reductive. The data indicated a good deal of self-deprecatory behaviour, which you would hardly associate with monarchy; and her robot imitation wasn't exactly regal either! Another female workplace persona, most definitely stereotypical, is the 'battleaxe'. As I noted earlier, Gwyneth Dunwoody – a British politician who fought her corner in the unreconstructed masculinist community of Westminster for over forty years – claimed to embrace this term.

The thing is, women are relative newcomers in many professional contexts, particularly in positions of authority. Interview and discussion-group data in a Spanish study indicate that they continue to be regarded with suspicion and are considered to be ineffective leaders. Spanish women in authority are criticized for giving orders using indirect forms, for example. In using them, they are perceived as lacking self-confidence or as manipulative, yet men's use of indirect forms in a similar fashion is not evaluated negatively (Martín Rojo and Esteban 2005: 69). The study reveals some rather depressing attitudes towards women in authority, suggesting that old prejudices and negative associations prevail: 'Spanish women in positions of responsibility often find themselves obliged to perform juggling acts to minimize and conceal their authority at the same time as exercising it' (2005: 74). Like Hillary Clinton perhaps, women bosses have to cope with a continuous balancing act using displays of toughness and likeability. In downplaying institutional authority, as many women in charge do (e.g. Kendall 2003: 621; Martín Rojo and Esteban 2005: 68), they run the risk of being seen to lack it.

In attending to how women in positions of authority are evaluated, I have shifted from women's talk in the workplace to talk about women in the workplace; in other words, how they are represented. Representations of working women in the media are the subject of the next section.

Media representations of working women

Here are some disparate observations about the media and women in work. In the run-up to the 2008 elections in the United States, the National Organization for Women (NOW) set up a Media Hall of Shame. At their annual conference, the worst offenders were presented with mock awards. Among the absent 'winners' was Rush Limbaugh (MSNBC) for the doubts he expressed about Clinton's suitability for the presidency: 'Will Americans want to watch a woman get older before their eyes on a daily basis?' A 'Lifetime Achievement' award went in absentia to Chris Matthews (also MSNBC) for his 'dedication to sexist commentary' (Bennett 2008); among his 'achievements' was calling Clinton a 'she-devil'. In Europe in the same year, Carme Chacón took up office as the first female defence minister in Spain. The media marvelled at the collision of archetypes – mother and soldier – in the image of a woman, seven-months pregnant, reviewing the troops (Day 2008). Early the following year, British press coverage of a report on the Good Childhood Inquiry ran with headlines like this: 'Kids "damaged" by work mums' (*Sun*, 2 February 2009).

NOW's mock awards ceremony humorously highlights prejudices encountered by women who dare to enter the media spotlight. The impact of the Chacón photograph highlights traditional gendered expectations of a public event. And the press coverage of the Good Childhood report is a woeful example of how eager journalists can be to blame mothers for society's ills. The Good Childhood Inquiry was commissioned by the Children's Society, a charitable organization affiliated with the Church of England. Published as *A Good Childhood: Searching for Values in a Competitive Age*, its scope is enormous, with chapters on family, friends, lifestyle, values, schooling, mental health and inequalities (Layard and Dunn 2009). It touches on a huge range of issues about growing up in the modern world, from the need for high-quality youth centres to the potential effects of junk-food advertising, to peer pressure to have the latest mobile phone. Its key suggestions are wide-ranging, including measures designed to support working mothers, such as greater availability of high-quality, affordable childcare and extended parental leave after the birth of a child. Yet the newspapers focused exclusively on family break-up, for which women are held responsible:

> Kids 'damaged' by work mums (*Sun*, 2 February 2009)
>
> Working women 'fuel family splits' (*Daily Telegraph*, 2 February 2009)
>
> Mum's cash 'leading to split home' (*Mirror*, 2 February 2009)
>
> Children 'suffering for lack of two-parent family' (*Daily Mail*, 2 February 2009)

The complex of social issues explored in the report is ignored. Instead we are offered a simple scapegoat: the working mother.

In 2003, an article entitled 'The opt-out revolution' generated a media storm (Belkin 2003). Appearing in a *New York Times* Sunday magazine, the claims that it made were faithfully copied in subsequent coverage – articles with titles such as: 'Power: do women really want it?' (Sellers 2003, cited in Vavrus 2007: 51). Stories about women opting out of the workforce and returning to a full-time domestic role are a staple of media coverage. They have been a hardy perennial since the end of World War II, if not before. The coverage initiated by the *New York Times Magazine* article was investigated by Mary Douglas Vavrus. The phenomenon has since been reified with the neologism of 'off-ramping'. Vavrus, a feminist who specializes in political economy of the media, focuses particularly on two recurring elements. These are a rhetoric of choice – the articles are peppered with the terms 'opt' and 'choice' and their variants – and lack of attention to social factors impacting on women. All the articles conclude by blaming individual employers for not implementing family-friendly policies, but they engage in 'privatising rhetoric about social activities (like mothering)' (2007: 48) rather than following the argument through with critical discussion of such issues as lack of childcare provision, state support and so on. The 'opting-out moms' themselves are represented as self-satisfied, concerned only for themselves and their own families. Their lifestyles are represented as freely chosen, without any discussion whatsoever of the actual circumstances that have generated them. Vavrus identifies a caricature of feminism in this framing, since it implies 'because what they're doing is based on their choosing something – anything – that they are therefore upholding a feminist principle' (2007: 52). Missing from the media accounts of women leaving paid employment to bring up children is any mention of relations of power and social inequality. Vavrus quotes from Ann Crittenden's *The Price of Motherhood* to underline the major problem with the rhetoric of choice. In neoliberal fashion, it omits power:

> Those who benefit from the status quo always attribute inequalities to the choices of the underdog. To most women choice is all about bad options and difficult decisions: your child or your profession; taking on the domestic chores or marital strife; a good night's sleep or time with your child; food on the table or your baby's safety; your right arm or your left. No wonder many mothers talk about 'surrendering' to motherhood, as if it were a gigantic defeat that it is better to accept than to fight. (Crittenden 2001, cited in Vavrus 2007: 54)

Women are not faced with genuine free choice, then, in contemplating motherhood.

The 'off-ramping' coverage is less crude than dire warnings about reduced fertility or threats about ticking biological clocks, but nevertheless it is ultimately a hostile misrepresentation of the female workforce. The net effect of the 'off-ramping' stories is to legitimize patriarchal beliefs about women and work. Despite their condemnation of corporate workplace practices, they legitimize 'dangerously archaic notions about women, work, and family used to justify sex discrimination and reproduce an unjust system of family labor and care. Ultimately they rationalize patriarchal power' (2007: 49).

Further reading

Politics

Within language and gender studies, there is little on individual women as public figures in the political sphere. Robin Lakoff has discussed Hillary Clinton both as first lady (Lakoff 2000) and as senator (Lakoff 2003). In the British context, media representations of Cherie Blair are the subject of Page (2003). In examining the experiences of women at Westminster, Walsh (2001) discusses the media's marginalization of Margaret Beckett as leadership candidate (briefly covered in Talbot 2007b). The communicative style of Annette Lu, Taiwanese vice-president, is explored in Kuo (2008).

Media

General overviews of media discourse and gender are chapter 5 of Litosseliti (2006) and chapter 11 of DeFrancisco and Palczewski (2007). Byerly and Ross (2006) examines women's activism within the media. The central theme of Gill (2007) is the impact of feminism on the media, with some reflection on the notion of a 'postfeminist media culture'. For details of how US news media scare working women, read Rivers (2007).

On media discourse more broadly, a range of theoretical and discourse-analytical approaches is offered by the following recent book-length studies: Hutchby (2006), Lorenzo-Dus (2009), Matheson (2005), Talbot (2007b), Tolson (2006).

Workplace

Here are some studies of women in leadership positions that I have not already mentioned in this chapter: Kendall and Tannen (1997); Martin (2003). Kendall (2006b) looks at women's self-representation as mothers in small-talk at work. See also ch. 6 of Litosseliti (2006) and chapter 9 of DeFrancisco and Palczewski (2007).

Religion

Bean (2006) examines the salience of religious discourse in US first-wave feminism, while Jule (2006) considers silent female students at a contemporary US theological college. Chapter 6 of Walsh (2001) looks at the marginalization of women clerics in the Church of England. See also chapter 10 of DeFrancisco and Palczewski (2007).

Education

Swann (2003) is an overview of language and gender issues in educational settings. See also chapter 4 of Litosseliti (2006) and chapter 8 of DeFrancisco and Palczewski (2007).

11

Language, gender and sexuality

This chapter focuses on recent work influenced by theoretical developments in language and sexuality, research underpinned by the idea that identity is performed. It centres on heteronormativity, with particular attention to displays of heterosexuality in all-male groups, to definitions of sexual consent and rape, and to marginalized non-normative identities.

Queering gender

In chapter 7, I suggested that we view a person's identity as a constellation of subject positions bestowed by discourses. To counter any impression of passivity I presented the notion of a gendered identity as 'a performative accomplishment' (Butler 1999: 179). Then, in discussion of consumerism in chapter 8, I considered some of the feminizing practices that women and girls engage in as they actively work on their feminine identities. In a consumerist society, the consumption of commodities from fashion and cosmetics industries is an important component in the accomplishment of gender. However, there is far more to gender performances than clothes and make-up. They also involve how people comport themselves, including posture and gesture. Consider the following extract from a Marge Piercy novel (*Small Changes*, 1987 [1972]), in which a theatre group is being taught about posture and movement:

> She demonstrated how men sat and how women sat on the subway, on benches. Men expanded into available space. They sprawled, or they sat with spread legs. They put their arms on the arms of chairs. They crossed their legs by putting a foot on the other knee. They dominated space expansively.
>   Women condensed. Women crossed their legs by putting one leg over the other and alongside. Women kept their elbows to their sides, taking up as little space as possible. They behaved as if it were their duty not to rub against, not to touch, not to bump a man. If contact occurred, the woman shrank back. If a woman bumped a man, he might choose to

"It's a Lesbian."

interpret it as a come-on. Women sat protectively, using elbows not to dominate space, not to mark territory, but to protect their soft tissues. (Piercy 1987: 350)

In public spaces, we are performing gender even in the way we occupy a seat in the subway or a park bench. And, of course, part of the gender performance is an enactment of power relations.

From the perspective of performativity, gender is a ritual act and everyday gender performances are policed: 'Gender is the repeated stylization of the body, a set of repeated acts within a highly rigid regulatory frame that congeal over time to produce the appearance of substance, of a natural sort of being' (Butler 1999: 43–4). The regulatory frame is the 'cultural matrix through which gender identity has become intelligible' (1999: 23). For Butler, the naturalized categories of masculine and feminine are 'truth effects' of a hegemonic discourse on gender, which sets them up in asymmetrical opposition (1999: 174). This exposes the falsity of the perception that some forms of gender expression are more authentic than others.

Butler argues that when a newborn infant enters the world it is forced into a sex/gender category in the gender binary. The proclamation of 'It's a girl!' is not constative (a statement of fact) but a performative utterance that sets off the whole process of 'girling' (Butler 1993: 232). In her denaturalization of hegemonic conceptions of gender, Butler uses the example of drag queen performances. She argues that drag exposes the artifice behind femininity. Drag demonstrates that what generally appears natural and spontaneous is in fact constructed and endlessly reconstructed: a repeat performance. 'In imitating gender', she says, 'drag implicitly reveals the imitative structure of gender itself – as well as its contingency' (1993: 175). The gender binary of masculine/feminine is the scaffolding that props up heterosexuality (Sinfield 1994: 169, cited in Richardson 2009). Exposing it poses a threat to heteronormativity.

Drag's exposure of the artifice of femininity is nicely demonstrated in a study of African-American drag queens. In it, Rusty Barrett, a US linguist, makes use of the hegemonic construct of 'ladylike' behaviour identified by Lakoff (and discussed in chapter 3). In this extract, the performer shatters his illusion of middle-class feminine respectability with taboo language that is entirely unladylike:

> Are you ready to see some muscles? [audience yells]. . . . Some dick?
> Excuse me I'm not supposed to say that . . .
> Words like that in the microphone . . .
> Like shit, fuck, and all that, you know?
> I am a Christian woman.
> I go to church.
> I'm *always* on my knees.
> (Barrett 1999: 324)

The humorous double entendre in the last line ostensibly indicates religious devotion, but spoken by a drag queen in a gay bar it carries a clear meaning of performing fellatio, which, like the swearing, is also distinctly 'unladylike'. As Barrett says, by 'creating two contrasting voices within a single discourse, the performer plays off of the disjuncture between performed ("female") and biographical ("male") identity' (1999).

Drag queens, then, can be said to 'queer' the apparent naturalness of femininity. For Butler, as Bucholtz and Hall put it, 'drag queens are foot soldiers at the vanguard of the gender revolution, combating the perception that gender is biologically constituted' (2004: 501). However, as they go on to point out: 'drag is practice as well as theory, and . . . drag queens may be at least as interested in constructing their own identities as in challenging the identities of others' (2004). The drag performance may have the effect of denaturalizing gender but the performer is articulating gay desire.

Heteronorms

A study at an elementary school in northern California has examined the entry of pre-adolescents into the 'heterosexual marketplace' (Eckert 2006). This is a transition that affects both boys and girls, but in different ways, since within the heterosexual social order the resources available to them differ. Boys can continue to cultivate essentially the same accomplishments as in childhood whereas girls, if they are to invest in heterosexuality, must abandon the preoccupations of earlier years. From being vigorously active in the playground, for example, girls tend to become observers of the boys' games. Their new preoccupations relate to feminizing practices, including the stylization of the body and a flamboyant linguistic style:

> The transition into a heterosexual social order brings boys and girls into mutual and conscious engagement in gender differentiation, in the course of which girls move into the elaboration of flamboyantly stylized selves. The development of flamboyant linguistic style is a key part of this elaboration, and inseparable from the emerging use of other aspects of gendered style such as nail polish, lip gloss, hair style and new walks. (Eckert 2006: 195)

Not everyone invests wholeheartedly in the heterosexual market, however. And gender is policed – punished if it's not done right. Like many things, it is often only learned through painful experience. Gender norms perform a 'mundane violence' (Butler 1999: xx). An anecdote in Barrett (2004) provides a relatively harmless example. On seeing a Shirley Temple movie for the first time as a small boy, Barrett recounts being greatly impressed by how seriously she was treated by adults. The surest way to win their respect, he determined, was to 'act as much like Shirley Temple as possible' (2004: 296). Sadly, however, his Shirley-Temple-inspired utterance of 'Oh, Father, they're *lovely!*' in the middle of a crowded supermarket did not achieve the desired result at all! On the contrary, it evoked sheer horror. Yet earlier the same summer he had, to his mortification, elicited laughter from adults when he naively uttered the taboo word **motherfucker**. He was confused and distressed by his father's vehement recoil from his Shirley Temple impersonation:

> I felt as though I had been tricked by some horrible grown-up conspiracy. How could my utterance of *fucker* (which was obviously something adults didn't want me to fully understand) produce laughter, but a seemingly harmless word like *lovely* create such fear and rage. (2004: 297)

He definitely wasn't performing gender right. (For another account of 'not getting it right', see Morrish and Sauntson (2007).)

The policing of gender norms continues in adulthood, although this may be noticed only by people transgressing them, such as crossdressers and transsexuals. Halberstam's discussion of the 'bathroom problem' (1998: 20) provides an illuminating account of the routine questions and challenges besetting people who cross gender boundaries in public facilities.

The conversational backdrop: a clamorous heterosexuality

Celia Kitzinger, a British feminist working with conversation analysis, argues for its usefulness for studying the taken-for-granted in daily interactions. For evidence, she has trawled through CA data collected over two decades. She found the most telling and interesting data when heterosexuality was the taken-for-granted backdrop (Kitzinger 2006: 173). Family categories such as 'husband' and 'wife', 'in-laws', etc., were routinely used for the daily business of 'doing being ordinary' – that is to say, presenting oneself as an ordinary, normal and acceptable person. These categories perform interactional work. For example, a man phoning in to a suicide prevention helpline states that 'I just lost my wife and I feel awfully depressed.' No account or explanation of the link between these two statements is necessary, since he 'evokes the culturally-understood inferences of an intimate and caring relationship, such that the loss of such a category member renders understandable the caller's depression' (2006: 175). In another sample, a woman expressing grave concern about her husband has no interactional need to provide any justification for her call. In contrast, a caller phoning on behalf of 'just a friend' finds herself explaining why she is the one making the call rather than a family member. The point Kitzinger is making here is that these family categories are not readily available as a resource for same-sex couples: 'Lesbians and gay men do not have easy access to a person reference term like "husband" or "wife" that renders no longer appropriate the need for an account (Sacks 1995: 23–4) as to why they are the person calling' (2006: 176). Such occurrences, 'banal and commonplace' as they are, amount to 'a clamorous heterosexuality' (2006: 187) for lesbians and gay men.

Similarly, the kinship system in which a marital heterosexual relationship is embedded supplies categories such as **daughter-in-law**, none of which are available as resources for same-sex couples. Kitzinger notes the invention of terms that draw attention to the exclusion of same-sex couples from this system, such as her own parents' invented category **daughter-**

out-of-law as a 'non-recognitional referent' for her partner (2006: 179). Consider also a lesbian writer's wistful reference to her lover's brother as **brother-if-there-were-a-law** (MacLean 1995, cited in Kitzinger 2006).

I continue to attend to heteronormativity in the two sections that follow and turn next to the impact of heterosexual ideology in all-male groups.

Homosociality among male university students

In chapter 9, I outlined the importance of heterosexuality for hegemonic masculinity, illustrating the issue with examples from a US study of young men's cooperative talk about absent classmates and a Catalan study of verbal duelling. Central to both were men's implicit assertions of their own heterosexuality. Here is another example, this time some Chinese students studying in Britain who were chatting over dinner. The sample of talk was part of a set of data recorded by the participants for a fellow student, Pei Tian, who transcribed it and translated it from Mandarin. In lines 1 to 6, two of the three men are unambiguously displaying a heterosexual orientation. They are doing this by shared recollection of a woman they had both been eyeing up on the town bridge. The third is unwilling to participate and expresses disapproval (lines 7 and 8), which creates a problem for him:

```
1   A:  Remember one day we saw a cute girl on the bridge?
2       (..) Bloody hell she was hot
3   B:  What girl Oh I remember (.) the girl with giant tits (.)
4       those tits were like blown-up balloons (1.0)
5       What I miss most was her ass
6       it was almost showing when we walked past her    ·
        [
7   C:  Stop the dirty talk you perverts (.) don't you guys
8       have better things to do than talk about girls
9   A:  We are perverts? (..) no (.) no pretty face (.)
10      we are very normal with our sex and sex preference
11      (.) but now I have to question whether or not
12      your sex preference is different from ours
13      (.) I'm wondering what would th(h)at be
14  B:  heheheh he's only interested in men heh
15      enjoys being slapped like a bitch
```

(Adapted from Pei 2006: 22)

C does not join in their 'dirty talk', as he calls their ogling reminiscences, and brands them 'perverts' for engaging in it. This insult prompts a rebuttal from A. The address term 'pretty face' in line 9 hints at effeminacy and he follows it up by explicitly querying C's sexual orientation. C's unwillingness to participate in homosocial small-talk – when it involves objectifying a woman and her body parts – is sufficient to mark him as gay. If he won't participate in the sexualizing talk about women then he's not attracted to them, hence, as B makes explicit in line 14, he is 'only interested in men' (not only that but, it is suggested in line 15, he enjoys being abused – a violent suggestion which seems to have more than a hint of menace). C 'redeems' himself, however, by reviling someone else who is perceived as gay:

16 C: You two go to hell (.) I'm not Chris
17 A: What's Chris
18 B: He's that fucking gay boy=
19 A: =gay?
20 C: Yeah (..)
21   He's the guy who always wears skin-tight pants
22   talks in a soft voice (.) he even does the nail polish
23   (.) I can't fucking understand why there are such people
24   in the world (.) If I was wearing that stupid shit
25   I'd rather not step out of my room
26 B: Yeah I agree (.) I want to fucking puke when I see him
27   I can't stand those people
28 A: Fuck (.) can't believe we have this kind of person in our school

(Adapted from Pei 2006: 22)

C embarks on some verbal 'queer bashing', pointing to what he considers to be more significant signs of gayness: skin-tight pants, a soft voice and nail varnish. His dinner companions take up the topic enthusiastically, so that he successfully realigns himself with them.

In discussing hegemonic masculinity in chapter 9, I also looked at the hierarchical structure of a US college fraternity, focusing on dominance and control in male students' contributions to an election meeting. Here I return to the fraternity study, but this time I'm looking specifically at the maintenance of heterosexuality in all-male groups. As a Community of Practice, the fraternity is organized around sexual difference and heterosexuality (Kiesling 2006: 118). This is most strikingly evident in the stark segregation into male and female communities (that is, in fraternities and sororities). Practices include a range of activities, regular rituals and verbal strategies of dominance that are heavily dependent on a heterosexual ideology. When female and male students do socialize together, they are seen as engaging in distinct social events known as 'mixers'. Fraternity members follow up these parties with regular 'gavel' meetings, where participants recount their activities. The high point of gavel is the performance of distinct genres known as 'fuck stories' and 'drunk stories'. Kiesling notes that he was not permitted to record gavel, indicating 'how important this story round is for the social cohesion of the group – it is a form of ritual gossip which may never leave the group. The stories are a powerful way of creating a cultural model and placing value on it' (2006: 122). The narrative performances in gavel valorize a particular kind of predatory heterosexuality. Narrators garner status in performing them, since in doing so they not only get to boast about their own sexual prowess but also provide their peers with a highly valued form of entertainment. From these events, it is interesting to see the extent to which heterosexuality can be homosocial.

The fraternity brothers are adept at using verbal strategies of dominance amongst themselves that draw on heterosexual social relations of a traditional and asymmetrical kind. In other words, they put other men down by casting them as women. The use of 'feminine' address terms in the homosocial group takes various forms. The address forms **bitch** and **bitch boy** are common; the latter subordinates not only by gender but by age and race as well. Pledges may be metaphorically positioned as subordinate by being named as women. For example, one pledge – given weeks of cleaning chores to do for several older students – was named Hazel, after a fictional domestic cleaner. On another occasion, a brother positions one of his peers as subordinate and female by declaring 'Honey I'm home!' at an appropriate point in a game of Monopoly. In both cases, popular-culture references are being evoked, drawing on shared familiarity with stereotypical representations of the family from fifties American sitcoms.

The sexual politics of consent

In this section I attend to a crucial aspect of heteronormativity: defining sexual consent and rape. Kitzinger and Frith (1999) point to the clumsiness of refusal training programmes ('Just say no') that are based on ignorance of how people actually perform refusals. In English, people vary rarely do just say no, since in most situations it would be extremely rude! Close analysis of spoken interaction involving refusal demonstrates this. Refusals tend to be indirect and they are frequently produced with hedges, hesitations and other mitigating elements (*well er that would be kind of nice but. . .*). With this in mind, the advice to 'just say no' is absurd:

> the insistence of date rape educators on the importance of just saying no is counter-productive in that it requires women to engage in conversationally abnormal actions and allows rapists to persist in their claim that, if a woman hasn't actually said no (in the right tone of voice with the right body language), then she hasn't actually refused to have sex with him. (Kitzinger 2000: 181)

Not only is such advice oblivious to the minutiae of spoken interaction, it does nothing to counter powerful heteronormative assumptions about sexual encounters.

Heteronormative sexual identities and relations are enshrined in the romantic fiction of Harlequin Mills & Boon. Men take the initiative. The romance hero is active and impulsive. Women are the passive recipients of male desire, outwardly resistant but inwardly yearning. The romantic heroine's desire emerges as a response to the hero's charismatic presence, and it must be repressed (Talbot 1995a, 1997a). With protagonists like these, it is inevitable that no eventually means yes.

However, heteronormative assumptions about male and female sexuality circulate in the real world as well, including in the justice system and in media coverage. In the dominant discourse on rape, 'real rape' is perpetrated by a stranger in public space. Rape committed by a known person, though most frequent, is rarely brought to trial. Stranger rape, though least frequently occurring, is most frequently prosecuted. Victims of stranger rape are most likely to be perceived as 'legitimate' victims, though, even when brought to trial, attackers are not necessary held responsible for their own actions. The rape trial can be viewed as a mechanism of disciplinary power, in Foucault's sense (Lees 1997, cited in Ehrlich 2002: 6). It prompts women to engage in self-regulation and self-surveillance. A woman subjected to rape by a known person may think twice about reporting it. Fear of assault instils a fear of public space and forces women's self-surveillance of their own mobility and conduct in it.

A Canadian tribunal case

A study of proceedings in a Canadian university tribunal provides a painful illustration of the difficulties that are likely to beset complainants of acquaintance rape (Ehrlich 2006). The disciplinary tribunal followed two complaints of sexual harassment taking place in student accommodation. Two female students brought charges against a male student. On each occasion, mixed groups of students were stopping over in a female student's rooms. The defendant's version of events – essentially, *his* definition of consent – dominated the proceedings. In his version of what happened, both instances were consensual sexual encounters, not the unwanted sexual aggression that the two female students claimed. Since he 'defines "consent" as the absence of vehement expressions of resistance in the wake of every sexual advance, he contends that his escalating sexual aggression is justified' (2006: 201–2). The complainants were questioned about how they 'signalled' their lack of consent. In the following extract, a member of the tribunal (a female faculty member) interprets the student Marg's account as evidence of poor communication of her wishes (lines 4–14):

MB: complainant
GK: tribunal member

```
 1  MB:  I kept saying 'let's just go to sleep'. I didn't honestly know what
 2        else in my mind to do at that time. For me that was all I could
 3        do to tell him I didn't want to do anything.
 4  GK:  And did it occur to you through the persistent behaviour that
 5        maybe your signals were not coming across loud and clear, that
 6        'I'm not getting through what I want and what I don't want?'
 7        Does it occur to you 'I need to stand up and say something'.
 8        'I need to move him to the floor?' This is the whole thing about
 9        getting signals mixed up. We all socialize in one way or the
10        other to read signals and to give signals. In that particular
11        context, were you at all concerned your signals were not being
12        read exactly and did you think since signals were not being read
13        correctly for you, 'should I do something different with my
14        signals?'
```

The tribunal member seems to have already decided that miscommunication is at the heart of the case; she evokes gender socialization to account for it (lines 9–10) and strongly implies that Marg's communication was deficient. In line 12, she presupposes that Marg's 'signals' were 'not being read correctly' (rather than that the defendant might have been disregarding them). Marg explains that she did try to 'do something different':

```
15  MB:  I did. He made me feel like I wasn't saying anything, that I
16        wasn't saying 'no' and that's why I asked to talk to Bob, thinking
```

17	if I couldn't tell him maybe Bob could tell him. Bob came in the

17   if I couldn't tell him maybe Bob could tell him. Bob came in the
18   room and said everything was okay just to forget about it and go
19   back to sleep. I tried that. I told Matt, I said if the circumstances
20   would have been different, maybe. It was a lie but I mean it was
21   another way for me to try to tell him 'no'. I mean obviously I
22   just wanted to go to sleep. It wasn't getting through so I tried
23   different approaches. And in my mind I hoped that they were
24   getting through. I mean. I was making it as clear as I could. I'm
25   not sure if that answers your question or not but. . .

(Ehrlich 2006: 205)

Her questioner seems unimpressed and again invokes gender socialization to account for differing interpretations of Marg's 'signals' (lines 31–2):

26   GK: No. it's because right from there to the end you, you had felt
27   that you hadn't made it clear because at the end you said you
28   were willing to lie and give him this phone number and get rid
29   of him. So all along the way you felt your signals were not read
30   correctly. But the whole thing is, you know, that concerns all of
31   us is that the signals of, you know, between men and women are
32   just, are not being read correctly and I'm not debating who's
33   lying and who's telling the truth because it's not mine to say
34   that. The substance is why, that signals, do you feel at that time
35   your signals were not being read correctly?

In lines 32–3 she states that she is not in a position to judge whether one party was lying, despite the nature of the case, which inevitably pitches one person's word against another (nevertheless, she has just doubted the veracity of the complainant's claim about her 'signals' in lines 29–30, saying that she knew 'all along' that they were not being 'read correctly'). As Ehrlich remarks, the tribunal member 'seems to subscribe to a "different-but-equal" model of miscommunication' at this point, according to which 'it is not a question of one person lying and the other telling the truth; rather, "signals" are interpreted differently by these individuals' (Ehrlich 2006: 206). She has determined on a neutral 'difference' explanation, which suppresses potential power issues and lets the defendant off the hook. But, in any case, Matt was not equally accountable for failure to interpret the women's intentions; in fact, he was fed the line that 'there's a communication thing' during the proceedings (2006: 207). Elsewhere the tribunal member seems to be operating with a 'deficiency' model, however (lines 4–14 and 26–30), which holds the complainant to blame for communicating her lack of consent ineffectively.

The complainants' versions of events did emerge in this case, but only with the greatest difficulty. Both responded to the questioning about their 'deficient' communication with accounts of their night-time ordeal: being paralysed by fear, humiliated. Marg reported that she was 'extremely afraid of being hurt' and 'didn't want to get into a big fight' (2006: 206). These justifications for passivity tended to be disregarded (2006: 212–13). Ehrlich found, then, that the victims of sexual aggression are liable to be blamed for ineffective communication in 'failing to signal their lack of consent clearly and unambiguously' (2006: 209). In this particular case, the defendant was eventually found guilty; however, the university's recommendation to expel him was not followed by the tribunal members, who decided merely to bar him from campus dormitories (2006: 210).

Contestation and struggle in indigenous African communities

In the context of shifting power relations between women and men in indigenous African communities, a highly charged issue is the concept of marital rape. This has been explored by a South African linguist, the late Puleng Hanong, who conducted a research project on gender issues in indigenous South African communities. She focuses particularly on discourses of sexuality and her study gives insight into the extreme difficulty faced by indigenous South African women in the face of men's reluctance to relinquish privileges bestowed by tradition. The data were collected from speakers of indigenous languages by means of focus-groups and interview sessions at three universities. What I present here is a sample from a single focus group discussion following viewings of television coverage of a marital rape court case. The participants are speaking Sesotho with some code-switching into English. In the extract, two men, Joe and Sipho, dominate the talk and they clearly consider the concept of marital rape to be highly contentious. Joe employs a forceful question–answer rhetorical style, loudly rallying the support of the other men in the group:

1	Joe:	.hh uhm na *monna* ya nyetseng	.hh uhm *can* a married man
2		a ka beta mosadi wa hae (.)	*rape* his *wife*? (.)
3		JWANG (1.0)	HOW? (1.0)
4		monna o na le TOKELO ya	a man has the RIGHT to sleep with

5	ho robala mosadi ha feela a rata	his wife whenever he *wants*
6	(0.2) haeba ke phoso uh uh	(0.2) if I am wrong uh uh
7	le tla nthiba ja? (.) that is why	you'll stop me yeah? (.) That's
8	lenyalong conjugal rights e leng	why in marriage conjugal rights
9	ntho ya bohlokwa	is an important issue
10	hantle conjugal rights tsa monna	in fact a man's conjugal rights
11	ke right tsa hae to sexual	are his right to sexual
12	intercourse (0.5)	intercourse (0.5)

(Adapted from Hanong 2006: 204)

He goes on to claim that denial of this alleged right is illegal; a wife, it seems, has only obligations. These are very traditional views. Thato, a woman, interrupts to object to them in lines 17–18 and 23–4:

13	Joe:	Jwale mpolelle (.) haeba mosadi	So tell me (.) if the wife
14		a hana ho phetha MOLAO le	disobeys the LAW and the
15		MOETLO	CULTURE
		((simultaneous noisy talk))	
16		E:: E:: ke hlile ke cho jwalo (.)	ye::s ye::s I mean exactly that (.)
		[	[
17	Thato:	Modimo o bua jwaloka	God you are speaking
18		ka monna wa Mosotho hantle	exactly like a Mosotho man
		[ ]	[ ]
19	Joe:	mpolelle hore na uhm ha a mo	tell me when uhm
20		hanela ka ditokelo tsa hae (.) o	she denies him his rights
21		lebeletse hote monna yeo wa	(.) how does she expect this
22		Modimo a phele jwang?	man of God to live?
		[	[
23	Thato:	athe mosadi yena	is the woman
24		ha se wa Modimo?	not of God?

(Adapted from Hanong 2006: 205)

Monna yeo wa Modimo (This man of God) is an endearment term. Thato's appeal to Joe to extend its use to women is a conciliatory gesture

(2007: 206). Hanong points out that women's contributions to discussions are sparse in her focus group data and largely limited to protestations and appeals for calm like Thato's above. The women are constrained by *hlonipa*, a linguistic repertoire of 'respect language' that hampers their contributions to talk. It is characterized by restraint, silence, euphemisms and vague expressions, including in reference to sexual matters. It is a repertoire that disempowers women in law courts, since it imposes severe constraints on their ability to speak out (Finlayson 1995; Moeketsi 1999; cited in Hanong 2006: 200). In the focus groups, women intervene to complain about the men's views and manner, in contrast with the haranguing style of debate with which the men dominate the floor. As the extract continues, Sipho takes the floor:

25	Sipho:	Arabang potso Bra Joe (.)	Answer Brother Joe's question
26		monna a lebe kae ha mosadi	(.) where should the husband
27		wa hae a mo hana?	go if his wife refuses him?
28		Moholwane o a bona hore	My brother do you realise
29		jwale BEIJI:::NG e re	that now BEIJI:::NG has
30		baketse mathata?	caused us problems?
31		jwale uhm (.) basadi ba se	now uhm (.) women are
32		ba re behela di-sanction	imposing sanctions on us

((murmuring and laughter)) (3.0)

Sipho is establishing solidarity among the men in the group in his use of the kinship terms **Bra Joe** (brother Joe) in line 25 and **moholwane** (older brother) in line 28. He blames Beijing (where the United Nations Fourth World Congress on Women took place in 1995) for the allegations of marital rape that are being discussed. Another woman intervenes:

33	Palesa:	Ka mantswe a mang molao ha	In other words the law says
34		o re letho ka ditokelo tsa	nothing about the rights of
35		basadi?	women?
36		haeba monna uhm (.) .hh a batle	if the man uhm (.) .hh wants
37		dikobo mosadi wa hae a sa	blankets but his wife does not
38		batle uh uh-	want uh uh-
		[	[
39	Sipho:	a ka hana wang (.) mosadi A	how can she refuse (.) a wife
40		NTSHEDITSWE DIKGOMO?	FOR WHOM CATTLE
41			HAVE BEEN PAID?

| 42 | ntle le haeba e se le yena | except if it is she who is now |
| 43 | hlooho ka tlung | the head in the house |

(Adapted from Hanong 2006: 204–5)

Palesa's **ho batla dikobo** (to want blankets) in lines 36–7 is a euphemistic expression for demanding sex. It's prefaced with hesitations and pauses that suggest it was uttered with some difficulty and her stance is conciliatory. In contrast, Sipho shouts in lines 40–1 as he evokes the institution of *lobola* (the bride price, traditionally paid in livestock). In evoking it, he 'constructs the gender hierarchical relationship in the African family – the wife for whom lobola has been paid has no right to deny her husband sex, thus she cannot make any claims to rape, and by implication her voice is silenced' (2006: 206). The men's sense of entitlement is strong and the women's self-imposed restraint does not equip them well to contest it. The women are disadvantaged in the argument arena by cultural expectations about their verbal behaviour.

It is very evident that the men are upset by disruption of the traditional gender hierarchy. In another focus group, the gender issues on the agenda are rejected as 'a new kind of cultural colonialism' and followed with the complaint that 'African women now behave like whites' (ibid.: 208). This is a view that is hinted at in Sipho's quip above about women 'imposing sanctions on us' (line 32). For these men, the international influence of feminism is pernicious and 'unfair', because it brings into play issues such as whether a wife should have any choice in the matter of sex with her husband. For women in indigenous communities, the cost of striving for social change may be so high that they have little choice but to collude with oppressive patriarchal traditions. Institutions such as *lobola*, or bride price, 'compel women to collude with men owing to fear of individual reprisals and breaking up of community cohesiveness' (Maitse 2000, cited in Hanong 2006: 210).

Resisting heteronormative identities

Amid all the clamorous heterosexuality in the world at large, lesbians and gay men carve out their non-normative identities. Identities are not produced by isolated individuals in a social vacuum; they are an 'outcome of intersubjectively negotiated practices and ideologies' (Bucholtz and Hall 2004: 493). The assertion and validation of non-normative sexual identities is the focus of this final section. A study of 'coming-out' stories on a website was undertaken by two British linguists, Liz Morrish and Helen Sauntson, and provides some straightforward examples as a starting point. Here are a few narrators constructing social sameness with others at university, in the media and via the internet:

> When I got to college I realised that I wasn't alone, and that many more people than I realised are gay. (Morrish and Sauntson 2007: 69)

> I finally realised I was gay when I was about 11 or 12. I just switched on the tv and 'Ellen' was on (thumbs up for the power of tv!), it was like an instant dejavoo. I was like omg, that's soooooo me! I felt so happy that I finally knew who I was. (2007: 78)

> At that time I had been making a lot of online friends and discovering that I wasn't weird or screwed up after all but a lot of others out there just like me. (2007: 80)

In other coming-out stories, narrators did the opposite; they established distinctness, as in these two examples reflecting on media representations:

> I only knew the stereotypical gay guy one sees in the movies and on TV so often which wasn't like me at all so I assumed I wasn't really gay.

> I think that the media . . . has made homosexuality look like one big orgy and full of deadly viruses and diseases. This is not the case. (ibid.: 79)

A pair of tactics, then, is to focus on degree of similarity: from total sameness to total distinction. Here Morrish and Sauntson are deploying Bucholtz and Hall's notion of 'tactics of intersubjectivity': analytical tools for examining assertions of identities that are non-normative in the larger society (Bucholtz and Hall 2004). Bucholtz and Hall identify three pairs of tactics altogether, relating to the assertion of degrees of similarity, degrees of authenticity and degrees of institutional validation. In other words, the tactics involve highlighting either sameness or difference, either genuineness or artifice, and either institutional recognition or marginalization.

In the next example, a narrator reports feeling compelled to feign a heterosexual identity with his family. In doing so, he is attending to lack of authenticity:

> My parents, brother, and lil sis all consider being gay 'disgusting' so I maintained a girlfriend to mask my true feelings. (Morrish and Sauntson 2007: 73)

A person's family is generally a key influence and a source of emotional stability, so that the risk in coming out to the family is particularly high. Another powerful regulator is religion and there are some stories 'in which

"Christianity" and "religion" are presented as being synonymous with homophobia' (2007: 75). In the following, two male narrators indicate that homosexuality is by no means authorized by the church:

> Gay = Sinful = first class trip to hell, right?
> I was always afraid to admit I was gay because of the religious upbringing I had. I grew up in a very conservative church and because of that was always told being gay is a sin. (2007: 76)

In Bucholtz and Hall's terms, it is illegitimated: 'Authorization focuses on identities that receive institutional sanction; illegitimation, in contrast, calls attention to identities that are denied such recognition' (2004: 504).

I turn now to a study of conversations among lesbians (Morrish and Sauntson 2007). In one of them, lesbian identities are explicitly and collaboratively asserted as distinct from the heteronorm. The participants are chatting while watching *Changing Rooms* (a British home improvement programme) on TV. They recognize and react to its heteronormativity. The extract opens with a 'distinction' tactic in line 1, then immediately switches to a focus on collective sameness:

1	C:	they're all so straight the people that go on this
2	A:	yeah I think we should all go on
3	B:	yeah we could do a lesbian changing rooms
4	A:	yeah and instead of telling the audience all about our children
5		we could tell them all about our cats
6	All:	(laughter)
7	A:	it would be like I'm ___ and this is my partner ___
8		and we live with our two children Fluffy and Tigger
9	All:	(laughter)

(Adapted from Morrish and Sauntson 2007: 36)

In this passage, the participants are foregrounding group lesbian identity using a tactic of 'adequation' (that is, highlighting 'adequate similarity'), achieved partly by means of inclusive **we** (lines 2, 3, 5 and 8). In their co-construction of an imaginary lesbian version of *Changing Rooms*, they assert lesbian identity by replacing children with cats and, later in the conversation, 'wallpaper' and 'pastels' with 'big dyke symbols all over each other's walls'. They are engaging in a playful subversion of heterosexual family structure: 'The most significant effect of this is humour – the speakers trivialise, and therefore undermine, the concept of the Western heterosexual family by inserting inappropriate or incongruous meanings into its structure.' (2007: 37). As Morrish and Sauntson point out, the incongruous insertion of some other pet – let's say, dogs – would not work half as well, as it wouldn't perform a lesbian in-joke.

In another extract, the same speakers are talking about their recent visit to a local gay bar. It provides an example of localized norms within a gay Community of Practice:

```
1   A:   Tania and her girlfriend didn't believe that that bouncer
2        in the Wow Bar was female the other night
3   B:   yeah they kept going it's a man it's a man
4   A:   and in the end it got really embarrassing because they went
5        right up to her and were making it really obvious and staring
6   B:   yeah and we were like thinking oh shit she's gonna beat us up
7        cos she's so hard and scary
```

(Adapted from Morrish and Sauntson 2007: 39)

What is interesting about this exchange is the fact that the incident is recollected negatively, as 'really embarrassing'. Far from being illegitimated, non-normative gender behaviour is authorized, accepted as appropriate in a gay bar:

> The ideology being conveyed here is that, in gay bars, it is acceptable and normal for women to look and behave in a culturally recognisable masculine fashion and vice versa. Furthermore, it is wrong to question or challenge these non-conformist attitudes towards gender if you are to frequent such establishments and especially if you, yourself, are gay. (2007: 40)

The extract of Wow Bar dialogue, then, is an example of an 'authorization' tactic.

I will finish with some observations from a study by a French linguist, the late Anna Livia, of personal ads in *Lesbia Magazine*. In personal columns, the styling of self and other is very much in focus. This makes them useful, and indeed intriguing, for attending to identity construction. Moreover, like the people frequenting the gay bar, readers of personal ads in a lesbian magazine are participating in a community that does not operate according to the heteronorms of the wider society.

The personal ads are usually in three parts, with a self-description first, followed by a description of the desired other and a list of exclusions. The three-part structure is marked with Roman numerals in this example:

(I) 30 ans, balance, andro, cherche contrepoids féminin pour équilibre harmonieux et calins. Souhaite (II) poids plume, mouche ou moyen. (III) Catcheuses, camionneuses, passez votre chemin.

(I) 30 years old, Libra, androgynous, looking for a feminine counter-weight for harmonious equilibrium and caresses. Want (II) featherweight, bantam weight or medium weight. (III) Female wrestlers, female truck drivers go on your way. (Livia 2002: 194)

This ad writer is seeking a prospective partner with a slim, feminine build. The majority of the ads have some reference to a masculine manner and build in the list of exclusions. In fact, many of them end with the formulaic exclusion: 'camionneuses s'abstenir' (women truck drivers need not apply). The dislike of masculine gender presentation is signalled in other ways too: for example, another ad writer asks the *ourse mal léchée* (badly licked she-bear) not to respond to the *marmotte* (marmot – figuratively a sleepy-head). In the context of the *Lesbia* personal column, the contrast between marmot and bear symbolizes gender difference, though no explanation is offered for the association of marmots, or sleepyheads, and femininity. The association of bears and masculinity, however, is quite straightfor-ward: 'The bear is considered not only uncultivated and blundering, but also aggressive and predatory, like a stereotypical man' (Livia 2002: 195). In the lesbian 'community' of this French magazine, an anti-butch discourse seems to be circulating. Butch lesbian identities are illegitimated, even within the marginalized group.

Interestingly, the converse of this rejection of female masculinity has been noted among gay men and identified as 'effeminophobia'. Niall Richardson, a British queer theorist, argues that fear of effeminacy is 'pred-icated on an anxiety about being anti-assimilationist and "not fitting in" with heteronormative culture' (2009: 536). Men who behave effeminately pose a problem for the gay population's need to 'fit in'. In violating the gender binary, 'queer' gender performances pose a threat to heteronor-mativity. Moreover, effeminacy is perceived as 'a lack of gay pride and is therefore in direct contradiction to the politics of gay assimilation' (2009).

It would seem, then, that the norms of dominant heterosexual culture just won't go away. To finish, a final observation about the assimilation of gayness into heteronorms in popular mainstream television. Consider the relentless heteronormativity of make-over shows – such as Gok Wan's *How to Look Good Naked* in Britain, or *Queer Eye for the Straight Guy* in the United States. Even with gay hosts, the restyling of the participants always has the goal of attractiveness for a hetero partner. The sexual identity of the hosts themselves is reduced to a matter of style.

Further reading

Language and sexuality

Several of the studies referred to in this chapter are reprinted in Cameron and Kulik (2006). This book provides a comprehensive survey and historical overview of the field. There is now a range of volumes available: Cameron and Kulik (2003), Campbell-Kibler et al. (2002), Livia and Hall (1997), Morrish and Sauntson (2007).

Performativity

Two useful general introductions to Butler's work are Lloyd (2007) and Salih (2002). For readings on performativity, try Jagger (2008) and five essays in part 1 of Salih and Butler (2004).

An interesting study of drag and performance not already mentioned is Barrett (1995, reprinted in Cameron and Kulik 2006).

Dating ads

Self- and other-commodification in personal ads is the subject of several studies that I have not already mentioned, including Shalom (1997), Coupland (1996, reprinted in Cameron and Kulik 2006). Hogben and Coupland (2000) looks at an intriguing variant on the genre: gay parenting ads for reproductive partners.

Sexual consent and rape

For further readings on rape trials and definitions of sexual consent, see Crawford (1995) and Ehrlich (2001, 2003). See also Cameron (2006b) on a US college's guidelines for students. Readings on doing refusals and date rape are Kitzinger and Frith (1999), Kitzinger (2000). There is also discussion in Speer (2005). For analysis of media reporting of rape, read Clark (1992, reprinted in Cameron 1998).

There are rape crisis websites catering for many countries worldwide; e.g. www.rapecrisis.org.uk for England and Wales, www.rapecrisis.org.za for South Africa and www.rapecrisis.com for USA (all accessed 9 Dec. 2009).

12

Reclaiming the language

This final chapter of the book examines struggles in and about discourse, with particular attention to attempts to eradicate sexism from English. It attends to processes of containment and struggle, including the discourse of 'political correctness', and the institutions where these processes have been taking place.

Sexism

Sexism is about discrimination on the grounds of sex, based on assumptions that women are both different from and inferior to men. It is a label for behaviour that systematically derogates women; in the words of *A Feminist Dictionary*:

> a concept, central to women's lives, which was wordless for many years.

> Behavior, policy, language, or other action of men or women which expresses the institutionalized, systematic, comprehensive, or consistent view that women are inferior. (Kramarae and Treichler 1985: 411)

The term itself was only coined at the end of the 1960s, probably on the analogy of **racism**. Earlier in the decade, the term **male chauvinism**, invented by women student activists, was used to criticize the attitudes of their male counterparts. We now have more *-isms* (**ablism, sizeism, ageism**) serving a similar function; that is, putting a label on a set of discriminatory assumptions and the social system based on them.

Feminist language-reform initiatives began in the United States, and the groundbreaking texts that I outlined briefly in chapter 3 were extremely influential. Other major resources were a collection on *Sexism and Language* (Nilsen et al. 1977) and an article on 'The semantic derogation of women' (Schulz 1975). The second of these was included in the first edited collection in the emerging field that has become known as 'language and gender' (Thorne and Henley's *Language and Sex: Difference and Dominance*).

Since the early 1980s challenges to sexist practices have been taking place in both public and private domains. These have involved struggle over all sorts of things, including over how men and women are represented in the press, in job advertisements, in everyday conversations and so on. For example, feminist critics have taken exception to the way women are often defined in terms of physical attributes, such as hair colour (**a blonde, a redhead**), attractiveness to men, or otherwise (**beauty, stunner, dog**). They have also taken issue with the extent to which women are defined in terms of home and family and, in particular, in terms of their relationships with men. If I ever have the misfortune to be reported in a British tabloid newspaper, I will probably be identified as a **working wife**, or perhaps as a **mother of two**. A man wouldn't get this treatment. Consider also the asymmetry of the traditional honorific titles **Mr** but **Mrs** and **Miss**: only women's marital status and 'availability' is marked. The new title, **Ms**, was intended to erase this asymmetry. In professional contexts in the United States it has largely succeeded. It has been less successful in Britain, however, and is widely used as a third option. In Britain these days a woman filling in a form has to choose from **Mrs**, **Miss** and **Ms**.

Another contentious issue has been occupational stereotyping and androcentric assumptions surrounding work generally. The use of the suffix *-man* in occupational names (**businessman, postman**) renders women in such occupations invisible. Even apparently gender-neutral agent nouns, like **driver** and **writer**, and unmarked occupational names like **doctor**, are assumed to refer to men, hence the need for the compound nouns **lady doctor** (but not **gentleman doctor**), **woman writer** (but not **man writer**), **woman driver** (but not **man driver**). This asymmetry implies that doctoring, writing and driving are somehow covertly gendered and perceived as male activities. It's interesting, and encouraging, that the compounds now sound slightly odd. You rarely come across similar compounds with **man** or **male**. In fact, the only two I can think of are **male nurse** and **male prostitute**, although there may be more, perhaps referring to workers in low-paid occupations. By pointing out asymmetries like these in terms of reference for women and men, critics of sexist practices have politicized classifications that were previously considered to be neutral. It has been argued that, in English, once words become marked as female they are systematically downgraded, often acquiring pejorative connotations (Schulz 1975). Compare **bachelor** and **spinster**, for instance.

Classifying people is part of the naming and ordering of experience; it both reflects and sustains existing social relations and identities. The categorization of people is a powerful normative force. Challenging the sexism in the way women are categorized requires a critical perspective on the 'labelling' practices of English, *critical* again in the sense of trying to show hidden connections between language, power and ideology.

Other asymmetries in the vocabulary of English have provoked feminist criticism. A man who hates women is called a **misogynist**. There is no equivalent impressive-sounding term for a woman who hates men. What is the male equivalent of a **nymphomaniac**, or a **slut**? It is difficult to find one. There are lexical gaps in English which, when exposed, betray widespread androcentrism. Women's experiences can be hard to talk about because terms for them aren't readily available (this was Dale Spender's argument in *Man Made Language*, aired in chapter 3).

Of course, sexism in language is more than a matter of vocabulary. Women have engaged in protracted struggles to be treated on an equal basis with men, especially in the workplace. This has involved challenges to sexist practices in interaction, including women's efforts to be taken seriously. This is the context in which **Ms** has come into use, as a way of placing women on the same footing as men. Marital status has never been an issue for men in the workplace; it need not be for women either.

Other terms of address used for women have also been a cause for concern. When you address someone, you choose from a system of address terms. The term you choose – and what the addressee says back to you – depends on whom you are addressing and your relationship with them. Close friends call one another by their first names and may use affectionate terms. Many people these days are on equally familiar terms with their employers. It is not always symmetrical, however. Employees are only 'familiar' if they have their employers' approval. Parents, and adults generally, tend to use affectionate terms like **love** or **pet** and first names with children, but, in addressing adults, children are generally required to 'show respect' in some way. Some years ago, a receptionist at my doctor's surgery used to address all patients indiscriminately as **flower**, even old men. I suspect it had something to do with the way patients are infantilized in medical care. The receptionist was being maternal, putting the patients at ease by addressing them as if they were children. I never heard her address the doctors in the practice in the same way; she addressed them respectfully as **Doctor**. Some of the patients may well have found her behaviour patronizing (or should that be matronizing?).

Address terms to women can also be used in a patronizing way. It is this kind of usage which feminists have identified as sexist. Terms of affection can be used, for instance, to diminish a woman's serious contributions to a discussion. At a business meeting, a solitary woman addressed as

honey is being put down, reduced in status in front of her male colleagues. Affectionate terms of address like **dear, honey, darling, sweetheart** or whatever – whether these are friendly or a put-down depends on the relationship of the people involved, on the power relations between them and their degree of social distance.

Other sexist practices involving language are the negative evaluation of women's voices (as shrill, strident and suchlike), of women's talk (as trivial, mere gossip) and folklinguistic beliefs about women talking incessantly. Guidelines drawn up in various institutional contexts for avoidance of sexist language are one limited example of organized resistance to sexism. The purpose of such guidelines, and of other attempts to curb sexist language, is to promote social change, to bring about changes in behaviour and equitable treatment for women.

This final chapter examines three things. I begin with the nature of struggles over sexism in English, where they take place, and the forms they take. I then consider the counter-resistance, that is to say, attempts to maintain the linguistic status quo. Finally, I turn to the phenomenon of so-called 'political correctness' and ask: what is it and how has it come to be a term of abuse?

Modes of struggle

Struggles in and over language are taking place all the time, in many different modes. Struggles over sexism in English include both individual contestations and organized resistance: objecting to being denied a say, to being defined in ways considered demeaning, to being treated in patronizing ways. In the public domains of the media, education and publishing there continue to be efforts to persuade 'gatekeepers' of language – the people in institutions who decide what counts as acceptable language and what does not – to use non-sexist alternatives. Not everyone is in a position to influence the gatekeepers of public language, however. And not all tactics are equally effective. But that does not leave them out of the struggle altogether.

Resistance and contestation

Sometimes I find myself being a resistant viewer when I'm watching TV. I have been known to shout at it and even, on occasion, to throw cushions (this is not recommended). In objecting to sexist stereotypes and weary old clichés, a viewer is drawing upon a feminist counter-discourse

Resistant viewer

in interpretation. One person at home shouting at the TV is giving vent to their irritation and this is no bad thing. It has the value of articulating resistance to sexism. It can serve as the bottom line in thinking about resistance and contestation: not very influential, but at least it's a start. More visible contestations by individuals can sometimes be seen in graffiti on posters. Some years ago, for instance, a car advertisement on a hoarding announced: 'If it was a lady, it would get its bottom pinched.' Under the caption someone had sprayed: 'If this lady was a car she'd run you down.'

Struggles over language are happening all the time. A British linguist, Linda McLoughlin, has interviewed some groups of schoolgirls and young women in a deprived inner-city area in north-west England, investigating how they subvert the language used by boys and men to 'define and confine them' (1993: i). They maintain, for example, that they use the term **slag** for males who 'sleep around' (1993: 43). This pejorative label is used by men as a form of social control, a constraint on women's sexuality. Not surprisingly, McLoughlin has found that the women are not politicized to the extent of identifying sexism as such. Their resistance frequently takes the form of retaliating in kind. Being subjected to frequent male taunts at school in the form of appraisals of their bodies, very often mocking their physical immaturity, they don't just suffer in silence. They retaliate by responding in kind ('pubes', used in the following, is a colloquial term for pubic hair):

C: I called all the lads at our school 'a desert'
R: Right come on explain that one (laughs)
C: There's no rain forests in a desert and like the rain forest is their pubes an a desert's got like only a few palm trees in it so there's only a few pubes

(McLoughlin 1993: 57)

Like young women in public places in many other communities, these women are subjected to frequent evaluative comments from men. Indeed, they are vulnerable to the sexist practice of harassment both in school settings and in the street. Their counter-abuse – that is, responding in kind – is a local solution which has its merits, but limited effectiveness. They often voice complaints about not getting any support from those in authority at school. Their strategy of counter-abuse does not work in their favour. It certainly does not endear them to their teachers. As 'C' below relates, they 'get in trouble' for it:

C: he's got a big nose an he always calls me a slag or a slut so I always call him 'big nose, small dick, no pubes' an he always gets like dead upset an things like that an he always tells his form tutor an I always get in trouble through it coz he's callin me a slag an I call him something back

(McLoughlin 1993: 57)

These beleaguered young women have limited resources available to them for identifying and challenging sexism. In their community, there is little escape from the oppressive practices of masculinity: 'the chat-up lines on Fitton Hill are the imperatives "Get your kit off" or "Get your tits out for t' lads". Such remarks are usually met with laughter or the comment "Dickhead", which again unfortunately shows that the women are not criticising males for their chauvinism head-on' (1993: 60). ('Get your kit off' means 'Take off your clothes.') These remarks, jokingly called 'chat-up lines' by McLoughlin, are of course not meant as such at all, but are yet more sexual taunting. The women resist and contest this taunting with the resources available to them.

Sexism is also resisted and contested in collective action. Some years ago, a familiar sight to travellers on the London Underground were stickers saying 'This poster degrades women', appropriately placed on offending advertising material on the escalators. One campaigner, Louise Graessle, recollects her stickering expeditions:

> we would meet at, say, five-thirty or six in the morning at Sloane Square underground station with our packets of these stickers . . . We would get on the District Line and would ride along to Dagenham and beyond, getting off every once in a while and riding up and down the escalators, putting stickers on the ads and trying not to get caught. (Wandor 1990: 130)

It was a highly effective campaign.

Struggles over access

Other effective kinds of collective action instigated by feminists have involved struggles over women's access to talk. For example, many women are not comfortable with forms of public talk traditionally characterized by competitiveness and self-display. Conscious resistance to traditional hierarchical modes of interaction, and pressure to change them, have succeeded in bringing about changes. Some collectives – trade unions, for instance – have shifted from formal chairing and orators / 'good speakers' in their meetings to good facilitation by the chair. The move away from a hierarchical mode of interaction to a more collective, cooperative one has helped women to find a public voice. The study of an American TV panel discussion, presented in chapter 7, showed two African-American women challenging the interview-like conventions imposed by the moderator. They were subverting his institutional authority, imposing more egalitarian, conversation-like conventions. Another strategy for helping women to find a voice is separatism. Sometimes the need for environments for talking about issues of importance to women has necessitated the setting up of women-only groups.

Women were excluded from the public domain for a long time (discussed in chapter 10). Until recently they were denied access to many privileged professional discourses; consider, for example, women's efforts to break into the medical profession. As I argued in chapter 7, entering into the medical profession is a matter of entry into medical discourse.

Women still do not have equal access to privileged professional discourses or to dominant speaker positions within them. Women are still under-represented in senior positions in the medical and university sectors, for instance. As a consequence, they still struggle to make themselves heard and to have their interests served. (However, having women in high places does not *necessarily* benefit women. Think of Margaret Thatcher: she is the only woman who has ever been prime minister in Britain, but there was nothing feminist about her policies.) Gatekeeping struggles within institutions – that is, over who gets allowed in – are also struggles over access. In a university department, for example, those who gain access to interviewing procedures are the ones who determine who gets employed. Gaining entry into employment is crucially about language, about entering into discourse, about positions of power held by (or withheld from) those already 'inside' it.

Interventions

The invention of the word **sexism** itself is an example of direct intervention. It was a neologism, coined to fill a lexical gap. Some feminist writers have exploited the creative potential of English, especially punning and other wordplay: for example, rewriting **therapist** as **the-rapist**, as Mary Daly memorably did in *Gyn/Ecology* (1979) (punning in the title of her book too). One new term which has quietly found its way into common usage is **parenting**, which has now replaced **mothering** in some contexts. This derivation – formed by wordclass shift, from noun to verb – brings fathers into the long-term business of childrearing (in contrast with **fathering**, the work of a moment!). Another possibility is to extend the scope of existing terms, as the Fitton Hill women have done with **slag**.

Experiments in fiction are another way of intervening in sexist language. Writers of fiction sometimes tinker with English, inventing alternative pronouns, for example, or coining new terms to fill in lexical gaps. Feminist science fiction is notable in this respect. In Marge Piercy's first SF novel, *Woman on the Edge of Time*, she utilizes a third-person pronoun that does not indicate the sex of the person referred to. In the novel, Piercy presents a utopian community, Mattapoissett, whose inhabitants have abolished gender. They never specify sex in pronominal reference, as we do with the pronouns **he, him; she, her**. In Mattapoissett, the third-person subject pronoun is **person**; elsewhere they use **per**. This does not eliminate sexual identity, but it does background it. Here are two examples of the third-person pronoun in operation:

'Sappho perself made that tale long ago.' Jackrabbit was watching the old woman with admiration. 'Many people now tell that story, but none better. At Icebreaking I taped per telling.'

'Person's way of insinuating into other people's beds was not always productive,' a young person said, standing on one foot. 'Jackrabbit came to me once after a dance and then never again. I felt I was an apple person had taken a bite of and spat out.'

'Person was so curious, began far more friendships than could be maintained', Bolivar said dryly, without raising his head. (Piercy 1979: 132, 312)

The characters in dialogue do not indicate the sex of the person they refer to but the reader can still distinguish between women and men, because the narrator (a woman from our world) uses sex-specific pronouns, nouns and possessives. So Piercy manages to have it both ways. As a result the reader has a glimpse of a community of men and women without gender differences. Such linguistic creativity and experimentation is a way of drawing attention to the status quo.

Another form of direct intervention in sexism in English is dictionary writing. Dictionaries tend to be treated as though they were inscribed in stone. People tend to think of them as repositories of facts about a language. This is inevitable if you are learning that language but native speakers of it tend to see dictionaries that way too. In fact, dictionaries are liable to reflect the prejudices of their compilers and the culture of their time. From a distance, these prejudices are clearly visible. Consider this entry for the verb **civilize** from a dictionary published in 1931: 'civilize: To bring from a state of barbarism to one of civilization, to introduce and foster social and moral improvement among: *savages have often been civilized by missionaries*' (cited in Moon 1989: 89). What kind of culture is **barbaric**, inhabited by **savages**? For most people nowadays, the views implicit in the definition and the example are highly problematic, if not downright offensive. They betray a narrow conception of civilization.

Lexicographers these days try to compile dictionaries that avoid such ethnocentrism, and also sexism. There are a number of issues involved in compiling new dictionaries. It is a convention in dictionaries for offensive or vulgar usages to be marked as such. Usages that are considered to be offensive by part of the population (such as **girl** for an adult woman, or **old woman** for a fussy man) need identifying. In compiling replacement dictionaries, lexicographers also need to avoid stereotyping in examples, such as in the entry quoted above. It is also important to compile the dictionary on the basis of a wide range of language use, not just using predominantly male written sources as has been the norm in the past. There are also various specialized dictionaries, not intended as replacements but as supplements providing terms omitted from conventional dictionaries (such as Maggie Humm's *Dictionary of Feminist Theory* (1989)) or as witty commentary (Kramarae and Treichler's *Feminist Dictionary* (1985)).

Another form of direct intervention is the monitoring of public language for sexism and racism. This is now widespread in the English-speaking world. Publishers edit potentially offensive material from manuscripts. Local government and social services engage in promoting gender equity by various means, as do a wide range of other bodies: employers in businesses, professional organizations and educational establishments. Most now have equal opportunities policies, codes of practice, complaints procedures and guidelines. Early examples in the United States were recommendations for curriculum reform and guidelines for the avoidance of sexism in publications drawn up by the National Council of Teachers of English. A British example is the National Union of Journalists' code of conduct for its members, which includes some guidelines for non-sexist usage. Here are a few of its suggestions:

Ford men voted	Ford workers voted
male nurse	nurse
woman doctor	doctor
housewife	often means shopper, consumer, the cook
mothers	often means parents
girls (of over 18)	women (especially in sports)
spinster/divorcee	these words should not be used as an insult

These guidelines also discuss stereotyping of various kinds, offering advice on how to avoid them, and point to the underrepresentation of women as workers, or as creative and decisive social beings.

Since the early 1980s, 'speakers of English have been in a position to observe a linguistic guerilla war raging all around them' (Cameron 1995b: 118). These military activities were instigated by feminists, but soon joined by others. In some ways, the linguistic guerrillas can be said to have won a major victory. Gatekeepers, in particular, are now very much aware of issues relating to gender, ethnicity and ablebodiedness. More generally, people are aware of giving offence by using certain terms and forms of address. What linguistic militants have achieved is the politicization of terms that previously seemed to be neutral. It is still possible for someone to use older forms, but they cannot be used in an apparently neutral way any more. For instance, a man – an old-fashioned traditionalist, let's say – might refer to a woman presiding over a meeting as the **chairman** (or even **Madam Chairman**!). But it is impossible for him to do so in a neutral way. In choosing **chairman** over **chairwoman**, **chairperson** or **chair** he says something about his attitudes towards women, for which he can then be held accountable. He no doubt finds this state of affairs very disagreeable.

Counter-resistance

Many people have complied, sometimes grudgingly, with the pressure to change brought to bear by the linguistic guerrillas. For some this has simply meant changing the potential source of offence, as in the attempts of a fantasy author to reuse his 'wog jokes' as 'troll jokes'. There are many instances of this sort of grudging compliance-without-understanding else-where, not least in the press. Not everyone has been such a pushover, though. In some quarters the fighting has been fierce.

The media

Resistance to linguistic intervention has been articulated in the media right from the start. Its critics have taken great delight in ridiculing proposed reforms, with newspaper journalists pouncing gleefully on its perceived excesses, regardless of their origins, scope or influence. The British press had a field day, for instance, when staff in a local supermarket relabelled their Gingerbread men as Gingerbread *persons*. This item of 'news' licensed subeditors' production of punning headlines like 'Gingerbread person takes the biscuit' (*Weekly Telegraph*) (if something 'takes the biscuit' it is an extreme example of absurdity).

There have been struggles within the institution of journalism as well. The National Union of Journalists' 'equality style guide', referred to above, was produced by a tiny minority within the NUJ and other members have put up considerable resistance to it. One journalist, Denise Searle, sug-gests that the main reason for the limited effectiveness of these guidelines is the union leadership's fear of being perceived as censors (1988: 255). A campaign to enforce non-sexist guidelines, or indeed for the removal of nude pin-ups, would be attacked as a threat to press freedom. If the code of conduct is imposed, it is at chapel (local branch) level and often ignored. In practice it is unlikely to be invoked at all because, to intervene, members of a union chapel at a newspaper would have to pitch themselves against their own editor. Searle gives an example of NUJ members working for the *Star* complaining that it had deteriorated to a 'porn sheet' and yet not interfering because the newspaper's content was the editor's business (1988: 255). Interestingly, the newspaper was eventually 'cleaned up' after pressure from advertisers. The threat of loss of advertising revenue forced Express Newspapers, the paper's owners, to remove the editor.

There are complaints procedures in place, with the NUJ's ethics council providing a channel for the views of the general public. This has had some success in dealing with the press's misrepresentation of lesbians, gays, ethnic minorities and the disabled. But complaints about sexism are rarely taken up and even more rarely succeed. Searle cites the example of a complaint about reportage in the *Sunday Express* of the first American woman in space, Dr Sally Ride. Searle paraphrases the complaint as follows:

> the story, headlined 'In orbit – with no lipstick', paid more attention to whether Ride took lipstick or perfume into space than to her achievements as a scientist. Reference to her qualifications and role did not appear until the last four paragraphs, whereas accompanying male astronauts' professional attributes and functions were clearly described at a much earlier stage. Ride, an astrophysicist, was also quoted as saying that the space flight was like a roller coaster ride at Disneyworld. . . . the article trivialised and glamorised the image of women and would therefore lead to discrimination. (1988: 256–7)

The complaint was rejected as trivial. More optimistically, Searle suggests that the presence of a number of women 'in the newsroom or on the subs desk, disturbing the "men-only" vacuum' is a strong force for bringing about change, since male colleagues find themselves feeling embarrassed. This increased female presence may eventually change men's perception of the anti-sexist guidelines as a form of censorship' (1988: 257).

Academia

Change has been, and continues to be, resisted elsewhere. There have been protracted struggles within education and the academic community. The counter-resistance has included linguists on both sides of the Atlantic. An early skirmish was a 1971 debate that took place in the letters page of a magazine, the *Harvard Crimson*, over the use of **he**, **Man** and **mankind** as generic pronouns and nouns (that is, to refer to humanity in general, both male and female). (The account and the extracts below are in Martyna 1983.) This affray began with the linguistics faculty taking it upon themselves to criticize an attempt made by a theology class to eradicate sexist language from its discussions:

> The fact that the masculine is the unmarked gender in English . . . is simply a feature of grammar. It is unlikely to be an impediment to change in the patterns of the sexual division of labor towards which our society may wish to evolve. There is really no cause for anxiety or pronoun-envy on the part of those seeking such changes.

The Harvard linguists were claiming that the generic masculine was simply a feature of grammar, unrelated to the issue of sex discrimination. Some linguistics students responded (rather bravely, I think!) to this letter. In their response they posed the following hypothetical situation:

> In culture R the language is such that the pronouns are different according to the color of the people involved, rather than their sex . . . The unmarked pronoun just happens to be the one used for white people. In addition, the colored people just happen to constitute an oppressed group. Now imagine that this oppressed group begins complaining about the use of the 'white' pronoun to refer to all people. Our linguists presumably then say, 'Now, now there is really no cause for anxiety or pronoun-envy.'

The 'R' presumably stands for 'racist'. The implication is that the generic masculine, far from being a feature of grammar alone, is an aspect of society's sexism and contributes to reproducing it. Unfortunately the media picked up on this debate. It was ridiculed in *Newsweek* in a column headed 'Pronoun envy'. Notice the use of wit to trivialize the issue and sexualize the reformers.

A more recent skirmish, over pronouns among other things, took place among members of the Linguistics Association of Great Britain. In 1984, LAGB members opposed proposals from other members to amend their own constitution. These proposals included the removal of generic masculine pronouns, proposals opposed on the grounds that it is not the business of linguists to engage in prescriptive practices. In introductory lectures in linguistics, students are often told that linguistics is about *description*, not *prescription*; about describing what is there in language, not laying down rules for how it should be used or making value judgements about other people's language use.

However, while this is fine for dismissing some of the snobbier pronouncements about 'bad' English, it is not entirely true. Actually, linguists lay down the law quite a lot, one way or the other (for detailed discussion, see Cameron 1995b). A classic work of language description, for instance, is Daniel Jones's *The Pronunciation of English* (1909). This phonetics text – essentially a description of received pronunciation (RP: the British upper-class accent) – was 'designed for the use of English students and teachers, and more especially for students in training-colleges and teachers whose aim is to correct cockneyisms or other undesirable pronunciation in their scholars' (Jones 1909: vii). Pronunciation dictionaries are still used in this way, as are grammars and dictionaries. They purport to be descriptions of a language, but they are treated as definitive and their contents are enforced. Such impositions of a particular pronunciation or grammar enforce language norms. They are examples of language politics in action, 'a form of social activity that aims at an authoritative manipulation of people's use of language by the use of prescriptive decrees and sanctioning measures' (Mey 1989: 334).

In recent years, denunciations of feminist language reforms are couched in terms of PC: that is, 'political correctness'. This curious phenomenon needs examining.

What is 'political correctness'?

It has been compared to the McCarthyism of the 1950s and the Nazi book-burnings of the 1930s and, as president, George Bush Senior swore to defend free speech from it (Annette 1994). In 1997, shortly before the onset of election campaigning in Britain, the health secretary announced on the radio that he was 'taking steps to remove political correctness from the adoption process'. PC has been likened to an amazing variety of cultural phenomena – Stalinism, the Cultural Revolution, the Great Plague – and has been held responsible for every imaginable restriction or form of complaint. Some time ago I saw a chalkboard outside a pub that proclaimed: 'If you think the music's too loud, you're too politically correct!'

So what on earth is PC? Well, perhaps a useful perspective to start from is how the 'proverbial Martian anthropologists' would see it, imagined by Cameron (1995b: 123). Inquisitive Martian scholars of Earth culture would get the impression that 'political correctness' was a powerful political movement based in universities and other cultural institutions, such as green organizations and public service professions. This powerful organization would appear to be committed to enforcing an orthodoxy, based on arcane systems of belief called 'deconstruction', 'poststructuralism', 'feminism', 'Marxism' and 'environmentalism'. It would appear to have two specific objectives in education: one being to replace the traditional, established core of the culture with marginal elements (teaching Alice Walker instead of Shakespeare, for instance) and the other being to privilege some groups (women, ethnic minorities, the disabled) over others. In education and beyond, another apparent objective would be to control and police all language used to talk about those same groups.

Cameron observes that these Martian anthropologists would become rather puzzled by the fact that the only sources they could find for all this mass of information seem to be the opponents of the movement being described (1995b: 124). They would eventually discover that this term 'PC' is not used by the supporters of this movement. Indeed, the people supposed to belong to it deny it even exists and reject the term 'PC' outright.

How can this be? Well, to make any sense of this peculiar state of affairs, it is necessary to look at where this anti-PC discourse is coming from and what is actually being objected to. In fact, this anti-PC discourse is part of the counter-resistance I've addressed already. Throughout the 1980s, there was a ground swell of hostility towards the interventions into discriminatory language of the kind outlined earlier in the chapter. The first major assault on the allegedly PC academy was a book with an apocalyptic title: *The Closing of the American Mind: How Higher Education Has Failed Democracy and Impoverished the Souls of Today's Students* (Bloom 1987). It became a bestseller. Following it, anti-PC fever burst into the pages of the American press. Another assault on the PC university was Roger Kimball's *Tenured Radicals: How Politics Has Corrupted Higher Education* (1990). A particularly outspoken opponent of PC in the US academic community is Dinesh D'Souza, whose bestseller, *Illiberal Education: The Politics of Race and Sex on Campus*, made him a media celebrity for a while.

All this anti-PC discourse comes from the political right. These books, among others, articulate the fierce resistance to changes being attempted in education since the 1960s. Consider the kinds of changes that have taken place. In some universities, affirmative action programmes have been set up encouraging minorities to enrol. The curriculum has been opened up, particularly the literary canon (Alice Walker *as well as* Shakespeare) and ways of teaching history, so that many arts and humanities faculties promote racial and sexual equality. Efforts have been made to stimulate social change by means of language reform measures intended to make people aware of discriminatory practices by recommending alternatives. These changes have taken place because of sustained pressure from 'below', not least from students. Recall the early Harvard debate over the generic masculine in the last section. It was student-led. Complaints about literature courses covering only the work of 'dead white men' also came from students.

These social programmes have many opponents, who have lumped together a wide range of issues, theoretical stances and political positions (deconstruction, affirmative action, feminism, multiculturalism . . .) and labelled them as PC in order to reject them. The label PC has become a way of casting aspersions, an easy way of dismissing challenges to the status quo. By crying PC, as Jeffrey Williams notes, a critic can 'dismiss these positions out-of-hand, as ridiculous or tyrannical, shortcircuiting any sort of more elaborated debate or discussion' (1995: 2).

Anti-PC discourse has an economic side too. Any research perceived to have the taint of the PC orthodoxy has no chance of funding from the National Endowment for the Humanities, a powerful funding body in the United States. Educational gatekeepers – notably Lynne Cheney, former chair of the NEH, and her successor, Sheldon Hackney – have denounced PC and all its minions (Scott 1995; Williams 1995).

In the United Kingdom, anti-PC discourse first really emerged in ridicule of the Greater London Council. In 1981, the Labour left-winger Ken Livingstone was elected as leader of the GLC. There followed a four-year period of concerted legislation and spending to foster multiculturalism, tolerance and affirmative action in the Greater London area. It also tackled environmental issues. Any visitor to London at the time would have been aware of the 'fare's fair' campaign about London Transport, for instance. This campaign was, among other things, asserting the importance of public need over private greed. All this began during Thatcher's first term of office, with a very different agenda: privatization. The GLC's headquarters were at County Hall, directly across from the Houses of Parliament on the opposite bank of the Thames; as Meera Syal, an actor-writer, remarks, 'it must have seemed to the Tories that after each policy they pushed through, the sound of hooting and loud raspberries would come drifting across the water' (1994: 129). Syal, as a British Asian, recalls the feeling of relief that flooded communities at having an elected council actually tackling racism and inequality head-on.

The press (more specifically the London *Evening News*) launched a massive anti-PC campaign, directed at the GLC. Syal's parody of the media sensationalism is so much funnier than the original absurdities:

> The screaming tabloid headlines: 'Council Worker Sacked For Ordering Black Coffee!' 'School Dinner Lady Hanged For Spelling Samosa Wrong!' And the photos of weeping childminders removing Noddy from their shelves, the TV footage of grimfaced women with cropped hair and boiler suits snatching golliwogs from the arms of wailing babes . . . The jokes about the physically challenged, follicularly challenged, vertically

challenged, usually told with great glee by the cerebrally challenged, making fun of the poncy lefties who couldn't let ordinary folk call a spade a bloody spade. Now granted, most of this press coverage is wedged in between Twenty Things You Never Knew About Parsnips and a pair of airbrushed nipples, but I know a backlash when I see one. (1994: 118)

The press smear campaign over PC spearheaded the destruction of the GLC (Hall 1994). The backlash has not been restricted to the GLC, by any means. There have been many other attacks on anti-racist measures in the press which have had seriously damaging effects. The training of social workers was singled out for a smear campaign, for instance, and the government subsequently instructed the Central Council for Education and Training in Social Work to remove anti-racist training from the curriculum because it was PC (Alibhai-Brown 1994: 67–8).

Anti-PC discourse is a response to the direct interventions into sexist and other discriminatory practices discussed earlier. Its effects are to undermine them. Let's just recall what are actually being attacked: the monitoring of public language for sexism and racism; the editing of potentially offensive material from manuscripts by publishers; the promotion of gender equity and suchlike by local government, employers, professional organizations and universities; the equal opportunities policies; the codes of practice and complaints procedures; the opening up of humanities curricula so that minority interests are less marginalized – all these have been thorns in the flesh for some, regardless of the effectiveness or otherwise of these interventions. All of them can be dismissed as PC.

The new frame of PC alters our perception of old issues. It reduces language reforms to absurdity. It reframes concerns for respect and consideration as forms of oppression. Just think: saying 'don't be so politically correct' sounds reasonable. But imagine saying 'don't be so anti-racist'! It presents an illusory choice between language reforms and real, important things, like equal pay (see, for example, Beard and Cerf's introduction to their parodic *Official Politically Correct Dictionary and Handbook* (1992)). Engagements with the literary canon, history curriculum, etc., are presented as attempts to destroy Western civilization as we know it.

The origins of the term itself are not entirely certain. It clearly didn't start its life as a stick to beat feminism with (along with anti-racism and other left-leaning tendencies). It seems to have sprung from American left-wing political movements and to have been used in an ironic self-mocking way rather than seriously. It came into wider circulation once the critics of 'PC' universities in the US started using it, pejoratively. Most people come across the term for the first time in the media, in genres that are unlikely to supply a definition and in the kind of context where you can't very well ask for clarification. Most examples of 'PC atrocities' in the media are either fabricated or grossly exaggerated: artefacts of media sensationalism. Its meaning has to be interpreted on the basis of very flimsy information. 'PC' has undergone a good deal of 'discursive drift' (Cameron 1995b: 127).

As I have already said, the new frame of PC changes people's perception of old issues. In the political climate dominating the industrialized West, socialist or populist critiques can be dismissed as PC. Egalitarian notions can be rejected as PC. As Williams rather grimly observes, 'the PC scare is a savvy ideological power play that negates any opposition or critique from the outset, a highly successful public relations campaign that cushions and justifies the current corporate redistribution of wealth and organization of life' (1995: 5).

To finish rather more light-heartedly, anti-PC discourse is now a widely available resource and is used in some bizarre contexts. This is one of the daftest I have come across; at least, it competes with the pub chalkboard I mentioned before. A small group of English comic creators – they called themselves the 'Graphic Terrorists' – produced a comic called *Bad to the Bone*, containing stories about men with large weapons and women with improbable bodies and very few clothes on. Now they are quite entitled to do this, if they wish, and it is good to see small-press publications being produced. But, sad to say, the results are not very imaginative (hardly groundbreaking stuff) and these days they might expect to get a lot of flak for being 'testosterone-heavy' or whatever. But now they have anti-PC discourse to draw upon. At a literary festival in 1996 they distributed handbills railing against their (anticipated) critics: 'Death to political correctness! Sworn enemy of creativity!'

To me this was a clear sign that they were cerebrally challenged. One thing about PC: it has provided a new kind of wordplay, new possibilities for linguistic inventiveness. Parodies of so-called 'politically correct' language are elaborate, convoluted euphemisms, exercises in absurdity. These playful flights of fancy often contain the structure pre-modifying adverbial + adjective – as in the well-known fairy tale: 'Melanin impoverished and the seven *vertically challenged* individuals'. Another thing about PC: it has to be said that it does add a certain finesse to verbal abuse, a genre in which finesse is often sadly lacking. 'Cerebrally challenged' sounds reasonably polite, doesn't it? So much better than 'stupid'.

Further reading

Sexism

For up-to-date accounts, see Mills (2008) and chapter 5 of DeFrancisco and Palczewski (2007). Hellinger and Pauwels (2007a) gives further detail and theoretical grounding. Also see Eckert and McConnell-Ginet (2003), especially chapters 2 and 7. The latter chapter is an account of categorization as a social practice. An interesting journal article on anti-feminist discourse and sexist 'hate speech' is Lillian (2007).

'PC' and language reform

Feminist language reform issues are covered in Pauwels (1998, 2003). Some recent readings on 'political correctness' are Talbot (2007a) and a special issue of the journal *Discourse & Society* (14 (1)(2003)).

References

Adams, Peter, Towns, Alison and Gavey, Nicola (1995) Dominance and entitlement: the rhetoric men use to discuss their violence towards women, *Discourse & Society* 6(3): 387–406.

Alibhai-Brown, Yasmin (1994) The great backlash. In Dunant 1994.

Andrews, Maggie and Talbot, Mary (eds.) (2000) *'All the World and her Husband': Women in 20th Century Consumer Culture*. London: Cassell.

Annette, John (1994) The culture wars on the American campus. In Dunant 1994.

Atkinson, Karen, Oerton, Sarah and Burns, Diane (1998) Happy families? Single mothers, the press and the politicians, *Capital and Class* 64: 1–11.

Azman, Azura (1986) Malaysian students' compliment responses. Unpublished term paper, Victoria University of Wellington, Wellington.

Bakhtin, Mikhail (1981) *The Dialogic Imagination*, trans. C. Emerson and M. Holquist. Austin: University of Texas Press.

Ballaster, Ros, Beetham, Margaret, Frazer, Elizabeth and Hebron, Sandra (1991) *Women's Worlds: Ideology, Femininity and the Woman's Magazine*. London: Macmillan.

Baron-Cohen, Simon (2003) *The Essential Difference: The Truth about the Male and Female Brain*. New York: Basic Books.

Barrett, Rusty (1994) 'She is *not* white woman': appropriation of white women's language by African American drag queens. In Mary Bucholtz, Anita C. Liang, Laurel A. Sutton and Caitlin Hines (eds.) *Cultural Performances: Proceedings of the Third Berkeley Women and Language Conference*. Berkeley, CA: Berkeley Women and Language Group, University of California.

Barrett, Rusty (1995) Supermodels of the world unite! Political economy and the language of performance among African American drag queens. In William Leap (ed.) *Beyond the Lavender Lexicon: Authenticity, Imagination and Appropriation in Lesbian and Gay Languages*. New York: Gordon and Breach.

Barrett, Rusty (1999) Indexing polyphonous identity in the speech of African American drag queens. In Bucholtz, Liang and Sutton 1999.

Barrett, Rusty (2004) As much as we use language: Lakoff's queer augury. In Lakoff and Bucholtz 2004.

244   *References*

Baxter, Judith (2003) *Positioning Gender in Discourse*. London: Palgrave Macmillan.

Baxter, Judith (ed.) (2006) *Speaking Out: The Female Voice in Public Contexts*. Basingstoke: Palgrave Macmillan.

Bean, Judith Mattson (2006) Gaining a public voice: a historical perspective on American women's public speaking. In Baxter 2006.

Beard, Henry and Cerf, Christopher (1992) *The Official Politically Correct Dictionary and Handbook*. London: Grafton.

Beetham, Margaret (1996) *A Magazine of her Own? Domesticity and Desire in the Woman's Magazine, 1800–1914*. London: Routledge.

Belkin, Lisa (2003) The opt-out revolution. *New York Times Magazine*, 26 Oct. pp. 42–7, 58, 85.

Bem, Sandra Lipsitz (1993) *The Lenses of Gender: Transforming the Debate on Sexual Inequality*. New Haven: Yale University Press.

Bennett, Lisa (2008) Media Hall of Shame calls out sexist offenders, *National NOW Foundation Times*, www.nowfoundation.org/news/fall-2008/hall_shame.html. Accessed 17 March 2009.

Bentham, Jeremy (1791) *Panopticon*. London: T. Payne.

Benwell, Bethan (2001) Male gossip and language play in the letters pages of men's lifestyle magazines, *Journal of Popular Culture* 34(4): 19–33.

Benwell, Bethan (2002) Is there anything 'new' about these lads? The textual and visual construction of masculinity in men's magazines. In Litosseliti and Sunderland 2002.

Benwell, Bethan (ed.) (2003) *Masculinity and Men's Lifestyle Magazines*. Oxford: Blackwell.

Benwell, Bethan (2004) Ironic discourse: evasive masculinity in British men's lifestyle magazines, *Men and Masculinities* 7(1): 3–21.

Benwell, Bethan (2005) 'Lucky this is anonymous': ethnographies of reception in men's lifestyle magazines', *Discourse & Society* 16(2): 147–72.

Benwell, Bethan and Stokoe, Elizabeth (2006) *Discourse and Identity*. Edinburgh: Edinburgh University Press.

Benyon, John (2002) *Masculinities and Culture*. Buckingham/Philadelphia: Open University Press.

Bergvall, Victoria (1996) Constructing and enacting gender through discourse: negotiating multiple roles as female engineering students. In Bergvall, Bing and Freed 1996.

Bergvall, Victoria and Remlinger, Kathryn (1996) Reproduction, resistance and gender in educational discourse: the role of critical discourse analysis. *Discourse & Society* 7(4): 453–79.

Bergvall, Victoria, Bing, Janet M. and Freed, Alice F. (eds) (1996) *Rethinking Language and Gender Research: Theory and Practice*. London: Longman.

Bing, Janet M. and Bergvall, Victoria L. (1996) The question of questions: beyond binary thinking. In Bergvall, Bing and Freed 1996.

Black, Maria and Coward, Rosalind (1990) Linguistic, social and sexual relations: a review of Dale Spender's *Man Made Language*. First published 1981, repr. in Cameron 1990 and 1998.

Bloom, Allan (1987) *The Closing of the American Mind: How Higher Education Has Failed Democracy and Impoverished the Souls of Today's Students*. New York: Simon & Schuster.

Bloor, Meriel and Bloor, Thomas (2007) *The Practice of Critical Discourse Analysis*. London: Hodder Arnold.

Blum-Kulka, Shoshana (1993) 'You gotta know how to tell a story': telling, tales and tellers in American and Israeli narrative events at dinner. *Language in Society* 22: 361–402.

Blum-Kulka, Shoshana (1997) *Dinner Talk: Cultural Patterns of Sociability and Socialization in Family Discourse*. Mahwah, NJ: Lawrence Erlbaum.

Bodine, Ann (1975) Sex differentiation in language. In Thorne and Henley 1975.

Born, Georgina (2002) Reflexivity and ambivalence: culture, creativity and government in the BBC, *Cultural Values* 6(1/2): 65–90.

Born, Georgina (2004) *Uncertain Vision: Birt, Dyke and the Reinvention of the BBC*. London: Secker & Warburg.

Brizendine, Louann (2006) *The Female Brain*. New York: Morgan Road Books.

Brockes, Emma (2008) After the tears and the triumphs, Hillary's last stand, *Guardian*, 1 March 2008.

Brown, Penelope and Levinson, Stephen (1987) *Universals in Language Usage: Politeness Phenomena*. Cambridge: Cambridge University Press.

Bucholtz, Mary (1996) Black feminist theory and African American women's linguistic practice. In Bergvall, Bing and Freed 1996.

Bucholtz, Mary (1999) Purchasing power: the gender and class imaginary on the shopping channel. In Bucholtz, Liang and Sutton 1999.

Bucholtz, Mary (2000) 'Thanks for stopping by': gender and power on the shopping channel. In Andrews and Talbot 2000.

Bucholtz, Mary and Hall, Kira (2004) Theorizing identity in language and sexuality research, *Language in Society* 33(4): 469–515.

Bucholtz Mary, Liang, Anita C. and Sutton, Laura (eds.) (1999) *Reinventing Identities: The Gendered Self in Discourse*. Oxford: Oxford University Press.

Butler, Judith (1993) *Bodies that Matter: On the Discursive Limits of 'Sex'*. London / New York: Routledge.

Butler, Judith (1997) *Excitable Speech: A Politics of the Performative*. New York: Routledge.

Butler, Judith (1999) *Gender Trouble: Feminism and the Subversion of Identity*, 10th Anniversary Edition. New York: Routledge.

Byerly, Carolyn and Ross, Karen (2006) *Women & Media: A Critical Introduction*. Oxford: Blackwell.

Caldas-Coulthard, Carmen Rosa (1996) 'Women who pay for sex. And enjoy it': transgression versus morality in women's magazines. In Caldas-Coulthard and Coulthard 1996.

Caldas-Coulthard, Carmen Rosa and Coulthard, Malcolm (eds.) (1996) *Texts and Practices: Readings in Critical Discourse Analysis*. London: Routledge.

Cameron, Deborah (ed.) (1990) *The Feminist Critique of Language: A Reader*. London: Routledge (2nd edn, 1998).

Cameron, Deborah (1992a) *Feminism and Linguistic Theory*, 2nd edn. London: Macmillan.

Cameron, Deborah (1992b) Review of Tannen 1991. In *Feminism and Psychology* 2–3: 465–89.

Cameron, Deborah (1995a) Rethinking language and gender studies: some issues for the 90s. In Mills 1995b.

Cameron, Deborah (1995b) *Verbal Hygiene*. London: Routledge.

Cameron, Deborah (1996) The language–gender interface: challenging co-optation. In Bergvall, Bing and Freed 1996.

Cameron, Deborah (1997) Performing gender identity: young men's talk and the construction of heterosexual masculinity. In Johnson and Meinhof 1997.

Cameron, Deborah (1998) 'Is there any ketchup, Vera?' Gender, power and pragmatics, *Discourse & Society* 9(4): 437–55.

Cameron, Deborah (2000) A self off the shelf? Consuming women's empowerment. In Andrews and Talbot 2000.

Cameron, Deborah (2006a) *On Language and Sexual Politics*. London: Routledge.

Cameron, Deborah (2006b) Degrees of consent: the Antioch College sexual offense policy. In Cameron and Kulik 2006.

Cameron, Deborah (2006c) Theorising the female voice in public contexts. In Baxter 2006.

Cameron, Deborah (2007) *The Myth of Mars and Venus*. Oxford: Oxford University Press

Cameron, Deborah and Coates, Jennifer (1988) Some problems in the sociolinguistic explanation of sex differences. In Coates and Cameron 1988.

Cameron, Deborah and Kulik, Don (2003) *Language and Sexuality*. Cambridge: Cambridge University Press.

Cameron, Deborah and Kulik, Don (eds.) (2006) *Language and Sexuality: A Reader*. London: Routledge.

Campbell-Kibler, Kathryn, Podesva, Robert J., Roberts, Sarah J. and Wong, Andrew (eds.) (2002) *Language and Sexuality: Contesting Meaning in Theory and Practice*. Stanford: CSLI Publications.

Carabine, Jean (2001) Unmarried motherhood 1830–1990: a genealogical analysis. In Wetherell, Taylor and Yates 2001.

Cheshire, Jenny and Trudgill, Peter (eds.) (1998) *The Sociolinguistics Reader*, vol. II: *Gender and Discourse*. London: Arnold.

Chodorow, Nancy (1978) *The Reproduction of Mothering: Psychoanalysis and the Sociology of Gender*. Berkeley: University of California Press.

Christie, Christine (2000) *Gender and Language: Towards a Feminist Pragmatics*. Edinburgh: Edinburgh University Press.

Clark, Kate (1992) The linguistics of blame. In Michael Toolan (ed.) *Language, Text and Context*. London: Routledge.

Clayman, Steven E. (2002) Tribune of the people: maintaining the legitimacy of aggressive journalism, *Media, Culture and Society*, 24: 197–216.

Clinton, Hillary Rodham (2003) *Living History*. London: Headline.

Coates, Jennifer (1988) Gossip revisited: language in all-female groups. In Coates and Cameron 1988.

Coates, Jennifer (1995) Language, gender and career. In Mills 1995b.

Coates, Jennifer (1996) *Women Talk: Conversation between Women Friends*. Oxford: Blackwell.

Coates, Jennifer (ed.) (1998) *Language and Gender: A Reader*. London: Routledge.

Coates, Jennifer (2003) *Men Talk: Stories in the Making of Masculinities*. Oxford: Blackwell.

Coates, Jennifer (2004) *Women, Men and Language*, 3rd edn. London: Longman.

Coates, Jennifer (2005) Masculinity, collaborative narrative and the heterosexual couple. In Thornborrow and Coates 2005.

Coates, Jennifer and Cameron, Deborah (eds.) (1988) *Women in their Speech Communities*. London: Longman.

Cockburn, Cynthia (1983) *Brothers: Male Dominance and Technological Change*. London: Pluto Press.

Collins, Patricia Hill (1990) *Black Feminist Thought*. Boston: Unwin Hyman.

Connell, Robert W. (1987) *Gender and Power: Society, the Person and Sexual Politics*. Cambridge: Polity.

Connell, Robert (2002) *Gender*. Cambridge: Polity.

Connell, Robert (2005) *Masculinities*, 2nd edn. Cambridge: Polity.

Cook, Guy (ed.) (2008) *The Language of Advertising*, 4 vols. London: Routledge.

Coupland, Justine (1996) Dating advertisements: discourses of the commodified self, *Discourse & Society* 7(2): 187–207.

Coupland, Justine (2007) Gendered discourses on the 'problem' of ageing: consumerized solutions, *Discourse and Communication* 1: 37–61.

Coupland, Nikolas and Jaworski, Adam (eds.) (1997) *Sociolinguistics: A Reader and Coursebook*. Basingstoke: Macmillan.

Coward, Rosalind (1984) *Female Desire: Women's Sexuality Today*. London: Paladin.

Cowhig, M. (1986) A quantitative analysis of phonological variables in the speech of Newcastle schoolchildren. Unpublished dissertation, Department of Speech, University of Newcastle upon Tyne.

Crawford, Mary (1995) *Talking Difference: On Gender and Language*. London: Sage.

Crittenden, Ann (2001) *The Price of Motherhood: Why the Most Important Job in the World is Still the Least Valued*. New York: Henry Holt.

Daly, Mary (1979) *Gyn/Ecology: The Metaethics of Radical Feminism*. London: The Women's Press.

Davies, Bronwen and Harré, Rom (1990) Positioning: the discursive production of selves, *Journal for the Theory of Social Behaviour* 20: 43–63.

Davies, Catherine Evans (2004) 'Women's Language' and Martha Stewart: from a room of one's own to a home of one's own to a corporation of one's own. In Lakoff and Bucholtz 2004.

Day, Elizabeth (2008) Mother-to-be who signalled the changing of the guard, *The Observer*, 20 April. Downloaded from www.guardian.co.uk on 20 April 2008.

DeFrancisco, Victoria L. (1991) The sounds of silence: how men silence women in marital relations, *Discourse & Society* 2(4): 413–23.

DeFrancisco, Victoria P. and Palczewski, Catherine H. (2007) *Communicating Gender Diversity: A Critical Approach*. London: Sage.

Delin, J. (2000) *The Language of Everyday Life*. London: Sage.

Dendrinos, Bessie and Pedro, Emilia Ribeiro (1994) Giving directions: the silent role of women. Paper presented at the 11th Sociolinguistics Symposium, Lancaster University.

Deuchar, Margaret (1987) Sociolinguistics. In John Lyons, Richard Coates, Margaret Deuchar and Gerald Gazdar (eds.) *New Horizons in Linguistics 2*. Harmondsworth: Penguin.

Donald, Robyn (1990) *No Guarantees*. London: Mills & Boon.

Donovan, Paul (1997) *All Our Todays*. London: Jonathan Cape.

D'Souza, Dinesh (1991) *Illiberal Education: The Politics of Race and Sex on Campus*. New York: Free Press.

Dunant, Sarah (ed.) (1994) *The War of the Words: The Political Correctness Debate*. London: Virago.

Dundes, Alan, Leach, Jerry and Özkök, Bora (1972) The strategy of Turkish boys' verbal dueling rhymes. In John Gumperz and Dell Hymes (eds.), *Directions in Sociolinguistics*. New York: Holt, Rinehart and Winston.

Dunn, Louise (1988) A study of tag questions in women's friendly interaction. Unpublished term paper, Lancaster University.

Eckert, Penelope (1989) The whole woman: sex and gender differences in variation, *Language Variation and Change* 1(1): 245–67.

Eckert, Penelope (1998) Gender and sociolinguistic variation. In Coates 1998.

Eckert, Penelope (2004) The good woman. In Lakoff and Bucholtz 2004.

Eckert, Penelope (2006) Vowels and nail polish: the emergence of linguistic style in the preadolescent heterosexual marketplace. In Cameron and Kulik 2006.

Eckert, Penelope and McConnell-Ginet, Sally (1992) Think practically and look locally: language and gender as community-based practice. *Annual Review of Anthropology* 21: 461–90.

Eckert, Penelope and McConnell-Ginet, Sally (2003) *Language and Gender*. Cambridge: Cambridge University Press.

Eder, Donna (1990) Serious and playful disputes: variation in conflict talk among female adolescents. In Allen D. Grimshaw (ed.) *Conflict Talk: Sociolinguistic Investigations of Arguments in Conversations*. Cambridge: Cambridge University Press.

Edley, Nigel (2001) Analysing masculinity: interpretative repertoires, ideological dilemmas and subject positions. In Wetherell, Taylor and Yates 2001.

Edwards, T. (1997) *Men in the Mirror: Men's Fashions, Masculinity and Consumer Society*. London: Cassell.

Edwards, Viv (1988) The speech of British black women in Dudley, West Midlands. In Coates and Cameron 1988.

Eggins, Suzanne and Slade, Diane (2005) *Analysing Casual Conversation*. London: Equinox.

Ehrlich, Susan (2001) *Representing Rape: Language and Sexual Consent*. London: Routledge.

Ehrlich, Susan (2002) Guest editorial: discourse, gender and sexual violence, *Discourse & Society* 13(1): 5–7.

Ehrlich, Susan (2003) Coercing gender: language in sexual assault adjudication processes. In Holmes and Meyerhoff 2003.

Ehrlich, Susan (2006) The discursive reconstruction of sexual consent. In Cameron and Kulik 2006.

Evans, Mary (2008) Why Hillary can't win, *Times Higher Education*, 13 March 2008, p. 26.

Fairclough, Norman L. (1992) *Discourse and Social Change*. Cambridge: Polity.

Fairclough, Norman L. (1995) *Media Discourse*. London: Edward Arnold.

Fairclough, Norman L. (1998) Political discourse in the media: an analytical framework. In Allan Bell and Paul Garrett (eds.) *Approaches to Media Discourse*. Oxford: Blackwell.

Fairclough, Norman L. (2001) *Language and Power*, 2nd edn. London: Longman.

Fairclough, Norman L. and Wodak, Ruth (1997) Critical discourse analysis. In Teun A. van Dijk (ed.) *Introduction to Discourse Analysis*. Newbury Park: Sage.

Fant, Gunnar (1966) A note on vocal tract size factors and non-uniform F-pattern scalings, *STL-QPSR* (4/1966): 22–30.

Farghal, Mohammed and Al-Khatib, Mahmoud A. (2001) Jordanian college students' responses to compliments: a pilot study, *Journal of Pragmatics* 33: 1485–502.

Fausto-Sterling, Anne (2000) *Sexing the Body: Gender Politics and the Construction of Sexuality*. New York: Basic Books.

Fausto-Sterling, Anne (2005) The bare bones of sex: part 1 – sex and gender, *Signs: Journal of Women in Culture and Society* 30(2): 1491–527.

Ferguson, Marjorie (1983) *Forever Feminine: Women's Magazines and the Cult of Femininity*. London: Heinemann.

Fine, Cordelia (2008) Will working mothers' brains explode? The popular new genre of neurosexism. *Neuroethics* 1: 69–72.

Finlayson, R. (1995) Women's language of respect: Isihlonipho sabafazi. In R. Mesthrie (ed.) *Language and Social History: Studies in South African Sociolinguistics*. Cape Town: David Philip.

Fishman, Pamela (1983) Interaction: the work women do. In Thorne, Kramarae and Henley 1983.

Fishman, Pamela (1998) Conversational insecurity. In Cameron 1998.

Fortune, D. and Fortune, Gretchen (1987) Karajá literary acquisition and sociocultural effects on a rapidly changing culture, *Journal of Multilingual and Multicultural Development* 8(6): 469–90.

Fortune, Gretchen (1995) Gender marking in Karajá. Paper presented at Lancaster University (Linguistics Dept), 10 March.

Foucault, Michel (1979) *Discipline and Punish: The Birth of the Prison*, trans. Alan Sheridan. New York: Random House.

Foucault, Michel (1986) *The Foucault Reader*, ed. Paul Rainbow. Harmondsworth. Penguin.

Foucault, Michel (1990) *The History of Sexuality*, trans. Robert Hurley. Harmondsworth: Penguin.

Freed, Alice (1992) We understand perfectly: a critique of Tannen's view of cross-sex communication. In Hall, Bucholtz and Moonwomon 1992.

Freed, Alice (1996a) Language and gender research in an experimental setting. In Bergvall, Bing and Freed 1996.

Freed, Alice (1996b) The language of pregnancy: women and medical experience. In Natasha Warner, Jocelyn Ahlers, Leela Bilmes, Monica Oliver, Suzanne Wertheim and Melinda Chen (eds.) *Women and Belief Systems: Proceedings of the 1996 Berkeley Women and Language Conference*. Berkeley: Berkeley Women and Language Group.

Freed, Alice (1999) Communities of practice and pregnant women: is there a connection? *Language in Society* 28 (2): 257–71.

Freed, Alice (2003) Epilogue: reflections on language and gender research. In Holmes and Meyerhoff 2003.

Frost, Julie A., Binder, Jeffrey R., Springer, Jane A., et al. (1999) Language processing is strongly left lateralized in both sexes: evidence from functional MRI, *Brain* 122: 199–208.

Gal, Susan (1979) *Language Shift: Social Determinants of Language Change in Bilingual Austria*. New York: Academic Press.

Gardiner, Judith Kegan (ed.) (2002) *Masculinity Studies and Feminist Theory: New Directions*. New York: Columbia University Press.

Gill, Rosalind (2007) *Gender and the Media*. Cambridge: Polity.

Goffman, Erving (1978) *Gender Advertisements*. London: Macmillan.

Goffman, Erving (1981) *Forms of Talk*. Oxford: Blackwell.

Goodwin, Marjorie Harness (1980) Directive-response speech sequences in girls' and boys' task activities. In McConnell-Ginet, Borker and Furman 1980.

Goodwin, Marjorie Harness (1993) *He-Said-She-Said*. Bloomington: Indiana University Press.

Goodwin, Marjorie Harness (2003) The relevance of ethnicity, class, and gender in children's peer negotiations. In Holmes and Meyerhoff 2003.

Goodwin, Marjorie Harness (2007) *The Hidden Life of Girls: Games of Stance, Status and Exclusion*. Oxford: Blackwell.

Gough, Val and Talbot, Mary (1996) 'Guilt over games boys play': coherence as a focus for examining the constitution of heterosexual subjectivity. In Caldas-Coulthard and Coulthard 1996.

Graddol, David and Swann, Joan (1983) Speaking fundamental frequency: some social and physical correlates, *Language and Speech* 26: 351–66.

Graddol, David and Swann, Joan (1989) *Gender Voices*. Oxford: Blackwell.

Guendouzi, Jackie (2001) 'You'll think we're always bitching': the functions of cooperativity and competition in women's gossip, *Discourse Studies* 3: 29–51.

Gumperz, John (ed.) (1982) *Language and Social Identity*. Cambridge: Cambridge University Press.

Halberstam, Judith (1998) *Female Masculinity*. Durham, NC: Duke University Press.

Hall, Kira (1995) Lip service on the fantasy lines. In Hall and Bucholtz 1995.

Hall, Kira (2003) Exceptional speakers. In Holmes and Meyerhoff 2003.

Hall, Kira and Bucholtz, Mary (eds.) (1995) *Gender Articulated: Language and the Socially-Constructed Self*. London: Routledge.

Hall, Kira, Bucholtz, Mary and Moonwomon, Birch (eds.) (1992) *Locating Power: Proceedings of the Second Berkeley Women and Language Conference*. Berkeley: Berkeley Women and Language Group.

Hall, Stuart (1994) Some 'politically incorrect' pathways through PC. In Dunant 1994.

Hall, Stuart (1997) The spectacle of the 'Other'. In Stuart Hall (ed.) *Representation: Cultural Representations and Signifying Practices*. London: Sage.

Halpern, D. F. (1992) *Sex Differences in Cognitive Abilities*. Hillsdale, NJ: Lawrence Erlbaum.

Hammersley, M. (1997) On the foundations of critical discourse analysis, *Language and Communication* 17(3): 237–48.

Hanke, Robert (1992) Redesigning men: hegemonic masculinity in transition. In Steve Craig (ed.) *Men, Masculinity and the Media*. London: Sage.

Hanong, Puleng (2006) Culture, voice and the public sphere: a critical analysis of the female voices on sexuality in indigenous South African society. In Baxter 2006.

Harrison, Claire (2008) Real men do wear mascara: advertising discourse and masculine identity, *Critical Discourse Studies* 5(1): 55–74.

Harvey, Keith and Shalom, Celia (eds.) (1997) *Language and Desire*. London: Routledge.

Hearn, Jeff (1998) *The Violences of Men*. London: Sage.

Hellinger, Marlis and Pauwels, Anne (2007a) Language and sexism. In Hellinger and Pauwels 2007b.

Hellinger, Marlis and Pauwels, Anne (eds.) (2007b) *Language and Communication: Diversity and Change*. Berlin: Mouton de Gruyter.

Henton, C. G. and Bladon, A. W. (1985) Breathiness in normal female speech: inefficiency versus desirability, *Language and Communication* 5: 221–7.

Herbert, James (1979) *Lair*. London: New English Library.

Hermes, Joke (1995) *Reading Women's Magazines: An Analysis of Everyday Media Use*. Cambridge: Polity.

Hewitt, Roger (1997) 'Box-out' and 'Taxing'. In Johnson and Meinhof 1997.

Higgins, Michael (2010) The 'public inquisitor' as media celebrity, *Cultural Politics* 6(1): 93–110.

Hogben, Susan and Coupland, Justine (2000) Egg seeks sperm. End of story. . .? Articulating gay parenting in small ads for reproductive partners, *Discourse & Society* 11(4): 459–85.

Holmes, Janet (1984) Hedging your bets and sitting on the fence: some evidence for hedges as support structures, *Te Reo* (27): 47–62.

Holmes, Janet (1986) Compliments and compliment responses in New Zealand English, *Anthropological Linguistics* 28(4): 485–508.

Holmes, Janet (1992) *An Introduction to Sociolinguistics*. London: Longman.

Holmes, Janet (1995) *Women, Men and Politeness*. London: Longman.

Holmes, Janet (2000) Politeness, power and provocation: how humour functions in the workplace, *Discourse Studies* 2(2): 159–85.

Holmes, Janet (2005) Power and discourse at work: is gender relevant? In Lazar 2005a.

Holmes, Janet (2006) *Gendered Talk at Work*. Oxford: Blackwell.

Holmes, Janet and Meyerhoff, Miriam (eds.) (2003) *The Handbook of Language and Gender*. Oxford: Blackwell.

Holmes, Janet and Schnurr, Stephanie (2005) Politeness, humor and gender in the workplace: negotiating norms and identity contestation, *Journal of Politeness Research* 1(1): 121–49.

Holmes, Janet and Stubbe, Maria (2003a) 'Feminine' workplaces: stereotype and reality. In Holmes and Meyerhoff 2003.

Holmes, Janet and Stubbe, Maria (2003b) *Power and Politeness in the Workplace: A Sociolinguistic Analysis of Talk at Work*. London: Longman.

hooks, bell (1984) *Feminist Theory: From Margin to Center*. Boston: South End Press.

House of Commons Information Office (2009) *Some Traditions and Customs of the House* (Factsheet G7). Downloaded from www.parliament.uk/about/how/role/customs/traditions.cfm on 19 February 2009.

Humm, Maggie (1989) *The Dictionary of Feminist Theory*. Hemel Hempstead: Harvester Wheatsheaf.

Hutchby, Ian (2006) *Media Talk: Conversation Analysis and the Study of Broadcasting*. Maidenhead: Open University Press.

Hyde, Janet Shibley and McKinley, Nita (1997) Gender differences in cognition: results from meta-analyses. In P. J. Caplan, Mary Crawford, Janet Shibley Hyde and J. T. E. Richardson (eds.) *Gender Differences in Human Cognition*. New York: Oxford University Press.

Jackson, Peter, Stevenson, Nick and Brooks, Kate (2001) *Making Sense of Men's Magazines*. Cambridge: Polity.

Jagger, Gill (2008) *Judith Butler: Sexual Politics, Social Change and the Power of the Performative*. London: Routledge.

James, Deborah (1996) Women, men and prestige speech forms: a critical review. In Bergvall, Bing and Freed 1996.

Jamieson, Kathleen (1988) *Eloquence in an Electronic Age*. Oxford: Oxford University Press.

Jenkins, N. and Cheshire, Jenny (1990) Gender issues in the GCSE oral English examination, part I, *Language and Education* 4(4): 261–92.

Jespersen, Otto (1922) *Language: Its Nature, Development and Origin*. London: Allen & Unwin.

Johnson, Sally and Finlay, Frank (1997) Do men gossip? An analysis of football talk on television. In Johnson and Meinhof 1997.

Johnson, Sally and Meinhof, Ulrike Hanna (eds.) (1997) *Language and Masculinity*. Oxford: Blackwell.

Johnstone, Barbara (1990) *Stories, Community and Place: Narratives from Middle America*. Bloomington: Indiana University Press.

Johnstone, Barbara (1993) Community and contest: Midwestern men and women creating their worlds in conversational storytelling. In Deborah Tannen (ed.) *Gender and Conversational Interaction*. Oxford: Oxford University Press.

Jones, Daniel (1909) *The Pronunciation of English*. Cambridge: Cambridge University Press.

Jones, Deborah (1990) Gossip: notes on women's oral culture. In Cameron 1990. (Reprinted from *Women's Studies International Quarterly* 3(1980): 193–8.)

Jugaku, Akiko (1979) *Nihongo to onna* (The Japanese language and women). Tokyo: Iwanami.

Jule, Allyson (2006) Silence as morality: lecturing at a theological college. In Baxter 2006.

Kendall, Shari (2003) Creating gendered demeanors of authority at work and at home. In Holmes and Meyerhoff 2003.

Kendall, Shari (2006a) 'Honey, I'm home': framing in family dinnertime homecomings, *Interdisciplinary Journal for the Study of Discourse* 26: 411–41.

Kendall, Shari (2006b) Positioning the female voice within work and family. In Baxter 2006.

Kendall, Shari and Tannen, Deborah (1997) Gender and language in the workplace. In Ruth Wodak (ed.) *Gender and Discourse*. London: Sage.

Kiær, Sarah (1990) The construction of motherhood in the discourse of antenatal care. Unpublished MA dissertation, Lancaster University.

Kiesling, Scott Fabius (1997) Power and the language of men. In Johnson and Meinhof 1997.

Kiesling, Scott Fabius (2006) Playing the straight man: displaying and maintaining male heterosexuality in discourse. In Cameron and Kulik 2006.

Kimball, Roger (1990) *Tenured Radicals: How Politics Has Corrupted Higher Education*. New York: Harper & Row.

Kimmel, Michael, Hearn, Jeff and Connell, Robert (eds.) (2004) *Handbook of Studies on Men and Masculinities*. London: Sage.

King, Oona (2005) Review of Somes et al. *Women in Parliament: The New Suffragettes*. Downloaded from www.oonaking.com/ on 17 March 2009.

Kitzinger, Celia (2000) Doing feminist conversation analysis, *Feminism and Psychology* 10: 163–93.

Kitzinger, Celia (2006) 'Speaking as a heterosexual': (how) does sexuality matter for talk-in-interaction? In Cameron and Kulik 2006.

Kitzinger, Celia and Frith, H. (1999) Just say no? The use of conversation analysis in developing a feminist perspective on sexual refusal, *Discourse & Society* 10(3): 293–316.

Knecht, S., Deppe, M., Dräger, B., et al. (2000) Language lateralization in healthy right-handers, *Brain* 123: 74–81.

Kramarae, Cheris (1981) *Women and Men Speaking*. Rowley, MA: Newbury House.

Kramarae, Cheris and Treichler, Paula (1985) *A Feminist Dictionary*. London: Pandora.

Kress, Gunther (1985) *Linguistic Processes in Sociocultural Practice*. Victoria: Deakin University Press.

Kuiper, Koenraad (1991) Sporting formulae in New Zealand English, two models of male solidarity. In Jenny Cheshire (ed.) *English around the World: Sociolinguistic Perspectives*. Cambridge: Cambridge University Press.

Kuo, S. (2008) A woman warrior or a forgotten concubine? Verbal construction of a feminist politician in Taiwan. In Doreen Wu (ed.) *Discourses of Cultural China in the Globalizing Age*. Hong Kong: Hong Kong University Press.

Labov, William (1966) *The Social Stratification of English in New York City*. Washington, DC: Center for Applied Linguistics.

Labov, William (1972a) *Language in the Inner City*. Philadelphia: University of Pennsylvania Press.

Labov, William (1972b) Rules for ritual insults. In T. Kochman (ed.) *Rappin' and Stylin' Out*. Chicago: University of Illinois Press.

Labov, William (1982) Objectivity and commitment in linguistic science: the case of the Black English trial in Ann Arbor. *Language in Society* 11: 165–201.

Labov, William (1990) The intersection of sex and social class in the course of linguistic change, *Language, Variation and Change* 2(2): 205–54.

Labov, William and Waletzky, J. (1967) Narrative analysis: oral versions of personal experience. In J. Helm (ed.) *Essays on the Verbal and Visual Arts*. Seattle: University of Washington Press.

Lakoff, Robin (1975) *Language and Woman's Place*. New York: Harper & Row.

Lakoff, Robin (1995) Cries and whispers: the shattering of the silence. In Hall and Bucholtz 1995.

Lakoff, Robin (2000) *The Language War*. Berkeley: University of California Press.

Lakoff, Robin (2003) Language, gender, and politics: putting 'women' and 'power' in the same sentence. In Holmes and Meyerhoff 2003.

Lakoff, Robin (2004) *Language and Woman's Place*. In Lakoff and Bucholtz 2004.

Lakoff, Robin and Bucholtz, Mary (ed.) (2004) *Language and Woman's Place: Text and Commentaries*. Oxford: Oxford University Press.

Lave, J. and Wenger, E. (1991) *Situated Learning: Legitimate Peripheral Participation*. Cambridge: Cambridge University Press.

Laver, John (1994) *Principles of Phonetics*. Cambridge: Cambridge University Press.

Layard, Richard and Dunn, Judy (2009) *A Good Childhood: Searching for Values in a Competitive Age*. Harmondsworth: Penguin.

Lazar, Michelle (2000) Gender, discourse and semiotics: the politics of parenthood representations, *Discourse & Society* 11(3): 373–409.

Lazar, Michelle (ed.) (2005a) *Feminist Critical Discourse Analysis: Gender, Power and Ideology in Discourse*. London: Palgrave Macmillan.

Lazar, Michelle (2005b) Performing state fatherhood: the remaking of hegemony. In Lazar 2005a.

Lazar, Michelle (2007) Feminist critical discourse analysis: articulating a feminist discourse praxis, *Critical Discourse Studies* 4(2): 141–64.

Lees, S. (1997) *Ruling Passions: Sexual Violence, Reputation, and the Law*. Buckingham: Open University Press.

Leman, Joy (1980) 'The advice of a real friend': codes of intimacy and oppression in women's magazines 1937–1955, *Women's Studies Quarterly* 3: 63–78.

Lillian, Donna (2007) A thorn by any other name: sexist discourse as hate speech, *Discourse & Society* 18(6): 719–40.

Litosseliti, Lia (2006) *Gender and Language: Theory and Practice*. London: Hodder Arnold.

Litosseliti, Lia and Sunderland, Jane (eds.) (2002) *Gender Identity and Discourse Analysis*. Amsterdam/Philadelphia: John Benjamins

Livia, Anna (2002) Camionneuses s'abstenir: lesbian community creation through the personals. In Campbell-Kibler et al. 2002.

Livia, Anna and Hall, Kira (1997) *Queerly Phrased: Language, Gender, and Sexuality*. Oxford / New York: Oxford University Press.

Lloyd, Moya (2007) *Judith Butler*. Cambridge: Polity.

Lorenzo-Dus, Nuria (2001) Compliment responses among British and Spanish university students: a contrastive study, *Journal of Pragmatics* 33: 107–27.

Lorenzo-Dus, Nuria (2009) *Television Discourse: Analysing Language in the Media*. London: Palgrave Macmillan.

McConnell-Ginet, Sally, Borker, Ruth and Furman, Nellie (eds.) (1980) *Women and Language in Literature and Society*. New York: Praeger.

Macdonald, Myra (1995) *Representing Women: Myths of Femininity in the Popular Media*. London: Arnold.

McElhinny, Bonnie S. (1995) Challenging hegemonic masculinities: female and male police officers handling domestic violence. In Hall and Bucholtz 1995.

McElhinny, Bonnie S. (2002) Armed robbers, assholes and agency: ideology in the interactions of police officers. In Sarah Benor, Mary Rose, Devyani Sharma, Julie Sweetland and Qing Zhang (eds.) *Gendered Practices in Language*. Stanford: CSLI Publications.

MacErlane, Siobhan (1989) The ideology at work in a feature article from *New Woman*: 'Learning to talk . . . to your lover', *New Woman* tells us how. Human Communication Research Project. Unpublished BA dissertation, Lancaster University.

MacGregor, Sue (2002) *A Woman of Today*. London: Headline.

Machin, David and Thornborrow, Joanne (2003) Branding and discourse: the case of *Cosmopolitan, Discourse & Society* 14(4): 453–72.

Machin, David and Thornborrow, Joanne (2006) Lifestyle and the depoliticisation of agency: sex as power in women's magazines, *Social Semiotics* 16(1): 173–88.

Machin, David and Van Leeuwen, Theo (2009) Toys as discourse: children's war toys and the war on terror, *Critical Discourse Studies* 6(1): 51–63.

MacKinnon, Catherine (1982) Feminism, Marxism, method, and the state: an agenda for theory, *Signs* 7(3): 515–44.

MacLean, J. (1995) An afternoon with my if-there-were-a-laws. In K. Jay (ed.) *Dyke Life: A Celebration of the Lesbian Experience*. New York: HarperCollins.

McLoughlin, Linda (1993) Reverse discourse: young women's sex talk. Coping tactics to deal with sexual harassment and challenges to displays of masculinity. Unpublished MA dissertation, Lancaster University.

McLoughlin, Linda (2000) *The Language of Magazines*. London: Routledge

McLoughlin, Linda (2008) The construction of female sexuality in the 'sex special': transgression or containment in magazines' information on sexuality for girls? *Gender and Language* 2(2): 171–96.

McRobbie, Angela (1978) *Jackie*: an ideology of adolescent femininity. Occasional paper, Centre for Contemporary Cultural Studies (CCCS), University of Birmingham.

Maitse, T (2000) Revealing silence: voices from South Africa. In S. Jacobs, R. Jacobson and J. Marchbank (eds.) *States of Conflict: Gender, Violence and Resistance*. London: Zed Books.

Maltz, Daniel and Borker, Ruth (1982) A cultural approach to male–female miscommunication. In Gumperz 1982.

Marra, Meredith, Schnurr, Stephanie and Holmes, Janet (2006) Effective leadership in New Zealand workplaces: balancing gender and role. In Baxter 2006.

Marshall, Harriette and Woollett, Anne (2000) Fit to reproduce? The regulative role of pregnancy texts, *Feminism and Psychology* 10(3): 351–66.

Martin, Patricia Yancey (2003) 'Said and done' versus 'saying and doing': gendering practices, practicing gender at work, *Gender & Society* 17(3): 342–66.

Martín Rojo, Luisa and Esteban, Concepción Gómez (2005) The gender of power: the female style in labour organizations. In Lazar 2005.

Martyna, Wendy (1983) Beyond the he/man approach: the case for nonsexist language. In Thorne, Kramarae and Henley 1983.

Matheson, Donald (2005) *Media Discourses: Analysing Media Texts*. Maidenhead: Open University Press.

Mesthrie, Rajend, Swann, Joan, Deumert, Andrea and Leap, William (2000) *Introducing Sociolinguistics*. Edinburgh: Edinburgh University Press.

Mey, Jacob L. (1989) 'Saying it don't make it so': the 'una grande libre' of language politics, *Multilingua* 8(4): 333–55.

Mills, Sara (ed.) (1994) *Gendering the Reader*. Hemel Hempstead: Harvester Wheatsheaf.

Mills, Sara (1995a) *Feminist Stylistics*. London: Routledge.

Mills, Sara (ed.) (1995b) *Language and Gender: Interdisciplinary Perspectives*. London: Longman.

Mills, Sara (2002) Rethinking politeness, impoliteness and gender identity. In Litosseliti and Sunderland 2002.

Mills, Sara (2003) *Gender and Politeness*. Cambridge: Cambridge University Press.

Mills, Sara (2005) Gender and impoliteness, *Journal of Politeness Research* 1(2): 263–80.

Mills, Sara (2008) *Language and Sexism*. Cambridge: Cambridge University Press.

Milroy, James and Milroy, Lesley (1993) Mechanisms of change in urban dialects: the role of class, social network and gender, *International Journal of Applied Linguistics* 3(1): 57–77.

Milroy, Lesley (1980) *Language and Social Networks*. Oxford: Blackwell.

Milroy, Lesley (1992) New perspectives in the analysis of sex differentiation in language. In K. Bolton and H. Kwok (eds.), *Sociolinguistics Today: International Perspectives*. London: Routledge.

Moeketsi, R. (1999) *Discourse in a Multilingual and Multicultural Courtroom: A Court Interpreter's Guide*. Pretoria: J. L. van Schaik.

Moon, Rosamund (1989) Objective or objectionable? Ideological aspects of dictionaries, *English Language Research Journal* 3: 59–94.

Morrish, Liz and Sauntson, Helen (2007) *New Perspectives on Language and Sexual Identity*. London: Palgrave Macmillan.

Mouffe, C. (1992) Feminism, citizenship and radical democratic politics. In Judith Butler and J. W. Scott (eds.) *Feminists Theorise the Political*. New York: Routledge.

Mullany, Louise (2007) *Gendered Discourse in the Professional Workplace*. Basingstoke: Palgrave Macmillan.

Murray, Charles and Herrnstein, Richard (1994) *The Bell Curve: Intelligence and Class Structure in American Life*. New York: Free Press.

Nakamura, Momoko (2005) 'Let's dress a little girlishly!' or 'Conquer short pants!' Constructing gendered communities in fashion magazines for young people. In Shigeko Okamoto and Janet S. Shibamoto Smith (eds.) *Japanese Language, Gender and Ideology: Cultural Models and Real People*. Oxford: Oxford University Press

Neff van Aertselaer, JoAnne (1997) 'Aceptarlo con hombría': representations of masculinity in Spanish political discourse. In Johnson and Meinhof 1997.

Nichols, Patricia (1983) Linguistic options and choices for black women in the rural south. In Thorne, Kramarae and Henley 1983.

Nilsen, Aileen P., Bosmajian, Haig, Gershuny, H. Lee and Stanley, Julia P. (eds.) (1977) *Sexism and Language*. Urbana, IL: National Council of Teachers of English.

Oakley, Ann (1972) *Sex, Gender and Society*. London: Temple Smith.

Oakley, Ann (1982) *Subject Women*. London: Fontana.

Oakley, Ann (1984) *The Captured Womb: A History of the Medical Care of Pregnant Women*. Oxford: Blackwell.

Ochs, Elinor and Capps, Lisa (2001) *Living Narrative: Creating Lives in Everyday Storytelling*. Cambridge, MA: Harvard University Press.

Ochs, Elinor and Taylor, Carolyn (1992a) Family narrative as political activity. *Discourse & Society* 3(3): 301–40.

Ochs, Elinor and Taylor, Carolyn (1992b) Mothers' role in the everyday reconstruction of 'Father knows best'. In Hall, Bucholtz and Moonwomon 1992.

Ochs, Elinor and Taylor, Carolyn (1995) The 'Father knows best' dynamic in dinnertime narratives. In Hall and Bucholtz 1995.

Okamoto, Shigeko (1995) 'Tasteless' Japanese: less 'feminine' speech among young Japanese women. In Hall and Bucholtz 1995.

Orton, Harold (1962) *Survey of English Dialects: Introduction*. Leeds: Edward Arnold.

Osterman, Ana Cristina and Keller-Cohen, Deborah (1998) 'Good girls go to heaven; bad girls. . .' learn to be good: quizzes in American and Brazilian teenage girls' magazines, *Discourse & Society* 9(4): 531–58.

Page, Ruth (2003) 'Cherie: lawyer, wife, mum': contradictory patterns of representation in media reports of Cherie Booth/Blair, *Discourse & Society* 14(5): 559–79.

Paugh, Amy (2005) Learning about work at dinnertime: language socialization in dual-earner American families, *Discourse & Society* 16(1): 55–78.

Pauwels, Anne (1998) *Women Changing Language*. London: Longman.

Pauwels, Anne (2003) Linguistics sexism and feminist linguistic activism. In Holmes and Meyerhoff 2003.

Pei Tian (2006) The performance of hegemonic masculinity in all-male conversation. Unpublished term paper, University of Sunderland.

Pelissier Kingfisher, Catherine (1996a) *Women in the American Welfare Trap*. Philadelphia: University of Pennsylvania Press.

Pelissier Kingfisher, Catherine (1996b) Women on welfare: conversational sites of acquiescence and dissent, *Discourse & Society* 7(4): 531–57.

Philips, Susan, Steele, Susan and Tanz, Christine (eds.) (1987) *Language, Gender and Sex in Comparative Perspective*. Cambridge: Cambridge University Press.

Piercy, Marge (1979) *Woman on the Edge of Time*. London: Women's Press. First published 1976.

Piercy, Marge (1987) *Small Changes*. Harmondsworth: Penguin. First published 1972.

Pilkington, Jane (1998) Don't try and make out that I'm nice! The different strategies women and men use when gossiping. In Coates 1998.

Polanyi, Livia (1985) *Telling the American Story*. Norwood, NJ: Ablex.

Pujolar, Joan (1997a) Masculinities in a multilingual setting. In Johnson and Meinhof 1997.

Pujolar, Joan (1997b) *De què vas, tio? Gènere i llengua en la cultura juvenil*. Barcelona: Editorial Empúries.

Pujolar, Joan (2001) *Gender, Heteroglossia and Power: A Sociolinguistic Study of Youth Culture*. Berlin: Mouton de Gruyter.

Richardson, Kay (1997) Twenty-first-century commerce: the case of QVC, *Text* 17(2): 199–223.

Richardson, Niall (2009) Effeminophobia, misogyny and queer friendship: the cultural themes of Channel 4's *Playing it Straight*, *Sexualities* 12: 525–44.

Rigg, L. (1987) A quantitative study of sociolinguistic patterns of variation in adult Tyneside speakers. Unpublished dissertation, Department of Speech, University of Newcastle upon Tyne.

Rivers, Caryl (2007) *Selling Anxiety: How the News Media Scare Women*. Lebanon, NH: University Press of New England.

Romaine, Suzanne (1994) *Language in Society: An Introduction to Sociolinguistics*. Oxford: Oxford University Press.

Romaine, Suzanne (2003) Variation in language and gender. In Holmes and Meyerhoff 2003.

Rúdolfsdóttir, Annadis Greta (2000) 'I am not a patient, and I am not a child': the institutionalization and experience of pregnancy, *Feminism and Psychology* 10(3): 337–50.

Sachs, Jacqueline (1975) Cues to the identification of sex in children's speech. In Thorne and Henley 1975.

Sachs, Jacqueline, Lieberman, P. and Erickson, D. (1973) Anatomical and cultural determinants of male and female speech. In R. W. Shuy and R. W. Fasold (eds.) *Language Attitudes: Current Trends and Prospects*. Washington, DC: Georgetown University Press.

Sacks, Harvey (1995) *Lectures on Conversation: Volume I*. Oxford: Blackwell.

Salih, Sara (2002) *Judith Butler*. London: Routledge.

Salih, Sara (ed.) with Butler, Judith (2004) *The Judith Butler Reader*. London: Routledge.

Sapir, Edward (1929) The status of linguistics as a science, *Language* 5: 207–14.

Schulz, Muriel (1975) The semantic derogation of women. In Thorne and Henley 1975.

Scott, Joan W. (1995) The campaign against political correctness: what's really at stake. In Williams 1995.

Searle, Denise (1988) The National Union of Journalists' attitude to controlling media sexism. In Gail Chester and Julienne Dickey (eds.), *Feminism and Censorship*. Bridport, Dorset: Prism.

Segal, Lynne (1994) *Is the Future Female? Troubled Thoughts on Contemporary Feminism*. London: Virago. First published 1987.

Segal, Lynne (2006) *Slow Motion: Changing Masculinities, Changing Men*, 3rd edn. Basingstoke: Palgrave Macmillan.

Sellers, Patricia (2003) Power: do women really want it? *Fortune*, 13 Oct., pp. 80–100.

Shalom, Celia (1997) That great supermarket of desire: attributes of the desired other in dating advertisements. In Harvey and Shalom 1997.

Shaw, Sylvia (2000) Language, gender and floor apportionment in political debates, *Discourse & Society* 11(2): 401–18.

Shaw, Sylvia (2006) Governed by the rules? The female voice in parliamentary debates. In Baxter 2006.

Silberstein, Sandra (1988) Ideology as process: gender ideology in courtship narratives. In Todd and Fisher 1988.

Simpson, Mark (2006) Here come the mirror men, *marksimpson.com*, Accessed 22 June 2008 www.marksimpson.com/pages/journalism/mirror_men.html.

Sinclair, Amanda (1998) *Doing Leadership Differently: Gender, Power and Sexuality in a Changing Business Culture*. Melbourne: Melbourne University Press.

Sinfield, Alan (1994) *The Wilde Century: Effeminacy, Oscar Wilde and the Queer Moment*. London: Cassell.

Smith, Dorothy (1988) Femininity as discourse. In Leslie G. Roman and Linda K. Christian-Smith (eds.) *Becoming Feminine: The Politics of Popular Culture*. New York: Falmer Press.

Smith, Philip (1985) *Language, the Sexes and Society*. Oxford: Blackwell.

Somerset, Laura (2006) Whose experience is it anyway? Unpublished term paper, University of Sutherland.

Somes, Boni with Moran, Margaret and Lovenduski, Joni (2005) *Women in Parliament: The New Suffragettes*. London: Politico.

Speer, Susan (2005) *Gender Talk: Feminism, Discourse and Conversation Analysis*. London: Routledge.

Spender, Dale (1985) *Man Made Language*, 2nd edn. London: Routledge & Kegan Paul.

Spender, Dale (1995) *Nattering on the Net: Women, Power and Cyberspace*. Melbourne: Spinifex.

Stubbs, Michael (1997) Whorf's children: critical comments on critical discourse analysis. In A. Ryan and A. Wray (eds.) *Evolving Models of Language*. Clevedon: British Association for Applied Linguistics / Multilingual Matters.

Sunderland, Jane (2002) Baby entertainer, bumbling assistant and line manager: discourses of paternal identity in parentcraft texts. In Litosseliti and Sunderland 2002.

Sunderland, Jane (2004) *Gendered Discourses*. London: Palgrave Macmillan.

Sutton, Laurel A. (1995) Bitches and skankly hobags: the place of women in contemporary slang. In Hall and Bucholtz 1995.

Swann, Joan (2003) Schooled language: language and gender in educational settings. In Holmes and Meyerhoff 2003.

Syal, Meera (1994) PC: GLC. In Dunant 1994.

Talbot, Mary (1992a) 'I wish you'd stop interrupting me!': interruptions and asymmetries in speaker-rights in 'equal encounters', *Journal of Pragmatics* 18: 451–66.

Talbot, Mary (1992b) The construction of gender in a teenage magazine. In Norman Fairclough (ed.) *Critical Language Awareness*. London: Longman.

Talbot, Mary (1995a) *Fictions at Work: Language and Social Practice in Fiction*. London: Longman.

Talbot, Mary (1995b) A synthetic sisterhood: false friends in a teenage magazine. In Hall and Bucholtz 1995.

Talbot, Mary (1997a) 'An explosion deep inside her': women's desire in popular romance fiction. In Harvey and Shalom 1997.

Talbot, Mary (1997b) 'Randy fish boss branded a stinker': coherence and the construction of masculinities in a British tabloid newspaper. In Johnson and Meinhof 1997.

Talbot, Mary (2003) Gender stereotypes: reproduction and challenge. In Holmes and Meyerhoff 2003.

Talbot, Mary (2005) Choosing to refuse to be a victim: 'Power feminism' and the intertextuality of victimhood and choice. In Lazar 2005.

Talbot, Mary (2007a) Political correctness and freedom of speech. In Hellinger and Pauwels 2007b.

Talbot, Mary (2007b) *Media Discourse: Representation and Interaction*. Edinburgh: Edinburgh University Press.

Talbot, Mary (2008) 'It's good to talk'? The undermining of feminism in a *British Telecom* advertisement. In Cook 2008, vol. III.

Talbot, Mary, Atkinson, Karen and Atkinson, David (eds.) (2003) *Language and Power in the Modern World*. Edinburgh: Edinburgh University Press.

Tannen, Deborah (1984) *Conversational Style: Analyzing Talk among Friends.* Norwood, NJ: Ablex.

Tannen, Deborah (1986) *That's Not What I Meant*. New York: Dent.

Tannen, Deborah (1990) Gender differences in conversational coherence: physical alignment and topical cohesion. In Bruce Dorval (ed.), *Conversational Organization and its Development*. Norwood, NJ: Ablex.

Tannen, Deborah (1991) *You Just Don't Understand*. London: Virago.

Tannen, Deborah (1994) *Gender and Discourse*. Oxford: Oxford University Press.

Tannen, Deborah (1995) *Talking from 9 to 5*. London: Virago.

Tetlow, Helen (1991) The re-invented man: constructions of masculinity in one issue of *Arena* magazine. Unpublished MA dissertation, Lancaster University.

Tew, Marjorie (1990) *Safer Childbirth? A Critical History of Maternity Care*. London: Chapman and Hall.

Thomas, Beth (1988) Differences of sex and sects: linguistic variation and social networks in a Welsh mining village. In Coates and Cameron 1988.

Thornborrow, Joanne and Coates, Jennifer (eds.) (2005) *The Sociolinguistics of Narrative*. Amsterdam: John Benjamins.

Thorne, Barrie (1993) *Gender Play*. Milton Keynes: Open University Press.

Thorne, Barrie and Henley, Nancy (eds.) (1975) *Language and Sex: Difference and Dominance*. Rowley, MA: Newbury House.

Thorne, Barrie, Kramarae, Cheris and Henley, Nancy (eds.) (1983) *Language, Gender and Society*. Rowley, MA: Newbury House.

Todd, Alexandra Dundas and Fisher, Sue (eds.) (1988) *Gender and Discourse: The Power of Talk*. Norwood, NJ: Ablex.

Tolson, Andrew (2006) *Media Talk: Spoken Discourse on TV and Radio*. Edinburgh: Edinburgh University Press.

Trömel-Plötz, Senta (1991) Review essay: selling the apolitical. *Discourse & Society* 2(4): 489–502.

Trudgill, Peter (1972) Sex, covert prestige and linguistic change in the urban British English of Norwich. *Language and Society* 1: 179–95.

Trudgill, Peter (1986) *Dialects in Contact*. Oxford: Blackwell.

Trudgill, Peter (1995) *Sociolinguistics*, 3rd edn. Harmondsworth: Penguin.

Trudgill, Peter and Cheshire, Jenny (eds.) (1998) *The Sociolinguistics Reader*, vol. I: *Multilingualism and Variation*. London: Arnold.

Turner, P. (1988) A quantitative study of sociolinguistic patterns of vowel variation in adult Tyneside speakers. Unpublished dissertation, Department of Speech, University of Newcastle upon Tyne.

Uchida, Aki (1992) When 'difference' is 'dominance': a critique of the 'anti-power-based' cultural approach to sex differences. *Language in Society* 21: 547–68.

van den Bergh, Nan (1987) Renaming: vehicle for empowerment. In Joyce Penfield (ed.) *Women and Language in Transition*. New York: State University of New York Press.

van Zoonen, L. (1998) One of the girls? The changing gender of journalism. In C. Carter, G. Branston and S. Allan (eds.) *News, Gender and Power*. London: Routledge.

Vavrus, Mary Douglas (2007) Opting-out moms in the news, *Feminist Media Studies* 7(1): 47–63.

Walsh, Clare (2001) *Gender and Discourse: Language and Power in Politics, the Church and Organisations*. London: Longman.

Walsh, Clare (2006) Gender and the genre of the broadcast political interview. In Baxter 2006.

Wandor, Michelene (1990) *Once a Feminist: Stories of a Generation*. London: Virago.

Weedon, Chris (1997) *Feminist Practice and Poststructuralist Theory*, 2nd edn. Oxford: Blackwell.

West, Candace and Zimmerman, Don (1983) Small insults: a study of interruptions in cross-sex conversations between unacquainted persons. In Thorne, Kramarae and Henley 1983.

Wetherell, Margaret and Edley, Nigel (1999) Negotiating hegemonic masculinity: imaginary positions and psycho-discursive practices, *Feminism and Psychology* 9: 335–56.

Wetherell, Margaret, Taylor, Stephanie and Yates, Simeon (eds.) (2001) *Discourse as Data: A Guide for Analysis*. London: Sage.

White, Cynthia (1970) *Women's Magazines 1693–1968*. London: Michael Joseph.

White, Michael (2008) Fond farewell to 'battleaxe' Dunwoody at Westminster, *Guardian*, 9 May. Downloaded from www.guardian.co.uk/politics/2008/ on 10 May 2008.

Whitehead, Stephen (2001) *Men and Masculinities*. Cambridge: Polity.

Williams, Jeffrey (ed.) (1995) *PC Wars: Politics and Theory in the Academy*. London: Routledge.

Willis, Paul (1977) *Learning to Labour*. Westmead: Saxon House.

Wilmot, Helen (1991) *Jackie*: an investigation of the text and the readers. Unpublished BA special study, Bristol Polytechnic.

Winship, Janice (1987) *Inside Women's Magazines*. London: Pandora.

Winter, Joanne (1993) Gender and the politics interview in an Australian context, *Journal of Pragmatics*. 20: 117–39.

Wodak, Ruth (2003) Multiple identities: the roles of female parliamentarians in the EU parliament. In Holmes and Meyerhoff 2003.

Wodak, Ruth and Meyer, Michael (2001) *Methods of Critical Discourse Analysis*. London: Sage.

Wolf, Naomi (1990) *The Beauty Myth*. London: Vintage.

Young, Linda Wai Ling (1982) Inscrutability revisited. In Gumperz 1982.

Young, Lynne and Fitzgerald, Brigid (2006) *The Power of Language: How Discourse Influences Society*. London/Oakville: Equinox.

Zimmerman, Don and West, Candace (1975) Sex roles, interruptions and silences in conversation. In Thorne and Henley 1975.

Index